WE GOT FIRED!

...And It's The Best Thing That Ever Happened To Us

HARVEY MACKAY

BALLANTINE BOOKS • NEW YORK

A Ballantine Book
Published by The Random House Publishing Group

Copyright © 2004 by Harvey Mackay

www.ballantinebooks.com

Library of Congress Cataloging-in-Publication Data
Mackay, Harvey.
We got fired! : —and it's the best thing that ever happened to us /
Harvey Mackay.— 1st ed.
p.   cm.
Includes index.
ISBN 0-345-47186-5 (hbk.) — ISBN 0-345-47187-3 (pbk.)
1. Employees—Dismissal of—Case studies.   2. Job hunting—Case studies.
3. Vocational guidance.   I. Title.

HF5549.5.D55M33 2004
650.14—dc22
2004047683

Jacket photo credits: Joe Torre (NYY/Mark Mandrake); Lesley Visser (Dave
Russell/CBS); Bill Belichick (John Zich/NewSport/Corbis); Mayor Michael
Bloomberg (Stephen Chernin/Getty Images); Harvey Mackay (Judy Olausen)

Manufactured in the United States of America

1   3   5   7   9   8   6   4   2

First Edition: October 2004

DEDICATION

This book is dedicated to the millions of people who have
lost their jobs, especially the victims
of
mergers, acquisitions, consolidations, downsizings,
restructurings, reorganizations, and so-called right-sizings.

Being fired wasn't your choice.
Whether you rise up from it . . . is.

All the winners—and winners they all are—who contributed
to this book have very personal stories to tell. I have relied
on them to recall the facts of their stories accurately. No
doubt these gifted and successful people have done that to
the best of their abilities. This is also a diverse bunch
of achievers. I'm simply amazed at the similarities in
their comebacks. There are differences, too. Most slight.
Some dramatic. We're not all built the same.
We all bounce differently when we take a tumble.

ACKNOWLEDGMENTS

Because of tight deadlines, Ron Beyma was a miracle worker for me. Ron's perceptions polished everything I wrote.

Margie Resnick Blickman was her yeoman self, as usual. With an eagle's eye for detail, she's not only my editor, she's my sister and my best friend.

Greg Bailey is my right-hand man. His phenomenal attention to detail coordinated the entire series of interviews and the overall book. I simply could not have done it without him.

Nancy Miller, senior vice president and editor-in-chief of Ballantine, and her assistant, Deirdre Lanning—a better editorial team you cannot replicate.

Due to his great intellect, Scott Mitchell is invaluable at bouncing off strategies and tactics.

My assistant, Kathy Hanlin, who is always in the wings to pick up the ball and isn't afraid to run with it.

Lynne Lancaster, for being an editing star in the Mackay "Kitchen Cabinet."

My agent, Jonathon Lazear, has been with me for six books, which spells L-O-Y-A-L-T-Y and trust through the years.

Neil Naftalin—"Mr. Results"—a sharp mind and key strategist with endless ideas.

Mary Anne Bailey helped enormously with research, fact checking, and proofreading.

Christi Cardenas is also a great agent at Lazear and a quick-wit and great personality.

Vickie Abrahamson is a major player on my creative team and never lets me down.

Pat Fallon delivered—as he always does—this book's jacket designer, Jim Landry. I love the cover, and Jim was spectacular.

Judy Olausen is known as one of the best photographers in the world. She again took my photo for the cover.

David Hahn is publicist extraordinaire. He has the moves of a true pro.

Kim Hovey is a publicist's publicist. A winner in my book.

In between interviewing Hollywood's biggest stars, Pat O'Brien helped gain access to some of the great names. Maybe that's why they call his show "Access Hollywood."

Bob Dilenschneider is truly the man with the golden Rolodex.

Dr. William Brody is another indispensable friend who knows where the keys to the kingdom are buried.

Mitch Modell is a friend who's a who's who—a great connector.

Al Annexstad—a man for all seasons and reasons—a spectacular guy.

Thanks to the Korn/Ferry Organization for sharing Tierney Remick with me, and to Don Spetner and Amy Saruwatari for helping oversee the Korn/Ferry survey in the book.

Special kudos to Kim Vidt, who is incredibly helpful and brilliant.

Ed Breslin is the best backup guy around.

Joel Rippel is a guy who knows that little things don't mean a lot . . . they mean everything.

Thanks to Lee Iacocca for my excerpting of his famous bestseller *Iacocca: An Autobiography*.

A big thank-you to the pros at United Feature Syndicate who send my column throughout the country.

To everyone at Mackay Envelope Company, as always,

you've taught me how far loyalty and dedication go, and I can't thank each of you enough.

Always, always, always, my wife, Carol Ann. Her inspiration and overall support have made my life happier than I ever dreamed.

Contents

CONTENTS

WE GOT FIRED!

My Secret

"How do you define a secret?
When one person knows it."

Right now, I know something you don't. I got fired, and it was the best thing that ever happened to me! I—Harvey Mackay, who has been sharkproofing the world against job loss with over 10 million books sold since 1988—was fired. I'm now out of the closet. It wasn't that I tried to hide a black spot on my career. It was that I didn't think the whole deal was all that important. Last year I thought about it further. And then I realized it *was* important. Not maybe the firing itself, but the lessons I learned as a result of it. It literally changed my life. But it was embarrassing. So I had dodged giving it any significance for more than half a century.

Here's the straight story. My father, Jack Mackay, was the Associated Press correspondent in St. Paul, Minnesota. He virtually had only one job his entire life . . . and yes, he stayed around for thirty-five years to collect his gold watch. He was the best of the best. He took a backseat to no one, especially when it came to delivering scoops . . . the lifeline of a reporter.

Growing up as a kid, I came from modest beginnings, and my father was insistent there was no substitute for working odd jobs during summer vacations and Christmas holidays. I had a myriad of short stints from setting pins at a bowling alley to delivering newspapers to working at a driving range.

It was summer vacation my junior year in high school and I had just landed a neat job at a downtown St. Paul men's clothing store . . . and, of course, my father with his connections got me the job.

Now, peddling pants, socks, underwear, ties, hankies, and occasionally a shirt or two may not sound like the most glamorous position in the world . . . but in retrospect, it was a great gig. At a young age, I had an opportunity to learn about business . . . having a boss to report to . . . showing up for work on time . . . handling money and credit . . . understanding how customers shop . . . and, learning a little about the retail clothing industry. Overnight, I was plying the tricks of the retail trade. My boss, Chris, hammered these principles into my brain bank:

1) *Before you could count to "one-Mississippi," you greeted a customer at the front door with a "million-dollar, megawatt smile" and said "Howdy . . . may I help you!" The "howdy" was a hammy slice of creativity in those days because the store I worked at was Howard's and their theme was "Howdy from Howard's." No way would that advertising theme win first place in the 2004 Cleo Awards!*

2) *Never put more than three ties on the counter . . . it will only confuse the customer.*

3) *Always, and I mean always, play to the spouse (female). She will make the buying decision 99 percent of the time.*

4) *Once you get the customer to try on the pants, consider it a done deal.*

5) *Never ring up a sale without asking: "What else do you have in mind?" and "Would you like me to introduce you to our best suit salesman?"*

6) *Walk the customer to the front door and sometimes even out onto Wabasha Street and look 'im in the eye . . . say "Thanks!" . . . and then say: "Be sure and bring it back if you are not happy with it."*

7) *Never, never, never start to lock up if a customer misses closing time by a few minutes.*

8) *And, don't come to work in competitor's clothes, even if you are just a young kid peddling men's accessories.*

The above eight points are the short list because my memory is what I forget with, and—be kind—it was many decades ago. Looking back, probably the greatest plus of the job was, whether I realized it or not, I was polishing my sales skills at a very early age.

When you are young, footloose, and fancy-free, you don't have a care in the world. You are always in the "comfort zone." You don't quite realize the responsibility of holding down a legitimate job. Better said, you don't realize the importance of holding down a job *legitimately*.

Because my dad paved the way for me, I never really appreciated that there were many kids clamoring for a sweetheart summer job like I had. This sugarcoated plum fell right into my lap.

Here is where it gets a little embarrassing. I didn't get this job due to my instant mastery of the eight commandments of selling. I got it because of my dad. He was not only a customer of the store, but was very good friends with the owner and many of the salespeople. The buzz on me was to treat Harvey like "Little Lord Fauntleroy."

They never disciplined me if I took extra minutes on my lunch hour, never chastised me for being a few minutes late, nor for leaving a few minutes early on occasion.

You know the old story, give him an inch and he'll take a mile! . . . well, that was Harvey in spades.

In retrospect, I am positive all these little pinpricks added up and there was probably a whispering campaign going on behind my back. The Lord became a Louse. Lords generally do in our democratic land. No doubt the buzz became a buzz saw about this unappreciative, spoiled brat whose daddy knew the owner. And that saw was relentlessly whirring toward the back of my neck.

The deal breaker came when I started to ask for days off. Why? I dreamed of becoming another Ben Hogan and had had lots of success on the golf links playing for good ole St. Paul Central High School. I also set my goal that summer to become the Minnesota State High School Golf Champion the following year. As it happened, I three-putted the 72nd hole to miss by one stroke. The sad news is that my pro-sports dream was a delusion. Although I went on to play golf for the University of Minnesota, I would never become a professional golfer. Reason? Simple. If you grow up in Minnesota, the number of golf-playing days you have in any given year is radically less than what your counterparts in Arizona or Florida have. It didn't take my golf coach to point this out to me. It was my mother.

But back to Howard's Men's Store. First it was leaving an hour early . . . then several hours early . . . then half days early . . . and then the whole enchilada . . . asking for a whole day off to play in this "big" golf tournament.

I really got blindsided because most of my colleagues in the store played golf. I figured they'd be happy and proud to see my name in the paper and where I finished in the tournament the previous day.

Wrong! Just the opposite!

How could I be so dumb?

How could I be so naïve?

The rest is history. The management, of course, never called me in. They went directly to my dad and said, "Too many distractions . . . too many favors . . . too many special requests . . . we can't rely on your son. He is a nice kid, *but* . . . !"

To say I was devastated was an understatement. There were very few times my father ever raised his voice at me while growing up. But his words ring out loud and clear to me this very day.

"Disappointed . . . let me down . . . let yourself down . . . look what will happen to your name and reputation around town when the word finally gets out . . . You will never work at Howard's Men's Store again."

My dad made me—no forced me—to write a letter of apology in my own words . . . not his.

They say you are supposed to learn from your mistakes, and wow did I ever. Being fired and unwanted, especially when you know it's 100 percent your own fault, is not easy to take. . . . I shamed my family and myself.

What exactly did I learn from my train wreck at Howard's? Eight indelible rules that can help you not get fired from a cushy part-time job . . . and more importantly, can help you succeed in a job you care about.

1) *When a relative or well-connected friend lands you a job, remember that you did not get that spot on your merits. No matter what anyone tells you in a moment of kindness, don't forget you are there because someone else has pulled strings.*

2) *Insist that you hump racks on the sales floor and clean out the back storage room. Dig into the dirty work and be part of the gang—or you are begging your co-workers to gang up on you.*

3) *Look for a chance to stay a few minutes late or come early, especially when you can help a co-worker out. Particularly*

when that co-worker has a family and you are young and single.

4) *Realize that getting the job is not the done deal.* Keeping *the job every day is* doing *the deal.*

5) *Always find a friend early on . . . one you can trust. Somebody you can ask for frank input: What do people here* really *think about me?*

6) *Even if it's a temporary or part-time job, never let the people around you feel that your work is an extracurricular activity. When you make colleagues feel that* your *extracurricular activities are more important than* their *work, you insult them.*

7) *Never, never, never ask for days off in a temporary job. If you are invited to work holidays or summers, chances are it's so regular employees can enjoy some time off.*

8) *Realize that the person you are likeliest to hurt by slacking off is not your employer . . . not yourself . . . but the person who stuck his or her neck out and packaged the cushy deal for you in the first place. Not only can this be painfully embarrassing, it can substantially short-circuit any chance for you getting any future cushions.*

Luckily I got these messages loud and clear. I vowed never, ever to let this happen again. Believe me, at every single subsequent job I got through the rest of high school and four years of college, I minded my p's and q's and worked my guts out to do the best I could.

Being fired was invaluable "tuition" in the school of hard knocks. I will be eternally glad it happened.

It was an expensive lesson.

It was a hurtful lesson.

It was an embarrassing lesson.

I want every reader of this book to get the message . . . especially the younger set. Don't ever let this happen to you. Why? Because life has many hard lessons. Do yourself a favor and try to learn as many of them as you can with the least possible pain. Of course, I was only a raw high school kid with no one counting on my monetary support. I'm not trying to compare my experience to an adult breadwinner whose spouse or children are dependent upon him or her. Looking back, I was lucky to have learned my career lessons, not in kindergarten like the title of the famous book by Robert Fulghum, but while I was still a callow youth in high school.

But the sun did come out again, and guess what?

Two years later, I got virtually the identical job six blocks down the street at Howard's competitor, and this time I graduated to the Suit, Jacket, and Overcoat Department. I made a bundle in commissions. I fitted corporate purchasing managers into plaid jackets. I sold suits to Minnesota state legislators to whom I would later successfully sell domed stadiums when I became very active in the community. I made friends, some of whom I am lucky enough to have to this very day. Fifteen years later, after I had started my envelope-manufacturing business, my firm was stocking their warehouses ceiling-high with envelopes. None of this would have happened had I not learned my lesson at Howard's and taken my medicine.

In this book, you will learn about the mean streets of the employment jungle. People who didn't have a clue and were fired out of the blue. People who saw it coming but couldn't turn the tidal wave headed at them. People whose companies thought they were engaging in treason. People who were let go and not even given a reason. Some victims were young. Others were nearing their golden years. Still others were at the midlife peak of their careers. The common thread: None of them saw themselves as victims for very long. And that takes spunk.

MACKAY'S MORAL:

The way to douse a firing is to use what you learned
for an even better hiring.

INNIES AND OUTIES:
THAT INANE ANNOUNCEMENT

When key managers get fired, the firm doing the firing—especially if it is publicly held—issues an announcement. Why? The Securities and Exchange Commission (SEC) says you must. Getting rid of a manager is material information, like shedding a copper mine in Peru or ditching a helicopter division in Idaho. In the heat of the moment, few managers use the public announcement to trumpet that they are available for work elsewhere.

- Pursue *particular* interests. Instead of saying you are leaving "to pursue other interests," insist that the announcement say "to pursue the development of aerospace components for weather detection" or "to pursue the development of new software programs in cardiac care." What will court a potential employer most? Saying that you are intending a stroll on the beach or "spending more time with your family" sounds like you are bruised and more interested in licking your wounds than licking the world.

- **Write your own obit.** If you give a direction, you are far more likely to convince people that you left with a direction . . . as opposed to being the victim of a shot out of the dark. If you were fired tomorrow, why would you say you left? Why not write it down now? It's like a final will and testament. You don't like to think about the day that they are shoveling dirt on your face. In the job world, a ready and well-crafted answer may mean the difference between big bread and the bread line.

- **Press flesh.** It never hurts to know the press, especially the trade press within your own industry. This is a cannonball to cultivate. When you get the boot—even better, when you know the boot is coming—consider contacting a trade reporter and letting him or her know about how you see the industry. Betray no secrets, but let the world know what a whiz you are on the turf you command.

- **Own the exit.** When you leave a job, you may not be the one to pull the trigger. But think of convincing reasons why you *might* have. Your reasoning could be so persuasive, others may well be convinced that leaving this job was really your decision after all.

That brings me to the most persuasive point of all. I call it the *Andy Grove Axiom.* Andy Grove is a cofounder of Intel, and Intel puts the punch in almost anything with a processor inside. Here's the setup. Intel "had been losing money on memories for quite some time while trying to compete with the Japanese producers' high-quality, low-priced, mass-produced parts," according to Andy Grove. "But because business had been so good, we just kept at it, looking for the magical answer that would give us a premium price." Then came the realization: "We had lost our bearings. We were wandering in the valley of death." Chips or no chips? Andy Grove tells it this way:

". . . In the middle of 1985, after this aimless wandering had been going on for almost a year . . . I was in my office with Intel's chairman and CEO, Gordon Moore, and we were discussing our quandary. Our mood was downbeat. I looked out the window at the Ferris wheel of the Great America amusement park revolving in the distance, then I turned back to Gordon and I asked, 'If we got kicked out and the board brought in a new CEO, what do you think he would do?' Gordon answered without hesitation, 'He would get us out of memories [chips].' I stared at him, numb, then said, 'Why shouldn't you and I walk out the door, come back, and do it ourselves?' "

Andy Grove and Gordon Moore transformed Intel from a chip manufacturer into the leading maker of integrated processors. They refused to cling to an outmoded identity. Today, Intel is synonymous with the hearts and minds of PCs and laptops worldwide. These two business giants "fired" their past business identity before the marketplace could decimate Intel first.

MACKAY'S MORAL:

When the winds are right, "fire" yourself first.

DONALD TRUMP
FIRING'S HIGH PRIEST

Real estate mogul, executive producer and star of
the #1-rated TV show *The Apprentice*

*"Whenever you fire someone, the result is always
the same. They will hate you."*

It wasn't until Super Bowl XXVI weekend in Minneapolis in
1992 that I actually met Donald Trump. I had heard of him long
before that. And I had actually heard *from* him in 1988. That's
when my first book, *Swim with the Sharks*, made its appearance.
His book, *The Art of the Deal*, appeared earlier in the fall of
1987. Sifting through my mail one day in 1988, I happened
upon a beautiful congratulatory letter on *Sharks*. It was from
Donald. Here am I, a little envelope peddler in the flyover state
of Minnesota who goes through his mail and finds a letter from
Donald Trump to say he had read my book. I actually put it my
pocket and couldn't stop reading it for two weeks because I
couldn't believe it was for real. Donald Trump was already a legend, and his praise was a high-octane jolt.

Four years later in 1992, things didn't have exactly the same
slant. In the early 1990s, Trump was in the red. Not millions.
But billions. He had guaranteed almost $1 billion in loans. *Per-
sonally*. At the time, the Gulf War had KO'd his tourism business, his former wife was suing him for a couple of billion bucks,

and the Atlantic City casinos he had built were floundering. On the Saturday before the Super Bowl that matched the Washington Redskins and the Buffalo Bills, my friend Larry King and I met with Donald Trump in Larry's suite in the Radisson Hotel. It was a casual breakfast. And there was no reason on God's green earth for Donald Trump to explain what he had on his mind to me, this little envelope entrepreneur in Minnesota.

"Harvey, news of my demise is greatly exaggerated," he said with no little passion. "Let me tell you that every single one of these articles will be proven wrong. The newspapers and the magazines will regret the fact they ever printed them. You just watch my comeback." Then he took an envelope out of his pocket and drew out the business plan for his turnaround. How exciting for him to do that! How exciting for an *envelope* guy that he did it on the back of an envelope!

Although he was never in his life actually fired from any job, Donald Trump experienced far worse. The financial community and the press pulverized him. This was an enormous setback. Yet, even in the darkest moments, the electricity flashed and flickered around him like a trillion fireflies. The next day, during halftime of the game, Larry King and I were sitting in my suite at the Hubert H. Humphrey Metrodome. Donald promised to drop by. He was watching the game at exactly the other end of the stadium. Through my binoculars, I witnessed an unforgettable sight. As Donald Trump walked through the aisles, people rose, peered, and pressed to see him. To get close to him. Never had I seen a crowd react this way. This guy made interpersonal magic, magic like Merlin the Wizard could only dream of. I have never seen anything like it before or since. He was the *real* halftime show of 1992 . . . in those tame days, when no part of Janet Jackson's anatomy was anywhere to be found.

How many billions does Donald Trump now have? More than dreams of avarice. He's certainly on that list of the top one hundred in the United States. In his book *Trump: The Art of the Comeback*, he chronicled perhaps the greatest personal rebound in financial history. Then he went on to share what he knew. In 2004, he launched an NBC reality-TV series called *The Apprentice*. It became the number-one-rated television show. Over fifteen weeks, sixteen contestants (drawn from 215,000 applications) pressed themselves to the max. The payoff: the one survivor would earn a $250,000 paycheck and the presidency of a Trump corporate division. One person would win. Fifteen folks got fired. Overnight the show positioned Donald Trump as the most perceptive and successful authority on the hiring and firing of talent in business.

Who better to ask advice of than the man who made famous the phrase "You're fired"?

Having a phone chat with Donald Trump is a little like a high-speed chase in a Bruce Willis movie. You put the questions fast, and he nails the answers even faster. If you can't keep up, you're fired!

Donald, what are the things you look for when you must decide if you will fire someone?

"First, I look for their level of energy. Next comes competence. Are they prone to making mistakes? Have they been making minor or major mistakes? Can they recover from those mistakes? Everyone is entitled to make mistakes, but you want people who make *recoverable* mistakes. Can you learn from them or are they very destructive? Then comes brainpower. A lot of times, you hire someone who you think is very smart, and then you learn that person isn't very smart at all. Energy level, drive, competence, and brainpower. Harvey, does anybody give you an answer like that so quickly?"

Donald, the amazing thing is that nobody gives me a really commanding *answer so quickly. How different are the firing criteria you use in real life from the ones you used in the TV show* The Apprentice?

"Same criteria. I use the measures I just mentioned. I also evaluate personality. Sadly, even looks are important. It's not a question of good-looking or bad-looking. Some people just can't get through the front door because they're stupid in the way they dress. It's not a question of money. They could spend less money and still dress better. . . . Are they home run hitters? Are they singles hitters? Harvey, the criteria will never change. Intelligence . . . drive . . . stamina. They never have in millions of years and they never will."

Do you have a particular style or method for firing people?

"Firing is an interesting thing. I've fired people slowly, letting them down very gently over a period of months and even years. And I've fired people on the spot. Whenever you terminate someone, the end result is always the same. They always hate you. There are certain people whom I've not only eased out over a period of months, I even got them new jobs. Then I found out that they still hate me."

Wow, that sounds like two important lessons for a young manager to learn—one, that you will have to fire people in your career, and two, you will be hated when you fire them.

"The one common element in firing: Whether you do it viciously or nicely, that person will always hate you. I've had people go totally ballistic when they got fired. Usually those people honestly think that they are doing a good job."

How about the final moment of truth when you actually give them the news?

"There are many different ways to fire people. I don't always fire people the same way. For instance, I fire people very severely if they are stealing. If I catch them with sticky fingers, I will fire them in the most vicious manner possible. They are literally taken by their neck and thrown out of the building. That's the offense that bothers me the most. The people you catch who are doing things they are not supposed to be doing are one sort. Then there are also people who make mistakes but try very hard."

Would you agree with this premise? It's not the people you fire who make your life miserable. It's the people you don't fire.

"That's a very good statement. Oftentimes the biggest mistake you can make is in not firing the person. It's keeping someone in the company and on the payroll who shouldn't be there. They can just become destructive. Sometimes the biggest error is not whom you fire but whom you keep."

You have a real gift for sizing people up on the spot.

"It's very hard to size people up on the spot, Harvey. Often you will think somebody is a superstar, and they turn out to be a stiff. You can think somebody is a stiff and they turn out to be a superstar."

How do you read a résumé?

"I often see a résumé where people list every little job that they ever had. Somebody might have twelve jobs in two years. They are doing themselves a tremendous disservice by stating their career that way. I like to see a résumé where somebody has been in a company for five years or more. I am suspicious of people who have changed jobs every six months or every year."

What advice would you give to a young person who has been fired?

"If I were a dishonest person, I would advise them not to show that they've been fired. But I'm an honest person, so I can never recommend that. The worst thing I can see on a résumé is when somebody jumps from job to job. The only advice I can give is to keep chugging. Get a good job. Then do a better job of performing it."

Where does your incredible drive to excel come from?

"I had a father who was a very strong, very tough guy, but a really good guy. He was a contractor, and I started out working for him. To be honest with you, he always loved my work. My father was a very smart man, but he was also a very hard worker. He didn't know about playing golf on Saturday or Sunday. He would be out checking buildings and construction. He worked seven days a week. By the way, that wasn't work to him because he loved what he was doing. He was a very firm man. There was no game playing with him. I did a great job for him, and he really dug me.

"Does that do it, Harvey?"

Donald, does Barry Bonds hit 450-foot home runs? I countered, knowing I had just interviewed the master.

Walk through a Trump high-rise, visit a Trump casino, tune in *The Deal Maker* on the tube, or talk to Donald himself. It's always the same experience. It's done right, confidently, fast, and larger than life. And Donald Trump's portfolio of talent just keeps getting bigger. That's partly because he surrounds himself with sharp people who are winners. When I last called him and spoke with his highly capable assistant, Rhona, she commented, "I used to work for a real estate developer who also was a media personality. Now I work for a media star who also is a real estate developer."

MACKAY'S MORAL:

When you're sized up by the best, dress for success from toe to head, especially head.

IT PAYS TO FIND OUT
ABOUT YOURSELF

In the last dozen years, major league sports have added a new spectacle to the events calendar: Draft Day. This spectacle has become huge, and fans gather by the thousands in local sports arenas to watch TV coverage of middle-aged men in suits fumbling with Ping-Pong balls, making solemn-sounding announcements, and scribbling on blackboards.

Who's getting whom? Who's trading? Who's standing pat? Who's expendable? Who's untouchable? What kind of talent is in demand, in decline? Who got snookered, who snatched a prize from under everyone's nose? Who's winning, who's losing? No one *really* knows because you can't tell the final score when no one gets the ball until the following season, but it's a great game for any fan who enjoys lots of controversy and strongly held expressions of opinion.

Most of the Draft Day hype and hope focuses on athletic skills, but sophisticated player personnel executives, who are responsible for these multimillion-dollar decisions, know they have to factor in other elements. They realize that the performance of their draft choices will depend as much on the athlete's personal qualities as on their raw physical talent.

Personal qualities are a lot tougher to get a handle on than the numbers for the forty-yard dash or the vertical jump. Is this player committed? What is his value system? Is she coachable? Will he be a team player? Will she be able to overcome her shortcomings? Will he choke? Does she quit? Has he established sound training habits? How about personal habits?

Sports franchises rise and fall on the answers to these kinds of questions.

So do businesses.

The real issue here? It's research about people.

For forty years, I have relied on industrial psychologists to help me sort out the complexities of a hire. According to the American Management Association, the number of U.S. companies using psychological testing is growing rapidly.

Fortunately for us business types, it's a lot easier to get your subject to test when she's a forty-five-year-old salesperson than a nineteen-year-old athlete . . . even though with the athlete you may be risking $10 million or much more on the results. Just imagine the fan reaction if you were able to get one of these kids to test for you and you came up with something like, "We decided not to draft Mr. All-American because, even though he can shoot the eyes out of the basket from forty feet, he has an unresolved conflict with authority figures."

Whatever the results, I never let the industrial psychologists make the decision for me. Their information is just another tool in the hiring process. . . . It's just another arrow in my quiver.

But it's also a tool you can use to your own advantage as a prospective employee.

In two ways.

If you suddenly find yourself scanning the horizon for a job, go to an industrial psychologist and get tested. On your own.

I'm not going to kid you; it's not cheap. It will cost you at least several hundred bucks, but the oral and written exams will uncover strengths you never dreamed you had (and a few weaknesses to work on also). If you're being let go, try to talk your employer into paying the tab as part of your outplacement package.

Remember, you're at a crossroads in your life. The next job you take could determine your future. Isn't it worth your while to know whether you're heading in the right direction? If there is ever a time to change careers, to rethink your goals, isn't this it? Fate has forced you into this situation, so take this opportunity to find out about yourself and what you're good at. Also, the stress of being fired can cause an outbreak of the emotional heebie-jeebies. A good psychologist will not only tell you your strengths and weaknesses, but how they are playing under the pressure of the moment.

Don't do it on the cheap. Go to a firm with an excellent reputation so you know you're getting a sound evaluation from someone who's a lot less biased about you than you are.

Another use for this information: You now have in your hands the kind of report that 99.9 percent of other job seekers—your competitors—don't have. It contains information every interviewer is trying to learn about a prospect before making the hiring decision. Armed with this psychological profile, you now have your own personal *Good Housekeeping* Seal of Approval. You probably don't want to mention that you've had the assessment done to a potential employer. You surely don't want to share the report you have. But you can anticipate the kinds of questions future bosses or *their* assessor are likely to ask. You also know far better how to present yourself. Maybe your report says that you anger easily or that you come off as arrogant. You know where you have to lighten up in your interviews.

Does it show that you are a less-than-perfect human being? Of course. Not to worry. We all are. What it also shows is that you have areas of strength, as well as creativity and imagination

in your job-seeking skills. And that may be just enough to resolve the decision in your favor.

MACKAY'S MORAL:

Know thyself to get thyself hired.

PAT MITCHELL

CEO of Public Broadcasting System (PBS)

*"The optimist sees opportunity in every danger;
the pessimist sees danger in every opportunity."*

" 'Pat, did you know you are unemployed?' "

" 'What in the world do you mean, Gabe? I'm sitting at my desk working on my story,' I replied as I pounded out a paragraph on that rackety black Underwood.

" 'No, no . . . you're unemployed. It just crossed the newsroom wire that you people are out of business.'

"I hung up the receiver. A casual acquaintance of mine, Gabe Pressman of WNBC-TV, had been on the other end of the line. When I looked around the room, it was clear that nobody else had the news. They were all happily working away. I was hesitant about saying anything. It was a good half hour till an announcement came over the loudspeaker for us to all report to the executive floor. I knew immediately what it was all about. There had been rumors that the business wasn't sound financially. When we got up there, there were huge barrels of Bloody Marys. It was 10:30 a.m.! Someone on the editorial staff announced that *Look* magazine was shutting down. Those reporters who wanted to own their stories would have to negotiate with the magazine. 'Have a Bloody Mary and we're sorry,' one of the managers said. That was it."

Pat Mitchell had made a risky decision to leave a secure teaching position at Virginia Commonwealth University, the only profession for which she was really trained. She had also loved her job. She had been one of a group of young turks all under the age of twenty-six in a team-teaching program. They were trying to keep students interested in literature, history, and art at a time when students on many campuses were marching, holding sit-ins, and from time to time, vandalizing administration buildings . . . common extracurricular activities in the late 1960s.

Look had sent a reporter down to do a story on the Virginia team teachers, and it turned out to be a guy Pat had gone to college with. She was fascinated watching the writer and photographer put their story together, and because of their friendship, Pat got to help write the story. Her reporter/friend passed this on to *Look*'s managing editor, David Maxey, who offered to meet the young college teacher. An invitation arrived. Without a moment's hesitation, Pat flew up to New York. She had no real idea of what she was planning, but she found herself asking Maxey for a job. "As what?" Maxey asked the teacher, whose only writing experience had been a master's thesis and a couple of academic articles in literary journals. But Maxey took a chance and hired her as a researcher/writer, promising her that she would have a crack at a byline for one good story in her first year with the magazine. That is, if she came up with a good idea for one. At the end of the semester at Virginia Commonwealth, Pat took a leave of absence, certain that she would return to teaching once she had this big-city dream behind her. Her colleagues were just as sure she would be back in the academic nest after her journalistic lark.

Pat moved to New York with her five-year-old son in tow, and she sublet a loft from a friend in Chinatown. Why Chinatown? Pat wanted something as different from the safe, sheltered world of academe as she could find. In her first six months at *Look,* she met and interviewed Mayor John Lindsay and helped report a piece on the antiwar protests. And she kept pitching Maxey on a story that was going on all around her neighborhood: teenage gang wars.

Maxey finally agreed to let Pat do a story on the gang wars in Chinatown. All kinds of dreadful things happened in the battle for turf as different immigrant groups surged into New York's Chinatown. These new residents didn't speak English; they had no jobs and often no place to spend the long hours on the streets. That's why they were literally killing each other on a stoop outside a restaurant. To learn about these kids and their stories, Pat volunteered at a neighborhood community center as an English teacher and got to know some of the gang leaders in the process.

Pat has natural curiosity. From her early days, she wanted to know about anything and everything. As to the gangs of Chinatown: Who owned what turf? What did they fight about? Why was it so important? Because she lived in the neighborhood and no one knew about her uptown job, she began to gain the trust of a few key gang members and the story developed into a profile of two "warring" teens and their families. In August 1971, *Look* sent a photographer down to illustrate the story. At one point, Pat and the photographer ended up in the middle of a street melee. One of the photos in the spread was to be a shot of this duo in torn jeans with skinned knees, "injured in the line of duty."

At the offices, the mocked-up story was pin-punched on the wall in ten-by-fourteen galleys. It was going to be an October–November 1971 cover story. Pat canceled her teaching option at Virginia Commonwealth. She signed a lease for an Upper West Side apartment. She anticipated her son starting school there and wanted to get out of Chinatown before the story broke and her cover was blown completely.

"All plans were blown completely on that October morning

when the news came that meant I no longer had a job," Pat recalls. "I had no money in the bank. I had been there so little time, my severance was practically nothing. I had no training for anything except teaching. My first call was to Virginia Commonwealth. They said the term had already started. Maybe they could look at the winter semester if anybody left. They had replaced me. For me, it seemed the dream of a career as a magazine journalist had ended before it really got started." Another job in journalism? Remember that a platoon of much more seasoned journalists from the ranks of *Look* had also been released. They would devour any openings on the streets of New York.

"Forget the Bloody Marys. I needed work," says Pat, remembering her frustration. "As I piled into the elevator down to the lobby with some like-minded colleagues, I remember thinking about that phone call with Gabe Pressman. How come he knew and I didn't know? A little click went off in my head: television!" In the lobby, exiting staff members ran into a gaggle of TV reporters and cameramen streaming in to cover the *Look* wake. One shoved a microphone in Pat's face and asked, "So, what are you gonna do now that you're unemployed?" "I think I'll go into television," she answered as a flip comment. Astonishingly, her little sound bite ended up on the evening news. Gabe Pressman called her the next day and said if she really wanted to be on the tube, he could get her an appointment with his boss. He did.

At the same time, Pat made an effort to find a job with other big magazines of the day. The great pictorial magazines had become dinosaurs in the burgeoning age of television, especially with the onset of color TV. Pat visited the offices of *Life* magazine. Her contact there told her that things weren't much better at that powerhouse of photojournalism. In fact, *Life* went out of business for the first of several times about six months after that. The only other similar magazine that was successful was *Cosmopolitan*. "I went to see Helen Gurley Brown," Pat recalls, "but I figured out pretty quickly I didn't fit the *Cosmo* girl mold.

At the time I was so broke, I had to borrow money from friends to pay the rent. Even though I had a master's degree, I was working as a waitress on the second shift while getting in line for interviews at every television station executive's office who would see me.

"I sat a long time outside Bernie Shusman's office at WNBC until he finally saw me. When I shoved the story on Chinatown gang wars that had been written for *Look* in front of him, he began to ask questions. 'Can you do this story for us?' he asked. Of course, I replied, having no idea what that meant.

"I didn't know a thing about television, but from my perspective, it looked a lot more financially secure than magazines at the time. And even though I didn't know what 'doing a story' for television really meant, I was ready to try. Even if I failed at it, it was better than doing nothing . . . or going home to Georgia. Besides, I have always lived by an adage favored by my grandfather: 'Sometimes falling on your face is your first forward movement.' So with a lot of help from a sympathetic crew, I got the story together and it was broadcast on the six o'clock news. I had done the research, I knew the kids, I was able to interview them and get through the on-camera bits. But I was terrible on camera. So they used the story without me in it. Didn't matter really. I was hooked on television and its ability to take a complicated story, put it together in a few days, broadcast it to millions, and have enormous impact. I was determined to find a job in television."

NBC shipped Pat around to many of their owned-and-operated stations to try to find a spot for her. Pat had promise, but they weren't going to let her start in New York City. While NBC shopped around for the right fit, Pat went to work for New York Mayor John Lindsay's Republican presidential bid. She feels that brief excursion into politics gave her campaigning and consensus-building skills that helped shape her style forever. When she finally landed a job at the Boston NBC affiliate, she started as a political producer. Politics was, after all, an arena she had recently dipped her toe in. About two months after arriving in Boston, Pat went on the air with the eleven o'clock news team. She had a top-tier career there between 1972 and 1977. Then she went to Washington for eighteen months working on a show named *Panorama*.

At various times over twenty-five years, Pat worked for NBC, ABC, and CBS. She was on-air talent as well as producer, including being the substitute host for Jane Pauley on *Today,* and the arts correspondent for CBS's *Sunday Morning.* She was an NBC staffer for three separate stints. Along the way, she founded her own production company. She had the first woman-produced and -hosted Emmy-winning show on television, the daytime talk show *Woman to Woman.* It won that Emmy in 1984. Once again, Pat was pinching herself and asking: Can life get any better than this? In no time, she was asking another question. Could it get any worse? "Our financial partner in *Woman to Woman* sold us out. We were left high and dry and ended up disbanding the company," Pat says ruefully. "I had to pay off eighty-five people who were working for me at the time. None of us could afford to keep the production going without financial backers, and time was not on our side. People say to me today, if you had only kept your show going you would have been Oprah Winfrey. Maybe. I do know this: Oprah inherited many of our stations when we dropped out of syndication. I went back to NBC, taking the *Woman to Woman* format and title to the *Today* program."

The third stopover at NBC led to another leaving. It's common in this merry-go-round industry. That third and final departure from NBC was decisive in several ways. "I was working for the *Today* show and I disobeyed a direct order." Pat spells it out in black and white. "If I hadn't resigned, I probably would have been fired. At the time, I was both on the air and also producing special reports. I really wanted to do a story on a group of Arab and Israeli women in the Middle East who were banding together to try to find a way to peace. The *Today* show producers first agreed I could travel over and do the series, but when I got to Jerusalem, NBC changed its mind and decided it wasn't that important a story. They wanted me to return to New York with whatever we had done so far and abandon the bigger idea of documenting women on the front lines of conflict. I had already started this story and decided these women deserved awareness and attention. With my grandfather's admonition about falling flat on my nose ringing in my ears, I decided to stay and keep the camera crew going. I knew the odds were overwhelming that I would be fired. So I resigned. As I saw it, I would figure out how to pay for shooting the story when I got back. We returned with an amazing story, including the first American television interview with Hanan Ashrawi, the Palestinian leader. A friend of mine got interested in the program and she gave me the money to finish it. Ironically, I sold it back to NBC and they ended up airing it."

After NBC, Pat established a second independent firm, VU Productions, and created and developed series, specials, and documentaries. From there she moved to Turner Broadcasting. When she entered Turner, she arrived as an executive and at a very different career level as the head of a whole division. "I was no longer either talent or a producer," Pat emphasizes. "I had sworn I would never enter a big company as either of these. On-air talent are highly paid people, but they have no control over their lives. I went in as senior vice president of Turner Productions and reported directly to Ted Turner from the get-go. This was his independent documentary division. After the merger with Time Warner, I became president of CNN Productions and moved over to the news division and, ironically, also took on responsibilities at Time, Inc. for developing television extensions of magazines. That was like going full circle."

Pat's views on CNN founder Ted Turner are admiring and respectful: "Ted is the most out-of-the-box, inventive, risk-taking person I ever worked for. If he had a vision, he just went for it. It didn't matter how many doubters and detractors he met along the way. He was the only person whom I ever worked for who operated with the following standard: Take all the time you need and spend as much money as you need to, but get it right. It only matters that it's right and then it has value."

"But surely Ted Turner must have been concerned about ratings?" I asked Pat.

"Harvey, the work I did was evaluated differently," Pat answered. "He wasn't motivated by the conventional broadcast measurements of how much money will it make and how big an audience will it get. He cared about those things but not to the exclusion of the impact on society. He gave me different yardsticks. Then as now, he puts his money where his values are." Documentaries produced under Pat's leadership have won more than one hundred major awards and forty-one Emmys—most garnered during those banner years at Turner Broadcasting and CNN.

In March 2000, Pat became president and CEO of PBS—the Public Broadcasting System. PBS is a $2 billion organization, and it's what Pat calls a "pure democracy" with each of the 349 PBS stations having equal votes on issues from budget to governance to program schedules. The job takes diplomatic skills. During the past financially challenging years, this meant some strategic reorganization at PBS, too. Through three rounds of budget realignments, Pat has reduced overall staff and operating expenses by nearly 30 percent, and streamlined the number of her direct reports from fifteen to just five—a move any gifted manager would make.

"Where did you get most of the skills you use today?"

"The funny thing is, Harvey, at PBS I use the whole range of skills from every other job I have done. I didn't plan it that way, but that's how it worked out. In this position, I'm in the public eye, making speeches and presenting the case for public broadcasting in front of Congress, corporate America, foundations, and, of course, 'viewers like you.' My ability to do that was groomed in my on-air work.

"My producer experience is vital for overseeing the 2,100 hours of programs PBS commissions and schedules. Managerially, having run my own company, I can appreciate the demands of the 349 separate general managers running their own stations. It requires consensus building every day. You rule by consensus, not by control. I keep trying to describe the job I do so my successor will have a better understanding of it coming in than I had coming into PBS," Pat adds with a smile.

"Is PBS another chance to fall forward on the old schnoz?" I asked.

"Harvey, I'm fond of a quote by Winston Churchill: 'The optimist sees opportunity in every danger; the pessimist sees danger in every opportunity.' I'm an optimist. And as another world leader, Fidel Castro, pointed out in an interview I did with him several years ago, 'You have to be an optimist in order to create change.' I would agree with that statement."

"Pat, what would be your advice to people looking for a job today?"

"Be determined. When you have been unemployed and broke as I was during those months in New York in the 1970s, you learn lessons you don't forget. I was determined not to give up. I figured it would all come around if I could find a way to survive financially while I stayed focused on what I wanted. It didn't come easily. If you look at my résumé, it seems like one exciting jump from one rung to the next. Every one of those moves was somewhat of a risk. Some didn't work out as I planned or hoped. I didn't follow a straight line to get where I am, but I never went backward either."

Morals from Pat? There are plenty. . . .

- Seize every chance you have to learn. It's amazing how many skills we seem to acquire by accident. You know what's more mind-boggling than that? How much of this know-how becomes unexpected but indispensable pluses later on.

- When you get knocked down, don't spend a lot of time lying on the pavement. Pound the pavement instead.

- Talk to any highly paid entertainer or athlete who lives in the glass bubble of the public eye: The people who make the most money often have the least real control over their lives.

- Resigning on principle is a gateway to standing on your own.

MACKAY'S MORAL:

If you want to get to the top, getting it right can be a lot more important than just getting it done.

DOWN AND UP #1

- **Joanne Kathleen Rowling,** aka J. K. Rowling, was fired from some secretarial jobs because she was found writing creative stories on her computer. She used her severance to write *Harry Potter and the Sorcerer's Stone* while her daughter took naps. When she ran out of money, she received a grant to finish the book. Today, due to the popularity of Harry Potter books, movies, action figures, and more, she is a billionaire.

- President Richard Nixon fired the late **Archibald Cox** as the first Watergate prosecutor. He returned to Harvard as a distinguished law professor.

- **David Halberstam** was fired as a reporter for the *Daily Times Leader* in West Point, Mississippi. He went on to win the Pulitzer Prize.

- **Daniel Barenboim** was fired as the head of the Bastille Opera in Paris. Today he is the music director of both the

Chicago Symphony Orchestra and the German National Opera in Berlin.

- The U.S. secretary of the interior fired poet **Walt Whitman** when he found a copy of Whitman's *Leaves of Grass* by his desk. Once considered an obscenity, *Leaves of Grass* is today ranked as a masterpiece of American poetry. Wealthy Europeans who recognized his genius during his lifetime rescued Whitman from poverty.

- **Wolfgang Mozart** was fired as a court composer by Archbishop Colloredo of Salzburg. The composer moved on to Vienna, where he completed the mature masterpieces among his forty-one symphonies and twenty-seven piano concertos, along with several of the greatest operas of all time—including *Don Giovanni* and *The Magic Flute*.

- **Shirley Temple Black** was fired as a "washed-up" child star by Hollywood mogul Lew Wasserman. When she started crying, Wasserman shoved a box of Kleenex her way and said, "Here, have one on me." She went on to become the first female chief of protocol at the White House and an ambassador to first Ghana and later the Czech and Slovak Republics.

- **Jack Kemp** never would have run for Congress if the San Diego Chargers hadn't cut him. After a stellar thirteen-year professional football career, including a Most Valuable Player Award in 1965, Kemp represented the Buffalo area and western New York for eighteen years in the United States House of Representatives, then served four years as secretary of housing and urban development. He was picked by Senator Bob Dole as the Republican Party's vice presidential candidate in the 1996 presidential election.

LOU HOLTZ

Head Football Coach, University of South Carolina

*"Don't let people wallow in self-pity, but don't let them
be dishonest with themselves either."*

They say the rough is a tad longer at Estancia in Arizona these days. And look at the size of those mammoth bunkers! Bogeyed and beleaguered, it was time to divert my opponent, Lou Holtz. So I whipped out my classic razz: "If Arkansas hadn't fired you, Lou, we wouldn't be buddies today."

It's true. Coach Lou Holtz chalked up the best win-loss record in the history of University of Arkansas college football. Not just that. It was the second-best win-loss record in the history of the Southwest Conference. But you know what they say: No whopping success goes unpunished.

On a Sunday afternoon just before Christmas 1984, Lou put John Gutekunst on a plane back to Virginia Tech. "I had just hired John as defensive coordinator for Arkansas," Lou recalls. "It was about noon, and I was barely in the living room door when the phone rang. Arkansas' athletic director Frank Broyles asked me to come down to the office. When I opened the office door, Coach Broyles got right to the point. He said, 'Lou, I'm going to have to ask for your resignation.' I was stunned. Then he went on to say something about severance. He offered some amount. Maybe it was $150,000. I went home and told my wife, Beth, and she didn't believe what had happened." Neither Lou nor Beth saw this coming. Not in a million years.

How could Lou possibly get the boot? The scuttlebutt was that Arkansas had lost key players to colleges in other states. Other schools were purchasing some athletes, and Arkansas wouldn't do that. (One of many reasons why my alma mater, the University of Minnesota, would have given anything to get someone like Holtz.) But it looked like either Arkansas was being outrecruited or athletes were being bought outright. Certainly Frank Broyles had nothing to do with this recruiting mischief. During Lou Holtz's seven-year tenure under Broyles at Arkansas, his was one of the few schools that was never investigated. Could it have been a jealous and influential alum who triggered Lou's exit? I wonder to this day.

"Beth and I talked over our predicament." As Lou eyeballs his putt, he opens a chapter of the story I've never heard before. "You know what we decided, Harvey? I'd go down and beg them for a second chance. 'Whatever you have to do to keep this job,' Beth said, 'you tell them you'll do it.' Except for one remote dream, we had committed to ourselves that Arkansas would be our home for the rest of our lives. Our daughter Liz was going into her junior year of high school, and we wanted to stay put in Fayetteville. Our other three kids were in college. The NFL game broadcasts started at 12:00 noon. By 12:30, the networks broke the news that I was out at Arkansas."

Lou called Broyles. Could things be patched up? No dice ... but no reason was given either.

I was an active alum for the University of Minnesota. Our football team had weathered seventeen consecutive trouncings. We were starving for a successful and experienced coach. I had previously been authorized to offer Lou the job. Life in the Minnesota tundra? Not for Lou. Coaching in Minnesota? Not a chance. When I saw the breaking news on TV that Sunday afternoon, I spotted a silver lining in Lou's rain cloud. Within minutes of the TV announcement, I was on the horn to Coach Holtz. Would he reconsider visiting Minnesota? In the background, Beth said he certainly would. When? Now!

The airlines were all booked because of Christmas. Finally, cancellations freed up three seats. Lou, Beth, and daughter Liz got up in the middle of the night to catch the flight. Snowdrifts clogged the drive from Fayetteville to Tulsa. They finally made it. I met Lou and family at the airport garage in—what else?—a raccoon coat! And when I got to my car I had a raccoon coat for each of them, hoping they wouldn't notice the minus-25-degree windchill outside.

Recruiting Lou wasn't easy. The University of Minnesota's athletic director Paul Giel lay in intensive care, mending from triple-bypass surgery. We knew we wanted Lou. It's not that Lou played hard to get. He played straight to get. At the very outset, he told us that he would leave Minnesota if Notre Dame, and only Notre Dame—his dream of dreams—offered him the top-coaching job. I'd learned a thing or two about negotiating. We wanted Coach Holtz. In a day or so, the very best schools would realize they wanted him, too. We told him the job was his, but we had to have an answer before he left town.

Lou Holtz had just been fired. But he's a remarkable guy. Early in his career in college coaching, he had been fired before from the University of South Carolina. Less than twenty-four months later, he was part of Woody Hayes' staff at Ohio State and national champions.

"Things aren't always going to go the way you would like them to go," Lou believes, "but I think it is important to understand how important your attitude is, and don't ever lose sight of your dreams. Whenever you face adversity, you can't let it discourage you from being the very best you possibly can."

Resilient! He never let go of his conviction. He knew—once

again—he needed a new job. At the same time, he wouldn't let go of his dream: to become football coach at Notre Dame. Could he make a commitment to Minnesota and still keep his dream alive?

We had booked the Holtz family a suite of rooms at the Marriott Hotel. After we made them the Minnesota offer, Lou, Beth, and Liz talked it out. "All of us had mixed emotions," Lou remembers. "Everyone had a different point of view. We all went into different rooms and prayed on what we would do for a half hour. We came back and all of us were on the same page. We would go to Minnesota," Coach says, "but the Notre Dame clause had to be in the contract. That's when the two conditions were hammered out: Notre Dame had to approach me (I could not approach them) and Minnesota must have accepted a bowl bid."

The rest is history. Not only did Lou Holtz get the Minnesota job and get us to a bowl game, he became a miracle worker. Attendance went sky high, apathy turned into ecstatic excitement, and he completely turned around our football program, virtually overnight. He then won the Notre Dame post and became a sports legend.

But if Lou hadn't walked out of Arkansas the right way, he wouldn't have gotten the Notre Dame call. Coach handled himself brilliantly. In fact, Notre Dame called Frank Broyles as a reference when they were staffing their head coach job. "Had I been bitter, Coach Broyles could have axed the deal in a flash. Two years after firing me, Frank Broyles was my ally and encouraged Notre Dame to hire me. A few years later we were playing Southern Cal on Thanksgiving weekend. He ran me down and asked what it would take for me to come back to Arkansas. That was the first of two times he tried to hire me after I had left Arkansas. 'Coach, I was there before and you had problems with me,' I answered. 'I don't know what they were.' He only said, 'I listened to the wrong people.' I continue to have great respect for Frank Broyles . . . he and I remain good friends to this day. It wasn't the firing that kept me from going back to Arkansas. It was the commitment I had then made to Notre Dame. Working for Coach Broyles was a very positive experience. He let you run your program in the manner you wanted to run it. Our relationship remained very positive. He did what he did, I felt, because he lacked the necessary information."

"Lou, you're the coach, the teacher," I said to him over the 16th hole at Estancia. "Your players say you're the best teacher they ever had. But it sounds like you were on the learning side of this Arkansas experience."

Lou nicked back his South Carolina baseball cap and answered, "Harvey, that Sunday afternoon, I was really upset and bitter. Beth would not allow me to stay bitter. No matter how I felt inside, that bitterness never showed. To this day, I have never said a negative word about Arkansas or Coach Broyles. Getting fired was the best thing that ever happened to me. My bitterness could have created a lot of problems for me. Bitterness would have done nothing to help me."

"Coach, that's plenty of restraint," I countered. "Are things really that simple?"

"Simpler than you might think, Harvey," he said as he bent over and grabbed his tee. "When you get fired, ask yourself first: Is it justified? If it is, then be sure not to make that mistake again. If it's not, don't crawl into a shell and lose faith in what you're doing or how you're doing it. Don't be bitter about something you can't control. Leaving Arkansas turned out to be a positive thing. I had a wonderful experience at Minnesota and then came Notre Dame."

"Lou!" I yelled, exasperated after I duck-hooked my tee shot. "This sounds like a chapter of *The Waltons*. Didn't this whole deal make you tougher and less trusting, too?" I asked as we clambered back into the golf cart.

"Sure, Harvey, the Arkansas experience caused me to look at security a little bit more," Lou admits.

"So, now you don't lift a finger without involving a lawyer?"

"Nope, Harvey," he says, pinning back his glasses, "one lesson I've never learned is getting a lawyer involved. I just do a handshake. Just like you and I did, remember?" Lou is the only major coach I know in America who doesn't run with a lawyer.

We're in the clubhouse. He nicked me for a couple of bucks. What did you expect? "When you get fired, what's the most important thing friends and family can do?" I ask.

"Encouragement," Coach says over his favorite drink . . . Diet Coke. "Don't let people wallow in self-pity, but don't let them be dishonest with themselves either."

"You've had to fire people. Did the way you were axed at Arkansas affect how you fired people later?"

"When you have to terminate someone, think through, 'What's the most humane way I can do this?' Maybe they're not suited for that job. That's often the case. If so, then nudge them to a different direction."

Is firing forever?

"Not always. One of our players—Alten Maiden—was asked to leave Notre Dame. He was not exhibiting the qualities that made Notre Dame special. The school gave him the chance to sit out for a year and rethink if he really wanted to be there. You don't go to a school like Notre Dame to change it, but to become like Notre Dame. Once he thought it out, he came back, earned a 3.0 average academically, and became a good football player."

Can firings ever be averted?

"I can remember one case," Coach says. "David Knight was the player. He and I had a disagreement over him getting in the huddle properly. This wasn't the problem; this was the issue. The problem was that he didn't feel we were throwing him the ball enough. He said no one could cover him and this was true. He wanted to win and I wanted to win so we didn't have a problem, we had a disagreement. You only have a problem if both parties involved have different objectives. Because we both wanted to win, we resolved the disagreement and David Knight led us to that championship and played several years in the NFL with the New York Jets. At that time, I was a young coach at William and Mary and just learning how to be a head coach. I was fortunate that common sense prevailed as this experience turned out for his benefit, mine, and William and Mary's also."

I asked Lou if he has ever helped another coach face the situation of being fired.

"Many years ago, Jerry Burns was relieved of his coaching duties at the University of Iowa. Jerry was a good friend of mine, and I felt I needed to call him, which I did. When he picked up the phone, I said, 'Jerry, I really don't know what to say except I feel very bad about the situation, and I felt I needed to call.' He said, 'Lou, you sound like this is a wake. This is the best thing that has ever happened to me.' He explained, 'I was in a no-win situation and was too dumb to realize it. Now, this is going to force me to do some other things.' A year later he was coaching the defensive backfield for the Green Bay Packers and Vince Lombardi and won the Super Bowl. He then went with Bud Grant of the Minnesota Vikings and went to four Super Bowls while there. Afterward he became the head football coach of the Vikings and enjoyed a great deal of success.

"I've thought about this situation an awful lot. Sometimes you are in a position where you are hanging on, but you have absolutely no future. Always benefit from whatever happens to you and use that as a motivational tool to go to another level," Lou adds.

"Coach," I asked, "imagine that you are in front of a graduating group that is about to go out the door. They could be college seniors ready to hit the gridiron of life for the first time in their lives . . . or they could be a bunch of fifty-year-old managers who were just downsized out of their jobs and have to rebuild their careers from scratch. If you had just one minute before the opening gun, what would you tell them?"

"I've always felt that to be successful in any endeavor, you have to do three things. Find something you like to do. Find something you do well. And find somebody to pay you to do it. I've never had anything happen to me that didn't actually turn out to be in my best interest in the long run, provided I reacted favorably to it. Yes, it can be difficult for a period of time, but eventually you will look back on the adversity you faced and say that it made you a better person and put you in a better position to succeed and achieve happiness."

MACKAY'S MORAL:

You can't saw sawdust.
There is no bittersweet in bitterness.

FIRING IS REJECTION

When you're fired, you're rejected. It's as simple as that. You didn't get the *Good Housekeeping* seal, the Hanes underwear inspection tag, or the big one from Publishers Clearing House.

If you want to beat rejection, remember these thirteen tips:

1) **When you're rejected, don't take it personally.** *It doesn't say you're bad. It says somebody thinks you're not good enough.*

2) **Don't waste time on bitterness.** *It will hurt you more than anyone else and hold you back from moving on with your life.*

3) **Accept rejection as a fact of life, especially in highly competitive endeavors.** *Every year, 748 major league baseball pros aren't named Most Valuable Player (MVP). Twenty-nine NHL teams didn't win the Stanley Cup last year. Last year, 14,125 candidates who applied to Princeton didn't get in, and of the 1,601 who got in—425 never en-*

rolled. Most went to other schools where they thought they would get a better education. See, it works both ways!

4) **Don't let go of your dreams.** *Although Lou Holtz was flattened by disappointment in Arkansas, he made a success of his Minnesota experience, then went on to his dream job at Notre Dame.*

5) **Figure out why you were fired.** *Many—perhaps most—people who lose their jobs are mistaken about the real reason for which they lost their jobs. Some will say that they're failures, others that their boss had it in for them, and others yet that they were sure their career ended because of a stupid faux pas they made at the company picnic. Often firing is a straightforward cost-cutting measure. When you're fired, it's easy to weave fantasies and imagine villains. If you are going to spend even an hour feeling miserable, make sure that you are miserable for the right reason.*

6) **Don't burn bridges.** *Lou Holtz's ability to maintain a civil relationship with Frank Broyles enabled him to get a positive job recommendation when he needed it. And two more offers from Arkansas later on!*

7) **Don't wallow in failure, even when you're clearly responsible for it.** *The surest way to beat a setback is to get back on your horse. As Harry Truman put it: "As soon as I realize I've made one damned fool mistake, I rush out and make another one."*

8) **Visualize acceptance.** *Psychiatrist Victor Frankl was able to survive Nazi concentration camps by visualizing that he would one day give a speech describing how he survived a Nazi concentration camp. Focus on a time when you'll be*

working again in a job you love and where you feel great. Trust me, you can, and will, make this come true.

9) **Do doable things.** *One of the things that they teach soldiers who might become prisoners of war is to focus on small, doable things. Your helicopter may have been shot down, you have a broken arm, you're dining on caterpillars, and a bunch of thugs are regularly pounding the stuffing out of you at interrogations. So what do you do? Focus on washing out one of your socks! That's what one survivor in an international peacekeeping venture did. The next day, it was the other sock. The third day, it was beginning to map out an escape plan. In no time at all, it was planning where he was going to have his welcome-home party when his transport plane landed back in the States. And that's exactly what happened.*

10) **Do some work for charity.** *It's a no-brainer that charitable organizations can't demand a lot of your time when it's volunteered free of charge. What's astonishing is the number of great contacts that can be built through charitable work, and how often this network can lead to a well-paid position, as well as much-needed help for a good cause.*

11) **Look for the doors opened up by losing out.** *Is the way now clear to work for the boss you admired so much who bolted to another job? Does being fired by a large corporation open the door for being your own boss? Is your company getting out of those mini-widgets because the outfit across town has become so dominant in them?*

12) **Seek out a winners' circle of people on the outs.** *It's good to have a positive group of colleagues who are going through the same thing you are. But be careful. So-called self-help*

groups often turn out to be demoralizing self-hurt gangs. It's very easy to hang out and share suffering with people who are committed to lose. Pick people who are practical and action-oriented. People actively engaged to make things happen for themselves.

13) **Find things that motivate you.** *Some folks feel so guilty about rejection, they deny themselves the very things that will keep them motivated. It could be buying a book or a ticket to a tennis match, and it needn't be extravagant. Working out, keeping yourself fit and healthy, participating in activities that make you feel good about yourself—all are sure-fire ways to fire yourself up after being fired.*

MACKAY'S MORAL:

Finding a job is a matter of direction and selection,
not rejection and dejection.

BERNIE MARCUS

Founder of The Home Depot

"If you don't want to live a hunk of your life sitting in a stack of documents, making lawyers rich, forget about suing and get on with living your life."

Bernie Marcus knows a lot about ball-peen hammers and buzz saws. But he never ran into the business end of either until twenty-four years ago. Many Americans dread April 15. Bernie's house of horrors started on April 14, 1978. He was ushered into a room packed with lawyers and stenographers. First a flood of accusations. Then down came the broadaxe. "It was a bad scene," he recalls. "They threw me out of my office and put bars on the door. They searched my files. It was pretty terrible—one of those corporate things. You hear about them, but you don't really know what they are like until you live through one."

Bernie Marcus was forty-nine years old on that day when he was fired as CEO of the Handy Dan Home Improvement Center chain—an offshoot of the old-line hardware store. "I had never been fired in my life and had never experienced anything like this," Bernie says. "It was the low point of my life." Today, Bernie believes people should expect this kind of thing might happen to them in the bloodthirsty jungle of big business. "In the corporate world, when someone doesn't really like you, that's what happens. Sanford C. 'Sandy' Sigoloff ran our parent corporation, Daylin. Well, Sandy really didn't like me. By the way, I really didn't like him a lot either. He called himself 'Ming the Merciless.' He even had a sign put up over his door to announce it."

I asked Bernie how he ever got together with Sigoloff in the first place. It turns out Bernie didn't have any say in the matter. Daylin was in tough straits and had filed Chapter 11. Sigoloff was the turnaround artist picked by the board to pull the corporation out of the ditch. Among other gambits, he got rid of Daylin's drugstore division. When Sandy came in, he was leading Daylin through a bankruptcy. Here's the nub according to Bernie: "We were 80 percent owned by Daylin, but we at Handy Dan were not in bankruptcy. I ran my company, and I had a majority of its board. I was the only one in Daylin Sandy couldn't control."

Daylin might have been Disease City, but Bernie was committed to keep Handy Dan healthy. The chain had grown to sixty-six stores, and Bernie went after financing on his own. "A lot of vendors did not want to ship to us because Daylin was in bankruptcy," he recalls. "I had learned to deal with bankers—the people who loan you more money than anybody else. I had one banker who had invested a lot of money in Handy Dan. The guy was really good to our company. I made sure he was kept up to date on everything. Sandy and I used to have these terrible arguments. He would say you have to treat bankers like they're idiots. They don't know what they're doing." Bernie was sharp as a tenpenny nail in looking after his own business. He also built relationships that would help him mightily in his next life.

Turnaround types are known as gunslingers by executive recruiters. They come in and shave the fat off an organization. Sometimes they take some muscle along with it. Hired guns have a certain type of personality. "Sandy Sigoloff loved the fact he could fire people because he was in the bankruptcy mode," Bernie remembers. "I've never seen anybody treat people the way he did. Sooner or later, he was going to get me. He just was. And he did. He created a trumped-up deal that I was supposedly involved with, and he just fired me and created all kinds of havoc. He went to the SEC. He tried to ruin me physically, financially, and emotionally. Undercover people watched my house. It was a horror story—like something out of a James Bond novel."

Bernie learned a lot about how to size up the kind of boss you're likely to run into. He has spotted three species of corporate creatures during his spectacular business career. "Some are genuine, bright, hardworking . . . real. They make it on their own," he says admiringly. "Other top managers fake their way through with a board of directors they rope in. Sometimes you wonder how this type makes it. Then you have people like Chainsaw Al Dunlap and Sandy Sigoloff who are just vicious—presiding over people's bodies."

Just after he was terminated, Bernie met with Ken Langone, a large shareholder in Handy Dan and an investment banker. When Bernie revealed to him he had been fired, Langone told him, "My God! You've just been hit in the ass by a golden horseshoe. We should open that store you told me about three years ago." Bernie painted the big picture for him again. "Someday, somebody's going to open the store," Bernie explained, "that would put these small-scale hardware shops out of business." Langone asked him to fill in the blanks, but Bernie wouldn't share the details. He still wasn't prepared to listen to anybody at that point . . . or to trust the people he needed in a positive way. What had hit him in the ass sure didn't *feel* like a golden horseshoe.

Bernie was wounded and aching. His first and only thoughts were about getting even. "It's interesting when you have a low like this," he says philosophically today. "You reach one point where you have a chance of coming out or not coming out. If you come out, you're better than you ever were. If you don't come out, you become what they commonly refer to as a loser. *If* you come out, it's usually because of the influence some-one has on you." Bernie chose to come out by putting himself "under the influence" of a titan in modern retail history. "In my case," Bernie says proudly, "it was Sol Price who brought me around. Sol was the founder of Price Club, which has since be-come part of PriceCostco. I had known Sol for quite a number of years. He was a wonderful guy who shared his philosophies with a lot of people. Wal-Mart founder Sam Walton—to name another—was also befriended by Sol Price."

Bernie's personal turnaround got off the ground when Price called him up and invited him to dinner at his home in San Diego. Bernie went right to the point and told Price: "I've made a lot of money for everybody I worked for, but never really made any money for myself. My contract with Daylin was worth a million dollars. Sandy broke the contract. I want to get back at him. I want to prove that I'm not what he says I am. Right now, I'm suing Sandy for that million. Sandy has said: 'Sue me. And, you're not going to do it with my money. You're going to do it with *your* money.' "

To wage the suit, Bernie said, "I was eating up cash like it was going out of style. Eventually I would be broke." Everybody said he had a great case, but the truth was the money was getting him nowhere. After dinner, Sol said to Bernie, "Come with me. I want to show you something." They walked into a room with virtually no furniture in it. Instead there were papers stacked five to six feet high. Bernie was stunned when he learned, "They were all depositions from a lawsuit Sol had been involved with. He said to me, 'Here, Bernie, are three years of my life.' Mean-while, during this litigation, Sol had opened up Price Club and a son was running it. The lawsuit was consuming all of Sol's en-ergies, all of his strength. He told me, 'Bernie, I think you're a great retailer. I think you could be very successful and make a lot of money. Why are you spending your young life suing some-body? Why don't you just forget about it and go on and live your life? Otherwise, you're going to end up with a room like this.' "

Bernie headed back to Los Angeles that night. During the two-and-a-half-hour drive, he thought about Sol's advice. "By the time I got home," Bernie reflects, "I had decided he was right, and I made that turn. I just closed the book on that part of my life as much as I could. There is a certain kind of emotion that doesn't ever go out of you, and I still carry some of it today, after all these years. But the truth is, that was the turning point in my life. At that moment, I decided I *did* have the talent and the ability. I wasn't the smartest guy in the world, but I knew how to be successful and how to create things. From that point on, I began to look for opportunities in a very positive way. In L.A. the next morning after visiting Sol, I woke up. I mean really woke up! I called the attorneys, and said, 'You're off the case. End the litigation. I'm going on with my life.' "

Just where did Bernie go? To the launching pad for Home Depot. The rest is a colossal success story. For years, Home Depot has been the hottest specialty retailer—a Wall Street darling. A $60-plus-billion-dollar business today, it consistently ranks in the top echelon of the *Fortune* and *Forbes* lists. It now has around 1,700 stores. Home Depot became a public company in 1981, just over twenty years ago. In 2001, an investment guru calculated where an investor would be sitting today if he had anted up $1,000 to buy Home Depot stock in 1981. He'd be lounging on a nest egg of $1.9 million!

Did Bernie roar out of the box and do it all on his own? "One advantage I've had all of my life is that I always *knew* I wasn't the smartest guy in the world," as Bernie puts it. "That's very helpful. When you know that, then you are not ashamed or embarrassed to reach out to somebody. I have always been a totally entrepreneurial retailer and a people person. Loosey-goosey. That's the way I operate. I'm a 'people person' and a merchandiser. It wasn't till I was about thirty that I really understood a balance sheet. I needed somebody who was a strict financial type, someone who was smarter than I was who could watch the numbers and control the money. I wanted the smartest financial guy I could find. Arthur Blank, who had worked for me, was that guy. So I brought him aboard. He's the first guy I hired. I turned over the COO reins to Arthur in 1997. Surround yourself with the best possible people. That's advice I'd give anyone who has been fired."

Bernie was axed from a top spot in hardware retailing and went on to redefine that industry. But can you beat this? Hardware was not even a blip on his screen when he started out. Nor was retailing. Bernie wanted to be a doctor, but he couldn't get into medical school. Two strikes were against him—prejudice and poverty. Back then medical schools had a quota for Jews. Still, he studied pre-med for two years. Then his dean told him he *could* get into medical school. All he needed was $10,000! "Our family was poor as hell," Bernie says, still shaking his head today. "All of our relatives—aunts and uncles included, everybody: tip them upside down and we couldn't raise $10,000 together. So, I ended up going to pharmacy school so I could live at home in Newark. I never wanted to be a pharmacist."

Bernie Marcus is a soft-spoken guy with a warm smile. Underneath that exterior beats the heart of a cougar. He's a knock-your-socks-off competitor.

Where did he get the gumption to come back and stick with building the world's "Temple to Home Improvement"?

Certainly, Sol Price gave his attitude a boost, but Bernie's mother had a great influence on him, too. "My mother was one of the great optimists of all time," he reminisces. "We were very, very poor, but I didn't know that. I didn't have a clue. Even though we lived in a tenement, my life was idyllic. My mother was afflicted. I was born seventy-three years ago while she was bed-ridden. Her hands and feet were gnarled like trees. Doctors told my mother the only way she could ever walk again was to have another child. She didn't understand why. After all, she'd already had three children and her youngest child at that point—my sister—was eight years old. Then she had me. Lo and behold, my mother walked. They called me the 'miracle baby.' My mother still was gnarled, but she went on for many, many years after that. She was a great believer that everything was *beshert*—blessed by a happy fate. Even when people suffered, she would always find a bright side to things. She would rationalize events to their best possible result. I grew up believing, perhaps foolishly, that there's a bright side to everything. With that attitude, there's nothing that really couldn't be overcome. Other people will rationalize that God is punishing them. For her: it was meant to be for a reason. And the reason was always good."

I asked Bernie if there was any other person or experience that showed him the way back. He paused and then he said, "Sandy Sigoloff was a wonderful experience for me. *Not* when I was going through it, but he taught me a lot. He taught me the things you should never *ever* do. It was always my belief that you deal with people in an ethical fashion. Sandy was just the opposite of the way I have managed my own life." By the way, I forgot to ask Bernie if he ever dropped in for Handy Dan's blockbuster "Going Out of Business" sale.

MACKAY'S MORAL:

Going out to "fix" someone isn't the best way to fix yourself.

GETTING A JOB
Is A JOB

You're fired. You want to get back in the game. The most important thing to accept is this: Once you're fired, you already have a job. The job you have is tougher than the last one. It's more demanding. And it has greater potential. After all, weren't you just canned from the last job you had?

Your job now is to get a job:

- **Create a routine and stick to it.** If you have a job, then you might have the luxury of working 9:00 to 5:00. If you're getting a job, then plan on twelve to sixteen hours a day. Maybe you telephone from 9:00 to 11:00 and 2:00 to 4:00 each day. Freshen up old contacts. Create new contacts.

- **Make yourself accountable to a plan.** Plan out each week with a set of objectives. Set goals for each day. How did you do against last week's goals? If the measurement was a bust, maybe you are setting the wrong kinds of goals.

- **Expect drudgery.** Having a job is the lighthearted part of life. Getting a job is grueling work. The image of "landing" a job is nutsy. Finding a job isn't the lucky cast of a fishing rod or punching in the right lottery numbers. Most jobs are carefully assembled through painstaking and methodical effort. You get to "go to work" again through a series of carefully made contacts and impressions. American companies are spending billions just to let people go. How carefully do you think that they will invest their money to hire someone new? With more forethought than ever before!

- **Find a mentor.** Ask someone who has faith in you to serve as an advisor. Note: I said advisor, not shrink. Sol Price helped Bernie Marcus get perspective on his situation and set him on track for solving it.

- **Get online and toss that line to others.** Surf the web for industry information. Keep abreast of current events. Key business publications should lead your list of favorites and be regularly visited. Find opportunities to copy others on articles of interest from major publications. Let's say you are a salesperson who got the boot. Maybe you had a customer who is a diehard Los Angeles Clipper or Detroit Tiger fan. Maybe you stumble on some trivia you can send. Perhaps the head of your trade association is a passionate outdoor barbecuer, and you pass on the recipe for the greatest ribs in history. I used to tell people to go to the library. Now the card to the biggest, most current library in the world is sitting on your laptop.

- **Get online to prepare for every job interview.** Don't even bother to go to a job interview if you haven't (1) visited your potential employer's website beforehand, and (2) used a search engine like Google to call up as many articles and reports on your prospective employer as possible.

- **Get online to get a line on yourself.** Find out what is out there about yourself on the web. It may be more than you think, and it may not be what you want people to think of you. Socrates may have said "Know thyself." In our age, the ticket is "Search thyself." Have no doubt, prospective employers will be doing exactly that.

- **Stay in shape.** The easiest thing in the world if you're out of work is to sit in front of the tube, grazing on DVDs and carb bombs. Work out. Stay lean. Those tennis doubles may be with your next boss. And when Fortune presents its smiling face, be reasonable about how hard you try to ace the next serve.

- **Don't bed down with a single option.** So many people who have been fired pursue one single option after another. Finding a job is not "connect the dots." Why not ten options? Why not twenty? And don't make them all the same sort:
  If I stay in this industry, I could do this . . .
  If I retrain myself, I might do this . . .
  If I become self-employed, I have these chances . . .

- **Keep your "board" in touch.** Have a group of outside advisors, people who are senior (and *employed!*) who know all the details of where you are and what you are trying to achieve. Share your short-term plans and methods with them. Without making a pest of yourself, help them feel a vested interest in their investment in you.

MACKAY'S MORAL:

Having a job puts bread on the table. But compared to getting a job, having a job is a piece of cake!

BILL BELICHICK

Head Football Coach of the Super Bowl Champion
New England Patriots

*"Ownership makes their decision, whatever their
reasons are. I don't worry too much about the decisions
I can't control."*

St. Valentine's Day Massacre—1996.

Cleveland Browns owner Art Modell called up Bill Belichick, the team's coach. The day before, February 13, the team had negotiated its way out of its lease with the city for the Browns' Cleveland stadium. The next day, Bill was fired.

"Art Modell told me, 'I'm going to go in another direction,' " Bill recalled. "Harvey, I was a little disappointed. I had worked for the guy for five years and had spent a few nights on the couch. Look, I understand this business. We lost the games, and I won't say my performance was perfect. At the same time, a phone call that they would 'go in a different direction' a month and a half after the season ended . . ." A little disappointed! That call might have left Bill high and dry for work the following season. Half the coaches I know would have hurled an icy bucket of Gatorade smack at that gilded photo of the owner's puss in the team offices' lobby.

Bill first learned about the franchise's possible move in September 1995. The late Will McDonough wrote about it in the

Boston Globe. Baltimore had been aching for a football team ever since the Colts franchise was uprooted and moved to Indianapolis. For months, no one else in the press picked up on the possibility that the Browns might be pulling up stakes. "There were a couple of internal meetings when Modell and his son talked about the possibility, but we were asked to keep it quiet," says Bill. "As you know, I am originally from Annapolis, Maryland. They had made some suggestions that I would be going home. I didn't learn the decision until the Thursday before the Houston game in November 1995. It was our ninth game. The public announcement came on November 6.

"The departure announcement put team morale in the tank. Leaving Cleveland was a huge factor," said Bill with his classically objective attitude. "I can't put it into words. We were 4 and 4 when the move was announced, and 1 and 7 the rest of the way. We ended up 5 and 11. I've seen a lot of football, but this situation was unique for me. All the sponsors and people who supported the Browns, even monetarily, totally withdrew. The sponsorship signs around the stadium vanished. The town and the people of Cleveland felt like they had been abandoned. If you were part of the Browns organization, you felt more like a deserter than an outcast. We were still there . . . but we were leaving, so it was worse than if we had actually left, because we were still stationed there. Tremendous animosity developed against the team. In no way is this intended as an excuse for our record, Harvey, because we didn't play well enough, and we had to fight through it. But it was a huge obstacle to overcome with no support system in place for the organization. The ownership left town and participated in the welcoming festivities in Baltimore. The players on the team felt abandoned with a lot of questions about their futures.

"So, even though better days lie ahead after my dismissal, it wasn't one of my fondest memories."

"Do you think that the owners had a right to do that?" I asked.

"I've been in this business for a long time," replied Bill in that impressively stoical manner that makes him such a citadel in a clinch. "Owners make their decision, whatever their reasons are. As owners, it is their right and their privilege. I don't worry too much about the decisions I can't control. It was up in the air if the city of Cleveland would allow the Browns to leave or if they would be held to their stadium lease and whatever contractual arrangement they had. Could the Browns buy their way out of it? We had a couple of coaches leave the staff. Woody Widenhofer went to Vanderbilt. I couldn't hire any new coaches. We were in purgatory. I wasn't going to Baltimore. I wasn't fired. I wasn't anywhere. Had the team been forced to stay and play in Cleveland another year, I would have been kept as the coach."

His next job required a step back. First, in 1996, Belichick became assistant head coach in New England, and the Patriots went to their first Super Bowl since 1986. Then, for the following three seasons, he was assistant head coach for the New York Jets under Bill Parcells. In 2000, New England Patriots owner Robert Kraft named Bill Belichick head coach of the Patriots.

"How would you characterize your relationship with Robert Kraft in New England?" I asked Bill.

"From a coach's perspective, ownership supports you by giving you the tools you need to win," Bill answered. "Our owner shows that by his personal commitment in building a stadium or a practice facility . . . and, being able to acquire the talented players and staff to put a competitive team on the field. But Robert has gone above and beyond that. He provides support as well as genuine friendship. Robert's the owner—the boss, but also a good friend. You can't ask for any more than that. After that, it's up to me as a coach to take those resources and be productive with them. Robert Kraft has been tremendous in supporting me both personally and professionally."

Methodically, Belichick built the existing New England franchise and added other pivotal team members. The result? Super Bowl championships in both 2002 and 2004. Both games—two of the most exciting in Super Bowl history—won in the final seconds of the contest. And yet, Bill has a face of granite through every tick of the clock. His manner reminds me so much of Bud Grant when he coached the Minnesota Vikings. When I looked at Bud's face on the sidelines, I could never tell if the Vikings were up 31–0 or down 0–31. "In my job, I have to make a lot of decisions," Bill observed, "and I don't have a lot of time to make them. If I'm emotionally caught up in a game, it's hard for me to calculate the information that I need to make the decisions. I try to remain calm and be analytical and to leave the emotional aspect of the game to the participants."

Analytical as always, Bill acknowledged that his coaching style had changed over the years, especially in the transition from being coach at Cleveland to ultimately becoming the head coach at New England.

"I've been a head coach for two teams: the Browns and the Patriots," Bill reflected. "I'm a detail-oriented person. I've delegated more with the Patriots than I did with the Browns. At times, I may have been too detail-oriented in Cleveland. Perhaps I should have put my time and energy into some bigger picture things. In Cleveland, I might also have been a little too 'football-oriented.' I felt that so much of the game was determined between the lines, and a high percentage of my focus is still there. But there are a lot of things that go on outside the white lines that affect the chemistry of the team. I'm trying to be more aware of and sensitive to those."

Bill has also had to ride out some tough personnel decisions on the road to building the team. The impact of those decisions spilled over onto the playing field in bizarre ways, even in the victorious 2003–2004 season. On opening day, the omens looked anything but rosy. New England was shut out by Buffalo 31–0. Bill even admitted, "We got outcoached. We didn't do anything well." The Buffalo quarterback was Drew Bledsoe, whom the Pats had traded to Buffalo in 2002. That threw salt on the wound. A sack and five tackles were chalked up by safety

Lawyer Milloy on defense. Milloy had been cut loose by the Pats and picked up by the Bills days before the game. He barely had time to speed-read the playbook.

"Bill, Lawyer Milloy's departure demanded kid-gloves treatment, didn't it?"

"I handled it like I handle everything else," Bill answered, "honestly and directly. We had negotiated for six months to try to restructure his contract. We did it in the framework of league rules. We had to make a move. We tried to keep him. We did what we could and made our best offer. In the end, it wasn't one he would accept, and that's business. We had to move on. I told the team that. We understand what the rules are and we have to abide by them. In this case, we had to make a difficult decision which we didn't want to make." By the way, the end of the season looked nothing like the beginning. Unable to win a playoff spot for three consecutive years, the Bills fired *their* coach, Greg Williams, in January 2004.

For most managers, firing people is an occasional experience. Not so for an NFL coach. "We go to camp every year with eighty players," Bill explains. "We have to cut to fifty-three. Every year, I fire twenty-seven players. The ones who don't try hard are the easy ones. They don't play up to their capabilities. They deserve to be released. The guys who bleed for you, who do everything you ask them to do as well as they can, who play through adversity and who play hurt—those are the hard ones. Then it's a matter of competition and they lose out. They come up short or another person is just better at a specific job than they are. For some, the time has come for them to step aside and they don't get to retire on their own volition. The coach has to tell them because you represent the interests of the other fifty-three players. You owe it to the team to make the decisions that are best for the team and the team's best opportunity to win. Still, it's certainly tough to tell people that you can't keep them."

NFL coaching is the supreme balancing act. On the one hand, you have the desire to hang on to your job. On the other, you have to do what's right for the team. Which to choose? It's like the choice between security and opportunity. If you choose security—as others have said—you lose both. "You do what's right for the team," Bill firmly believes. "If the team wins, you'll hang on to your job." Doing one's best for the team demands a deep sense of unselfishness. When you listen to Bill Belichick, the interesting twist is the order of the process. He tries to demonstrate it before it's expected in return. "I try to give respect and hope it's reciprocated to the same degree that it's injected into the team," he explains. "You have to be unselfish and put the team first. I would expect the members of the team to reciprocate in that fashion. Having one common purpose can be a very powerful force."

"And when a player faces a setback, Bill? How do you handle it?"

"I try to show them that I have confidence in them. Foremost, I instruct them on how to deal with the performance problem. The motivational speeches have a place, but the first priority is to do the tangible things you need to do to fix the problem. If you couple self-motivation with the proper coaching and guidance, there's a pretty good chance they will be successful in rebounding. It's my job to provide that direction."

"A professional football coach's job is often compared with that of a manager's in business, Bill. In fact, a football coach has to act faster and in more drastic ways, doesn't he? Why exactly is that so?"

"I have never run a corporation, Harvey. In business, you can make 18 percent and I can make 17 percent and the next guy can make 16 percent—we're all pretty happy. At the end of the day in athletic competition, one team wins and the other team loses. You both can't be happy. Sunday afternoon at four o'clock, there's a dominant attitude on every team that has played its game—either a real good one or a real bad one. That's different from business. In pro-sports competition, you have to make a lot of decisions in a very short amount of time. I see the business cycle moving at a slower pace—results are measured quarterly or annually. On a football field, that forty-second clock is on. You're on a certain down, you have to call the play, and you have to make a decision. You often have just ten or sixteen seconds to decide. Once it's made, the play is called and the quarterback goes to the line. In that forty-second time frame, you may have ten seconds to calibrate it, be decisive, and go with it. I'd imagine it's a little quicker than in business."

Bill Belichick recovered so steadily from his setback in Cleveland, I'm convinced, partly because of the tremendous depth of his personal background. I can't think of another NFL coach who has lived coaching more from the cradle forward. Bill's father was a fullback for the Detroit Lions and coached at the Naval Academy for thirty-three years. "As a kid, I was very fortunate to watch my dad coach and to watch those teams practice," Bill recalls. "I didn't realize it at the time, but those teams had some great young men, among them future leaders of our country. Guys like Roger Staubach and Joe Bellino and Pat Donnelly and Tom Lynch. People who have gone on to great achievements on the field and in the military. I didn't think what I was doing was very special at the time. I was just a kid watching football practice. Collectively, these people had a tremendous influence on me in terms of work ethic, teamwork, and their unselfish drive. I've never known team effort any other way."

"And you just filed these impressions away in your brain bank, one after another—didn't you, Bill?"

"In high school, I had a good coach, but I wasn't a great player," Bill admits. "At best, I was an average player. Lacrosse was a better sport for me than football, and I would actually diagram lacrosse plays with the coach when I was at Wesleyan University in Connecticut.

"A lot of the most important lessons I learned in coaching came from watching the flow of football coaches at the Naval Academy. They changed pretty regularly. A big asset was the volume of coaches I was able to observe from age twelve to twenty-five. I saw hundreds—Naval Academy, NFL, football camps with my dad. My dad let me break down game films when I was eleven years old. My dad ran a football camp and would bring in fifteen coaches to work the camp. During the season, he would scout and I would go on scouting trips with him and sit in the press box. I met members of the media like John Steadman, Shirley Povich, and Ron Menchine, and coaches like Bobby Knight and Frank McGuire (the coach at North/South Carolina), tremendous college basketball coaches. The spectrum of people I came across was amazing. It was an incredible opportunity. It was unbelievable to be able to observe all the different levels and styles of football and football coaching. A lot of those people would get me information because they knew I was interested in it—game plans, scouting reports, articles about different techniques."

Talk about leveraging a network for information! Talk about preparation!

"Harvey, it was a coach's paradise! In the NFL, I was with five different coaches my first five years. That's not only five coaches, that's five staffs. I was influenced by a lot of different people. The biggest value was seeing a wide range of coaching styles. Because I saw so many successful styles, I became confident that there wasn't just *one* style. I didn't try to be Vince Lombardi or Tom Landry. I tried to be Bill Belichick."

"Bill, you have three pieces of advice for people. I've never heard a better list. They have all the zing of a two-minute drill to march you over the goal line. Coach, let's have 'em."

"Harvey, we all make a lot of mistakes as we go through life. (1) Don't make the big ones. Take care of yourself and your own personal health. It can all end in a second with one stupid decision, and we've seen that happen too many times. (2) It's not what you know, it's whom you know. You build your relationships from your childhood through your adolescent years. *You* control your relationships, whom you maintain friendships with and maintain contact with. You can know sixteenth-century British history forward and backward. That's great. But you need more. To me that more is the network of relationships that centers around you, your friends, and your associates. Each one of us controls that. Some of your best friends are from high school, others are from college, still others are from your formative years after college. Those people form a framework through which you can build yourself both personally and professionally. By the way, you are never exposed to more people than you are in college. The greatest opportunity to know different types of people occurs at that age in the college environment. (3) It's the self-starter in each of us that's really important. I don't think you can count on somebody else to motivate you to do something. You have to want to do it personally, and you have to provide that energy. It's unrealistic and unfair to expect someone else to push you in a positive direction. So you better pick out something you really like to do, because you will have to be your own driving force."

We're all able to learn from a driving force like Bill Belichick. . . .

- If you choose the high-wire life of professional sports, file your vanity in your dresser drawer. When crunch time comes, you can bet your assets that you're nothing but a property. The only difference between you and a seat in the stadium is that you aren't bolted down.

- When you're talking career, how you manage things outside of the white lines has equal value to what you do on the playing field. Out of bounds is in bounds in the world of influence and opinion.

- The speed with which a manager must make decisions is driven by only one thing: the speed of the game being played.

- The best way to get respect from others is to start off by giving it.

> ### MACKAY'S MORAL:
>
> Observation is everything. Learning to be a great coach is the most demanding spectator sport in the world.

BOUNDING BACK
IN BOUNDS

- In 1989, his third season in the NFL, **Cris Carter** was third in the NFL with eleven touchdown receptions for the Philadelphia Eagles. Less than a year later, the Eagles placed Carter on waivers. When the Minnesota Vikings claimed him for the $100 waiver price, the twenty-five-year-old Carter arrived in Minnesota a troubled player with a self-admitted drug problem. In Minnesota he embarked on a potential Hall of Fame career. When he retired in 2002, he was the second leading receiver in the history of the NFL.

- As a college quarterback, **Jake Delhomme** was so unknown that he was not invited to the NFL Scouting Combine in 1997. That snub began a six-year odyssey in which he was cut three times, served two stints in NFL Europe, and spent most of two years on the practice squad. The low point may have come in 1998, when he was just a backup in NFL Europe. In 2003, Delhomme quarterbacked the Carolina Panthers to the Super Bowl.

- After five lackluster seasons—including a 3–6 mark in the strike-shortened 1982 season—the Kansas City Chiefs dismissed **Marv Levy.** After a two-season hiatus from coaching and one year of coaching in the short-lived USFL, Levy became the coach of the Buffalo Bills in 1986. In 1988, his second full season with the team, Levy and the Bills earned the first of six AFC Eastern Division championships. Levy, who has a master's degree in English from Harvard, led the Bills to four consecutive Super Bowl appearances. Levy was enshrined in the Pro Football Hall of Fame in 2001.

- Fired as coach by both the New York Jets and New England Patriots of the NFL and out of the college game for seventeen years, **Pete Carroll** wasn't the University of Southern California's first choice in 2000. (He had turned down USC in 1997, and some alumni objected to his hiring in 2000.) In the 2003 season, Carroll rewarded athletic director Mike Garrett by leading the Trojans to a 12–1 record and a share of the national title.

- Even the sixth winningest coach (with 201 regular-season and post-season victories) in NFL history was fired three times. Just three years after coaching the Denver Broncos to the third of three consecutive Super Bowls, **Dan Reeves** was fired. Four years later, Reeves was fired by the New York Giants after back-to-back losing seasons. Just two years after being fired by the Giants, Reeves coached the Atlanta Falcons to the Super Bowl. Reeves was fired by Atlanta late in the 2003 season.

- **Nick Lowery** was cut eleven times by eight NFL teams before making it with the Kansas City Chiefs in 1980. Even then, he jokes, "I had to beat out the greatest kicker (Jan Stenerud) in history to make it."

- **George Seifert's** first major head coaching position was with Cornell of the Ivy League. Cornell went 1–8 in Seifert's first season and then went 2–7 in his second season. Seifert was fired with two games remaining in the 1976 season. It would be twelve years before Seifert would get another head-coaching position. In 1989, his first season as the San Francisco 49ers' head coach, he directed the team to a victory in the Super Bowl. Over the next seven years, he coached the 49ers to the NFC championship game four more times and a victory in the Super Bowl following the 1994 season.

- Just four games into his second season as the coach of the Los Angeles Raiders, **Mike Shanahan** was fired. It would be six years before Shanahan would get another head-coaching position in the NFL. In 1995, Shanahan took over the Denver Broncos. In his third season as the Broncos' head coach, he directed the team to the first of back-to-back Super Bowl victories.

- A ninth-round draft choice of the Pittsburgh Steelers in 1955, **Johnny Unitas** was cut before he even threw one pass in a game. Still determined, he played semi-pro football for $6 a game. After the season, Baltimore Colts coach Weeb Ewbank learned of this "outstanding prospect" on the Pittsburgh sandlots. Ewbank signed Unitas for $17,000 on a make-the-team basis. Expected to be strictly a backup, Unitas got his chance in the fourth game when the Colts' starter was injured. His first pass was intercepted for a touchdown but from that moment on, he never looked back. He would eventually throw a touch-down pass in an NFL-record forty-seven consecutive games. He was named the league's player of the year three times and was named to ten pro bowls. The late Johnny Unitas was elected to the Pro Football Hall of Fame in 1979.

- **Kurt Warner's** pro-football career got off to a bumpy start. Warner was a starter just one year in college (his senior season at Northern Iowa) before being drafted by the Green Bay Packers. Warner was cut by the Packers in training camp. He then went back and worked for mini-mum wage as a stocker in a grocery store in Cedar Falls, Iowa. Warner hooked on as the quarterback for the Iowa Barnstormers in the Arena Football League. This earned him a tryout with the Amsterdam Admirals of the NFL European summer league. From there he played his way onto the St. Louis Rams, and, after a year as a backup when he played only eleven snaps, he became the starter after the first-string quarterback was injured. Warner went on to win two NFL MVP awards and led the Rams to two Super Bowls.

HUNTING HEADS IS SERIOUS BUSINESS

"People who really understand intense competition don't always win everything that they touch."

Tierney Remick is global managing director for the consumer/retail market with Korn/Ferry International. Korn/Ferry stands at the forefront of recruiting. And Tierney hunts the top brass among executive heads. Her specialty is what's known as the C-suite level. Chief executive officers, chief operating officers, and chief financial officers. In case you missed it, the operative word here is chief.

If you think chief is a great thing, well, think again. Sixty percent of all CEOs end up getting fired! A consulting firm study found that the number of CEOs fired in 2002 was 70 percent greater than in 2001. The top is a risky place to be. . . .

"How does a fired CEO get back in the game?" I asked Tierney. "What traits must top executives have, if they are to rebound from being fired?"

"Harvey," she said, "the first thing one looks at is, has the executive learned from the experience. Have they grown personally as a result of being fired?"

"That's interesting," I said. "Firing is a *learning* experience?"

"It all starts with figuring out what didn't work, what went wrong," she continued. "Did the executive suffer from a leadership flaw? Was it an inability to understand what was going on around him or her? Did the executive have blind arrogance regarding a particular project? Does the executive understand and have a handle on the negatives? What is the individual doing to actively transform their leadership strategy? At the end of the day what didn't work and why, and how is the executive accountable?"

"That kind of makes the individual take the blame for the situation, doesn't it?" I asked.

"You've hit on a problem that arises more often than not, Harvey . . . making executives fail to look inward. The tendency is to blame others. It's human nature to make mistakes. At the CEO level, however, the mistakes happen to be a lot more visible, and have the potential for more serious consequences."

"I don't quite understand yet. Whose fault should it be, Tierney?"

"It isn't a matter of fault. The best positioning for an executive who's facing a job change is: 'I was hired to do X. My strategy to do X was as follows. At the end of the day, this strategy either didn't work or wasn't going to. I understand the reasons why. Or, we agreed to disagree. That company and I were moving in different directions. Here's what I learned.' This position is honest, and it also lets the individual rise above the situation."

"Sounds pretty humble, doesn't it?"

"We all make mistakes, Harvey. We all acknowledge that some managerial opportunities don't always go as well as we would have hoped. People are often a bit shell-shocked when something like this happens. Being excessively humble would be out of character. People don't arrive in the C-suite by being humble. People who get to this leadership level are confident.

But if they're successful, it's a confidence of knowing exactly what they are really good at."

"So, which kinds of executives have the right balance of confidence and realism?"

"That all hinges on the Empathy Factor."

"The what?" I asked as my eyebrows went up.

"How high is the manager's Empathy Factor . . . or do they even have one? These are all high-performing executives. Some of these people don't hit a wall and fail until very late in their careers. Then, wham! People like this have a much harder time rebounding than those who have grown up in sports or other competitive situations. People who really understand intense competition don't always win everything that they touch. They learn that young. They know what it's like to lose. They accept it. They have a high level of empathy for themselves and others as well. It's a built-in mechanism allowing them to pick up and keep moving forward. They can draw the positives out of a negative situation."

"You hear a lot of executives say, 'I never saw it coming.' " I asked Tierney next, "They never heard that cruise missile with their name on the nose cone whistling toward the back of their head. Is 'I didn't see it coming' for real?"

"Not very often. Consciously or subconsciously, most people at the C-level are not totally surprised when they are fired. Usually, there has been some dialogue that their performance is not what it used to be, that something's not working out as anticipated."

"So, you're saying, listen to your boss's or your board's words very carefully."

"Not just words. Absorb all the communications signals. A CEO is routinely asked questions by the board of directors at meetings. A CEO should listen to the *ways* those questions are asked. Were they once casual and familiar? Are the same questions now put in a more distant and guarded way? Then there's body language. . . ."

"A top executive should pay attention to body language?" I asked.

"Body language is a huge indicator. Firing someone is not an easy thing to do. If an individual knows they are about to fire someone, they tend to carry themselves and act toward that person in a different way. Words, gestures, carriage—they all change. . . . And, then there is the frequency of contact. Communication either increases at a rapid pace and there's micromanagement. The boss is suddenly on top of an executive. . . . Or, the exact opposite. There's no communication and that silence is unusual."

"In short, the chill is on."

"Harvey, it's a very difficult task to tell an individual they aren't performing and that they need to move on. It's human nature to create cues and send signals. These lay the groundwork for the communication that's going to take place."

"What else?"

"Certain responsibilities may be eliminated or a role is narrowed in scope."

"Tierney, how about promoting an heir apparent who will squeeze the unlucky person out from below?"

"That's another way to communicate."

"Do some executives have an inner drive to self-destruct? They might deny it, but do they actually try to get themselves fired?"

"That happens, too. In some cases, their worsening performance creates the opportunity to leave. In a high-threat environment—let's say a very troubled business or a highly competitive category—the executive is so burned out that they just want out."

"So, are they angry when the axe falls?"

"Harvey, you'd be surprised. Time and again it happens. They are *relieved*. For a number of executives, once it's decided they have to leave, they are actually relieved when it happens. They anticipated something had changed. They were uneasy. Getting fired at least answers the question: What's different? Their subconscious has been telling them, the ground is shifting."

"That's a different picture of top executives than most people have," I contended. "After all, these are the leaders. These are the guys who guide the team out of the jungle. You mean these leaders are just like everybody else? They can't tolerate ambiguity either?"

"It's not the same thing. Strategically they can be pathfinders and visionaries. Remember, these are high performers. High performers need that feedback loop as much if not more than most people. They are constantly asking: How am I doing? How am I doing? How am I doing?"

"Wow, Tierney," I wondered aloud, "there are so many complications. How does anybody get fired at all?"

"There's one interesting dynamic in corporate America that has made firing top executives a little less personal, Harvey. The mobility of executives throughout their careers has definitely increased. Executives don't believe they will be in a particular industry or company their entire career. In fact, many executives will work for five or so companies during a thirty-year career. Given that, if you haven't worked alongside the same people for twenty or thirty years, it makes for a different corporate experience. The act of firing people becomes more of a business strategy and a little less personal. It doesn't mean the executives don't care about the firing, but the relationships are different."

"So, if these old loyalties to the firm and inside the firm are dying out, what's an executive to do?" I asked.

"Network." The tone of Tierney's voice brightened. "Networking gives the person a strong personal advantage to build a new world. That's what you've been telling people in all your books and columns."

"Who will you call at 3:00 a.m. when you need a hard favor

like a lead to a job?" I asked, beaming as only a networking junkie could.

"That's very true, but that's just half of it. I've seen a number of dynamic, strong executives who need their network for more than favors. It goes beyond setting up contacts. They need emotional support."

"You mean fired CEOs should have a *support group*?" I asked with some amazement.

"The contact favors and the professional side are only part of it. You need to have people around you who know you, support you, respect you, and will be honest with you. When you go through this kind of rejection, your confidence is hurt. You begin to question some of your skills and abilities. You need supporters to 'put their arms around you' and reassure you that 'Everything will be okay. This will turn out just fine.' They can help orient you as to where you should point yourself next. In what kind of industry, environment, or culture will I be more successful?"

"Then—for lots of reasons—a CEO or any top executive better build that network before they need it?"

"Being a CEO is a very lonely job. CEOs need to have an advisory group. These are peers from their own network. They can actually ask these executives frank questions and get honest answers. There is a developing trend for CEOs to reach out to other active CEOs or retired CEOs as part of their own personal network. They need contact with other executives who aren't necessarily looking for someone to do something for them. A good network is diverse, supportive, and also challenging. The result: Some sort of personal as well as professional relationship develops."

"Okay, Tierney, tell me this: What types of people should be in a person's network?"

"A strong network should probably include executive recruiters," Tierney answered. "For one thing, they can serve as spokespersons for that executive within their respective industry—especially if they have a strong relationship with the executive over a period of years. I suggest keeping those relationships going even when you don't need them. When people are out of a job, they suddenly realize that they don't have the very base of contacts they need the most. Executive recruiters can help put something like a firing into context, so it isn't seen as an isolated event. Recruiters are also important because they understand trends. They have a broader eye for what's happening in an industry, and how skill requirements may change."

"This *is* interesting. The executive inside the company is too busy tending to the knitting. He or she doesn't pay enough attention to what it takes to do the job. Can you give me a for instance?" I asked, my curiosity piqued.

"I met with the CEO of a multibillion-dollar consumer durables company last week," Tierney recalled. "He had been aggressively promoted throughout his career in major Fortune 500 firms. He had been promoted to CEO of this particular company two years ago. Clearly, it was a stretch, but the board was very confident he could grow into the job. This company relied on certain raw materials. In the ensuing two years, the commodity prices went through the roof. This strangled their ability to make money. The business now had to divest certain assets. The CEO had been fired about a month ago. Upon reflection, he understood the learning experience. It was the first major failure in his career. He explained the situation very openly: 'My skills are in marketing and sales and growing revenues. The business needed an executive with mergers-and-acquisitions experience. I am not skilled in this area. In order for the company to achieve its goals, they really did need a different leader. I didn't like it, but I understood it.' I was impressed. He was asking the right question as he anticipated his next move."

"Tierney, let's say I'm a freshly fired CEO. I'm going to meet the chairman of another company for my first interview. I think

I've recovered from the wounds of being fired, but I've not really explained my situation to anyone yet. What are the mistakes I'm most likely to make? How do I guard against them?"

"We already talked about being honest and about not blaming others. Have a credible explanation of what went wrong. Don't belabor this, but you need to acknowledge it. Next come the lessons you learned and how you are putting them to work to move forward. But STOP before you have that interview. Why haven't you tried your presentation out first?"

"You mean road test it?"

"Absolutely. Before they go out on interviews, it's important for fired execs to have conversations with people whom they trust. Ask yourself very hard questions about what you really want to do. Some executives who set their sights on being CEO are really not suited for the job. There is a difference between skills that are most important to run a company and the skills that a particular executive most enjoys using. Some chief executive officers would be better as chief operating officers. In a typical U.S. company, 90 percent of a CEO's time is spent managing relationships with the board of directors and communicating with Wall Street. These skills aren't necessarily the ones that *get* a CEO to that level. Nor are these tasks that appeal to many executives."

"So being the king or queen of the hill isn't for everybody. What happens to the guys who get knocked off the hill and are tumbling down to the ground?" I wondered. "I read in the papers about some of the severance arrangements that these fired C-suite people get. The deals are pretty lush. What do most executives do when somebody pulls the cord on their golden parachute? They could float away to the 16th hole of Pebble Beach and have enough dough to putt out the rest of their lives."

"There are different groups, Harvey. Some are determined to make an imprint on a business. They want to get right back into the game, either as a CEO or some other job for which they might be better suited. For them, the money may be important but not the most important factor. Others are not driven by money at all but by competitiveness. Still others have internal motivations that have nothing at all to do with the world of business."

"Such as?"

"One CEO for a major Fortune 500 consumer products firm left the business world altogether and became a published novelist. Another established a small business, and that company is now thriving. The third left a major ad agency and went into acting. He is now teaching drama at the college level."

"It takes all kinds."

"Harvey, if I've learned anything, it's that there *are* all kinds of CEOs. And the situation each of them faces is just as different. What's the same is the competitive numbers that Wall Street expects them to produce."

Wow, my conversation with Tierney Remick taught me more about how the top execs handle abrupt career changes than most CEOs could have told me! It's a lot more complicated than even most of us imagine.

- **Keep your antennae up.** The words may sound the same, but danger signals may be flashing at you in a thousand different ways. Don't be paranoid. Be perceptive.

- **When you make a mistake, acknowledge it and move on.** Dump the blame game. Explain to people the lessons you learned. Firing is a failure only if you fail to learn from it.

- **Use your network to boost your spirits.** But don't expect your allies to be phony. Encourage frank and honest input that can really help you map out an effective fresh course.

- **Before you discuss your career setbacks with prospective employers, present those explanations to trusted friends.**

Get a critique before you present your case to managers who will decide on the next steps of your future career.

- **Do what you enjoy doing, and you will do it well.** The name of the game isn't getting a job, it's getting a life.

MACKAY'S MORAL:

Life isn't always sweet in the C-suite. Be prepared for a bumpy ride when you travel at high altitudes.

BERNADINE HEALY, M.D.

**U.S. News & World Report Columnist and
Former President of the American Red Cross**

"Be careful in a crisis: You just might survive."

In May 2001, Dr. Bernadine Healy—the president of the American Red Cross—appeared before the U.S. Senate Appropriations Committee. Her topic was planning for "Disasters of the Future." Bernie outlined doomsday scenarios and how the Red Cross was planning for unthinkable devastation. It has a congressional charter requiring it to respond on multiple fronts in times of federally declared national emergencies. How would volunteers be transported? How would we have enough blood for mass emergency use? And how would blood supplies be moved safely and quickly to areas that needed them? Would we be prepared for hospital overflow and making triage decisions? Did the United States have the volunteer resources to help break down and distribute the pharmaceutical stockpiles? Did we have the nurse and doctor volunteer base, pharmacists, IT people—all the players who would be essential in a national emergency?

Four months later, 9/11 struck.

"Maybe you wanted more of Mary Poppins and less of a Jack

Welch," Dr. Bernadine Healy wrote in her letter of resignation to the board of the American Red Cross. Bernie headed the Red Cross from September 1999 through year-end 2001. Her departure from the Red Cross was announced on October 26, 2001, a month and a half after 9/11.

Bernadine Healy ruffled feathers, and she did it with unflappable class. She was the organization's first physician-CEO. Dr. Healy is a cardiologist who knew she wanted to be a doctor from the age of twelve forward. She graduated from Vassar summa cum laude and was one of only ten women in her class at the Harvard Medical School. She was a full professor at Johns Hopkins, headed the Research Institute of the Cleveland Clinic Foundation, and was also dean of the Ohio State University College of Medicine and Public Health.

In addition to her remarkable academic, administrative, and research work, she has actively treated patients throughout her career. She even headed the coronary care unit at Johns Hopkins for eight years.

During all my conversations with her, guess what Bernie *didn't* tell me? She had survived a brain tumor diagnosed in early 1999, one that initially came with a dismal prognosis measured in months. And in her remarkable recovery, she took on the task of leading the $3 billion American Red Cross.

In a *New York Times* analysis published in December 2001, Deborah Sontag compared Bernie's departure with that of her predecessor Elizabeth Dole. In the words of Red Cross chairman David T. McLaughlin, "both women were fighting a culture, a culture that had grown up over a long period of time."

In the wake of 9/11, an unexpected challenge arose. An outpouring of overwhelming generosity across the country brought in record donations to the Red Cross: record numbers of blood donations and people stepping up to volunteer, and over $500 million in six weeks. Bernie immediately had these dollars segregated into a separate Liberty Fund to assure that they would not be comingled with the National Disaster Fund.

This was a shrinking fund readily accessed by chapters for all sorts of purposes.

The imperative to move on all fronts seemed so obvious to her from the first breaking news on the morning of 9/11. "I was standing in the office of my executive vice president Kate Berry as we, along with much of America, watched the second plane hit the World Trade Center before our eyes," says Bernie. "Kate was on the phone with the head of our Blood Division, Jackie Frederick, in Virginia about mobilizing supplies for what might be tens of thousands of casualties. Suddenly, Jackie began to scream into the phone: Through her office window she saw a jumbo jet crash right into the Pentagon; Harvey, that day felt more like Pearl Harbor than it did the hurricanes or house fires that were our daily bread."

Attending to the victims of the terrorist attack was the first priority. The Red Cross was in full swing in New York working along side other rescue workers. They had been at the World Trade Center bombing in 1993, but 9/11 was incalculably worse. The magnitude of the task hit Bernie even harder when she went out to the Pentagon late in the evening of 9/11 to see how their relief work was proceeding. She told me the Pentagon, this great symbol of national defense, looked more like a battlefield.

"It was surreal. Brigades of mostly civilian firefighters looked so tiny silhouetted against the night sky as they swarmed that ghastly smoking cavern that engulfed the upper floors of one Pentagon wing. The plane was an unrecognizable mass of molten steel, killing most hope for survivors. But things got very real when a sweaty, exhausted firefighter covered in soot came up to my daughter, Bartlett, a volunteer who accompanied me that evening, and asked, 'Ma'am, you don't happen to have an aspirin in your purse, do you?' No, she didn't, nor did any of us standing there. And looking around neither did we have a cot for him or a pillow to rest his aching head, or Red Cross volunteers to serve him or others struggling so mightily in that rescue effort. Harvey, his plea spoke volumes to the preparedness task we had ahead."

A different kind of battle was brewing, mostly outside of Bernie's view, over the Liberty Fund. A few board members, chapter heads, and old-time disaster workers started behind-the-scenes grumbling over the broader fund-raising goals for 9/11. Some resisted the family-grant program and deeply resented that the Liberty Fund could not be tapped by chapters for unrelated activities and routine small disaster work once the dust settled at 9/11 sites. This was the policy in the past. The more the money came in, the more temperatures rose. "Whenever you face a crisis as entirely new and potentially transforming as 9/11, there is plenty of tension and strain. When money is involved, it gets worse. Yes, Harvey, this was a combustible time, for America, and for the American Red Cross," she says.

The London *Sunday Telegraph* says Bernie was "forced out of office by a behind-closed-doors vote by the governors." She told me there was no question this was true. "Several who were there told me it was a 'lynching,' a 'railroading,' and very ugly." Former secretary of state Larry Eagleburger resigned his volunteer position as ambassador-at-large with the Red Cross in protest, and many dedicated Red Crossers who had been on her team were forced out. Bernie's advocacy of the Israeli Mogen David Adom was another contentious issue behind her dismissal.

If she has any regret it is that the board, many of whom had just been elected, were convinced by a few not to meet with her directly either before or after the vote. She believes to this day that most of this large, rather unwieldy board were well-meaning people, but they simply did not have the full picture. "I did the best I knew how and what I believed to be right for an organization I came to love. It was heartbreaking, but I was then, and still am, proud to have served during that time. As are most of my colleagues who served along with me," she says.

What else is Bernie particularly proud of accomplishing during her stint as head of what is arguably America's most prestigious humanitarian organization? "With the heart and the mind of a doctor I was drawn to the Red Cross because of its powerful mission on behalf of the nation: to prevent and relieve human suffering."

As part of an effort to focus the organization on the magnitude of its work, Bernie and her management team worked on changing the motto—the catchy version of the mission statement—of the Red Cross. She did not favor the old motto, "We'll be there." "Well, to my mind, you could be there as a voyeur, an arsonist, or an accidental bystander with your hands in your pockets," Bernie contends. After a lot of analysis and some creative staff work, the motto became: "Together we can save a life," which it is today. "That places the medical mission in the center of a circle which encompasses the Red Cross volunteers, its employees, donors, and those vulnerable souls who suddenly and typically through no fault of their own are in desperate need of help." This statement also is sobering. "If you understand that you just might be saving a life by providing safe blood, giving disaster help, or teaching health and safety—you are forced to confront the magnitude of your task. Continuous improvement, diligence, and accountability are simply the natural thing to do. That's how I led the Red Cross."

Bernadine Healy lost another high-visibility national service job once before, but that time it was due to an orderly and aboveboard partisan change. She was appointed as the first woman director of the National Institutes of Health (NIH) during the George H. W. Bush administration in 1991. Bernie is a lifelong Republican, and President Clinton replaced her in 1993. Since the directorship is a presidential appointment, Bernie describes that departure as inevitable. She regards the NIH as a great American treasure. It has driven medical research in this country and the world for over half a century. "Recognizing the limited term of service, and with my long involvement with NIH as a medical researcher and advisory council member, I went to NIH with a keen sense of what I was there to do—and could do." One opportunity was moving along the agenda for women's health research, something sorely needed. Among other efforts, she began the Women's Health Initiative (WHI), the largest clinical trial ever undertaken by the NIH.

Bernie also faced some controversy at NIH by standing up for leading scientists like the Nobel laureate David Baltimore and the codiscoverer of the AIDS virus, Robert Gallo, who she contends were falsely accused and later cleared of scientific wrongdoing; for advocating gene patenting on behalf of tax-payers; and on fetal tissue research. Interestingly, on the latter, she advocated continuing the research, while the Republican position was opposed to it. She was committed to reforming NIH's thinking about its budget and its future, instituting the first-ever strategic plan. And she established a Human Genome Program on the NIH campus and moved a few mountains to bring in a cutting-edge scientist, Francis Collins, to become the Human Genome Center's first full-time head.

I asked her why she launched such ambitious campaigns. "There was a sense that NIH didn't need strategic thinking from its leaders, and that all scientific direction should bubble up from the individual scientists it supported," she replies. "Though I was one of those individual scientists, I also believe that when you're managing billions of taxpayers' dollars, you have to have strong and accountable leaders at the helm. The two are not mutually exclusive." Her view is that NIH is there to do good science on behalf of human health—not just to do good science. "I reminded my colleagues often that the National Science Foundation, which funds equally good research in physics, chemistry, biology, and the social sciences, has a budget less than a third of NIH. It's not the science that makes the difference; it's the human health imperative in the mission that does." Strategic plans are now required for NIH by the Congress.

Since she is a cardiologist, I asked Bernie to compare her departures from the American Red Cross and NIH to the sudden, painful experience of a heart attack. "It's similar, Harvey, in that we are really all the same in a hospital gown, so to speak. Fundamentally, we all have the same range of emotions in what seems to be a personal crisis. You feel sad, you stew for a while, wonder if you will ever recover, and then you move on and you do." She quickly adds with a proverbial wink, "Be careful in a crisis; you just might survive.

"But these life events are also quite different from a heart attack. Losing a job you love brings no permanent damage—if you left for good reason. It's not life-threatening. What we are talking about here is a momentary, painful part of life to which we are all vulnerable." As she sees it, being singed is the risk of taking on new challenges and sometimes going where no one else has. She reminds me that Margaret Mead called her autobiography *Blackberry Winter* for that very reason. Unless blackberries endure a winter frost, they aren't a very good crop. "You may have to stick your neck out, and sometimes get frosted. Some people may misinterpret your reasons for doing things; sometimes you may be wrong; sometimes you may be fighting wrong. It's tough in the arena. But if you have faith in your own judgment and the cause is important, and if you have done your homework and sought wise counsel, and if you are driven by the right reasons, you then must have the courage to take the personal risk of standing up and being counted." She adds: "Life isn't a straight-upward trajectory, but I think you will win more than you will lose if you stand for something." Bernie thinks we do a disservice to those who follow us to pretend that our successes have been so easy. A determined but open mind, a strong heart, lots of hard work, a ferociously supportive family, and the good taste to develop a talented team and trusted friends— that's what gets you through the rough spots, but more importantly, brings you some enduring wins.

Bernie developed resilience to what life can dish out very

early in her career. She was a scholarship kid from Queens, the first in her family to get a college degree. And she has made her way in a very male world. "I've handled sexism by never viewing myself as its target, never seeing myself as its victim," Bernie believes. "I was a rare breed as a woman in medical school in the sixties, Harvey. Some male classmates and even a few condescending professors saw us as creatures taking space from men who really *would* do something with their medical career. I usually laughed it off with a quiet thought, 'Eat your heart out, buddy; I'm here.'" In lectures she often saw unnecessarily pornographic pictures and other stuff that would induce heart failure in women today. At the time she didn't particularly focus on that as a problem. She saw herself as an interloper in a very exclusive male club, and was wide-eyed and often amused by her discoveries. "Is this the way guys really behave?" Occasionally she got herself into trouble by taking the boys on for some of their more outlandish anti-female behavior, "but somehow we all survived with goodwill and good humor in the end. Bottom line, don't get fixed on things you can do nothing about. Otherwise they will slow you down."

Slowed down is not the way Bernie has ever run her life. Did I mention she was a CBS medical correspondent for six years? That she wrote a book for the public on women's health and that she is writing another on Red Cross founder Clara Barton? That she was volunteer president of the American Heart Association between 1988 and 1989 and did much to expand awareness that heart disease actually kills more women than men? That she has been a science advisor to three White Houses? Heads a Medicaid Commission for the state of Ohio? And, that she is now a senior writer for *U.S. News & World Report* and does a regular medical column that is as stunning for its wordsmanship as it is provocative for its content?

Bernie's career may cause you to ask some provocative questions of your own.

- If you are considering a career in public service, are you willing to take the tough stances that will truly make a difference? Are you prepared to lose your job rather than compromise on fundamental values?

- Have you developed enough different skills so that you can always have a backup career to turn to at a time of crisis?

- Do you worry about the things you can do something about and try your best to laugh at what you can't change?

MACKAY'S MORAL:

Nobody pumps on more cylinders than
a cardiologist with heart.

Statistics Don't Lie . . . Yours Don't at Least

Mae West immortalized herself with the words: "Too much of a good thing can be wonderful!" Remarkable how a passion for excellence can quickly turn into a passion for excess. In our heart of hearts, we know moderation is the road to happiness. But we still believe excess is the highway to *happier-ness*. The truth is, more isn't necessarily better. Nor does more of a good thing necessarily mean some other bad thing will go away.

We have a similar obsession about jobs and the economy. "Create more jobs, and happy times are here again." The fact is, creating new jobs and firings are as different as cheese and chalk. It's great when the economy creates new jobs, but that doesn't mean that there will be fewer firings. There may in fact be more. The issue is change. And change will continue to speed up. Not slow down. Change is what churns people through jobs. Change—unavoidable as it is—dislocates careers.

In the spring of 2004, I approached the prestigious recruiting firm Korn/Ferry. I asked them if they would be willing to conduct a survey of people who visited their website—managers like you. Korn/Ferry responded by conducting a global survey of executives registered with the firm's online Executive Center, www.ekornferry.com. Respondents from sixty countries, representing a wide spectrum of industries and functional areas, participated in the survey. Over a period of five weeks, Korn/Ferry canvassed between 2,200 and 3,000 managers with a series of questions about how people like you felt about job security.

Here's what we learned:

- When asked "Do you expect to remain with your current employer through the entirety of your career?": A resounding 95 percent said no!

- When asked "How concerned do you think most employees are that they will lose their job unexpectedly?": 68 percent were either concerned or very concerned. An additional 27 percent were somewhat concerned.

- When asked "With regard to your career, are you satisfied with the degree of control you have over your future?": Only 38 percent were satisfied or very satisfied . . . and 29 percent were not satisfied at all.

- When asked "Do you think that companies do a sufficient job of sharing candid job performance review information with employees?": 82 percent simply said no.

Conclusions? There are a lot of funny numbers out there. But your statistics don't lie. People are no longer sticking around for the gold watch . . . as if they expected anybody to give them one. Most people are frightened they will lose their job out of the blue and aren't satisfied that they have control over their careers. And most don't feel that companies are giving them the straight scoop about personal performance. Feeling enrolled on the Victim's Waiting List? Ladies and gents, this is a call to arms. The weapons of choice are information and preparation.

Back in 1992, management guru Peter Drucker made a fascinating observation: in 1913, domestic servants "were the largest single employee group in any developed country. Thirty percent of all wage earners were domestic servants. They are all gone." After the recessions of the 1960s and 1970s, how would we know when gravy times were rolling again? My colleagues said to watch the number of secretaries big companies would be rehiring or adding on. That would be the clue. What happened? The secretary—especially the take-a-memo-get-me-a-cup-of-java sort—has all but vanished. Today everyone is on their own, tickling their laptop and making mocha treks down to Starbucks. Computer programmers were the next big group to vanish. If not altogether, then at least to Bombay and Shanghai. Jobs evaporate overnight, whether it's boom time or bust.

MACKAY'S MORAL:

Be prepared—you never know if you're the next to go.

JESSE VENTURA

Former Governor of Minnesota

*"You can't exceed the dream, unless you have
one in the first place."*

I sat with Jesse Ventura in the governor's office in the Minnesota State Capitol in St. Paul after a round of golf. He was enlightening me on his meteoric rise that took him from being a professional wrestler to the governor's mansion.

Jesse "The Body" Ventura leaned back to jaw about the old days. Not so far back as when he tumbled to the bottom of a dam and nearly drowned in a whitewater whirlpool as an elite Navy SEAL, but a little later when he worked the small-time professional-wrestling circuit. Many a moon before full houses at Madison Square Garden or governors' mansions.

"Harvey, as a wrestler it was my job to sell myself as being the most arrogant jerk in the world because I was a villain. The public paid to see the hero kick the villain's butt. You have to antagonize the public so they want to come and watch the hero boot the villain's rear-end. That's just the way it was," says Jesse. You can still see those pectorals ripple, even under a three-piece suit.

"I'm fifty-one. When I look back now, I realize certain

things happened for a reason," Jesse says wistfully. "Some of these bouts, you got paid 25 or 35 bucks. In those days, I lived in Portland, Oregon, and wrestled one match in Klamath Falls. They're 310 miles apart. My wife had gone home to Minnesota for a wedding, so I had time on my hands. I paid my own expenses. At the end of this eighteen-hour, 620-mile round-trip, I ended up netting two bucks. And, I even got back-dropped and body-slammed in the deal! I looked in the mirror and asked: 'Do I really want to do this?' I guess I did. In my mid-twenties, I once wrestled sixty-three consecutive nights. That's a bit obsessive, I admit. The promoter's wife said I looked exhausted, chewed her husband out, and made him give me two nights off . . . without pay! In those days, if you didn't wrestle, you didn't get paid. When you *did* get paid, you were at the whim of the promoter and how large he judged the gate to be."

The good comes with the bad. In time, Jesse would be selling out Madison Square Garden for three consecutive matches and make thousands, billed at the top of the card. "You have to pay a price to ultimately get to the goal you want," he exclaims. "I exceeded the dream, but you can never exceed the dream without having it in the first place. This was the price I had to pay to become proficient at my trade."

Was it body slams on the mat that prepared Jesse for the contact sport of politics? Wrestling actually trained him best for another walk of life—broadcasting. It was his success—and firing—in broadcasting and Hollywood that paved the way for his political career. A career that let him put a full nelson on the traditional Democratic and Republican Parties and get elected as an Independent Party governor. The tie between broadcasting and wrestling has been around since the days of Vern Gagne and Gorgeous George. Nowhere was it more important than in burgs like Klamath Falls. "In some of those towns, I took the microphone and drove the people in," he leans over and tells me with his eyes fired up. "Every Saturday, you did TV interviews to cover all the small towns where matches were booked. Years later that helped me become governor, too. I learned to speak in front of the mikes. It gave me the confidence and the skill to talk without a prepared script. If you couldn't sell those people to come and pay their hard-earned money to see you get your ass kicked, then you didn't make money."

Not many people in today's workforce escape being fired. Jesse's been fired at least three times and maybe five. It depends how you're counting. Fired, maybe, but never down for the count for long. In 1990, Jesse got the boot from the World Wrestling Federation, then known as the WWF. He had been wrestling in the ring and doing commentary before and after bouts. Then he added "Get a Grip" hosting for the Movie Channel and color commentary for the Minnesota Vikings. Earlier, Jesse won a lawsuit against WWF's top honcho Vince McMahon, so bad blood was already there. Jesse was "pushing the envelope" in the original Chuck Yeager sense of the term. Test pilot Chuck Yeager was the daredevil pilot of the X-15 rocket plane in the early days of the U.S. space program. Nobody "pushed the envelope" harder than he did. Meaning: to fly the plane so fast and hard the outer skin (envelope) verged on exploding. Jesse Ventura is cut of the same cloth.

The governor was bound and determined to market himself "outside of the WWF regime." Jesse's recollections are blunt: "Vince told me I couldn't. I told him I was doing it anyway. 'Vince,' I said, 'either you'll let me have my freedom, or you're gonna fire me.' I could have given in. I could have simply said, 'Vince, I won't market myself. I'm happy with you.' I had a pretty lucrative deal then. It was a bit of stubbornness on my own part. But today I wouldn't have done anything differently." He was also effectively banned by the other big league, Ted Turner's World Championship Wrestling. That was the price of being center stage both as an announcer and as a competitor.

Next, it was Hollywood and a role in the Arnold Schwarzenegger film *Predator*. Then came the offer of a TV series called *Tag Team*—about two wrestlers turned cops. "I had temporarily moved to L.A., where a midseason replacement program had been bought up by ABC for seven or eight episodes," Jesse says. "The network had already spent a million dollars on the set. The night before we were to go into production, they pulled the plug. In a way, I was fired again. You prefer to fail on your own, instead of having someone else failing you. I was extremely disappointed. But this was a play-or-pay deal, so they ended up paying me off for all the episodes. I got my money, though it was still frustrating, because it could have ended up a three- to five-year series. I could have made so much money, I wouldn't be here today in the governor's office."

Jesse Ventura's reaction to being fired time and again is: What's next? . . . and it better be good. He thrives on insecurity. When they pulled the plug on the TV series, he went back to Minnesota. Then he ran for and got elected to the post of mayor of Brooklyn Park, a Minneapolis suburb. Meanwhile, he supplemented his $10,000 mayoral salary with a morning show slot on a Twin City radio station: KSTP Talk Radio. After one term as mayor, he walked away and went back into broadcasting full-time. This time he fired *himself* from government. As Jesse puts it, "Our country was formed with the idea that you come and serve. After you're done serving, go back and do what you used to do or do something new. I don't believe you should make a career out of elected public office."

For two years, the hitch with KSTP ran as smoothly as Jesse's shaved pate. They renewed his contract for another two years. Right after the renewal, Ka-BOOM! "Management told me they were going to take the morning show in a whole new direction," Jesse explains to me. "It really didn't dawn on me at that moment, but they were actually saying: 'So you don't have to come in tomorrow.' At that particular moment, I felt huge disappointment and frustration. The fact that they had signed me to a two-year contract three months earlier made it even more confusing. Since I was giving it my all, I wondered why. My ratings were fine again. They paired me up with someone who didn't work out . . . who wasn't a choice of mine. They forced the person on me. There was no chemistry. In radio, you have to have chemistry when you team people together. The numbers dropped. The person had been let go, and the numbers were recovering. If something goes wrong in business, it's very easy to put it on someone else. They were backing out the door bearing problems that they more or less created themselves."

Did Jesse rant and rave the way he would have showed off in the ring? Hang on to your turnbuckles. He pattered away as soft as a kitty. "I wasn't going to show my emotions to them," he says. "I just said okay, thank you, turned around, and walked out the door. I didn't plead or argue for the job. I didn't shed a tear, but two of the people I worked with started crying when they heard. I called up my wife and said, 'Pack up the kids. We're heading to the lake.' I was thinking about my long-range plan as I drove out. But I wasn't fully upset, because I'd be getting a year-and-three-quarter paid vacation. I certainly was going to make them honor what they had signed. It was their choice to remove me from the air. I have great confidence in my lawyers. When I sign an agreement, I expect it will be carried through."

The kitty may have pattered out the door, but the lion in Jesse was crouched to pounce. "When I left, I didn't go public to defend myself. I felt there was really no reason to air my feelings in public on either side," he says, outlining his strategy to me. "I was still under contract and I didn't want to jeopardize the contractual arrangement by opening mouth A and putting foot B in it. I don't know if it changed my character, but it brought back a clear sense of reality of what the world is like." That's how Jesse the risk taker sums up the KSTP experience as a lesson learned about security and about himself. "Security is a day-to-day thing," he says. "You can be secure today and totally insecure tomorrow. It reaffirmed to me that there are no guarantees in this life. Sure, it made me suspicious. To this day, I can't understand why they signed me to a longer contract if they were going to make this change. I would have thought they would have let my first contract simply expire. It's very difficult to do the job in a controversial business, if you're looking over your shoulder all the time. There are some people who can have one eye focused over their shoulder and still plod ahead. I may not be that type of person."

Three-quarters of a year later, the sports–talk radio station KFAN hired Jesse. He calls it "very testosterone-driven radio." He was a barn burner—mixing sports commentary with a huge helping of hard-hitting politics. "Working for KFAN helped me to prove to myself that KSTP was just plain wrong," he observes. From that bully media pulpit, Jesse marched into the political arena and nailed down the governorship. Now, he's in the middle of firing number five by my count. He's doing his own termination and walking away from the governorship for the same reasons he left the mayor's job: time to move on.

So often down. Time after time, up higher than before. An unshakable belief in destiny has a lot to do with his ability to bounce back. "Each one of us has a destiny that we're driven to by certain decisions," Jesse says. "You may not understand why you're picking a direction in that fork in the road now, but years down the line it will come clear to you. At any given time, things happen in your life, and you haven't got a clue. I'm a great believer in fate and that things happen for a reason. Five to ten years later, you see the reason. You may not know it now, but it will become many times clearer to you as time goes by. Like the SEALs training incident where I almost drowned as a young guy, it took a couple of years for the significance of the KSTP firing to come clear for me. Think about it. The single most important thing that made me become governor was the failure of a television pilot."

If you believe Jesse Ventura is a wild man about risk, think again. Those sixty-three straight nights of hammerlocks say different. He's a worker. "If you are in a tough job situation and you enjoy what you're doing," Jesse says forcefully, "then I think it's better if you try to work it out. If you don't enjoy it, sometimes you have to bite the bullet to survive. You have to make the judgment if you can *afford* to move on. In wrestling, I reached a point where it didn't do me any good to talk with these promoters, so I just decided to move on. On the other hand, if something bad happens—like getting fired—you need to have two or three fallback positions you can go to." For folks further along in their careers but shoved into the sidelines, he has this to say: "My advice to people over forty who are out of work is to look back over the many accomplishments you have already had in your life and realize that destiny will play its role. As long as you keep a positive attitude and believe in yourself, good things will happen. You just may not recognize them right away."

So Jesse Ventura is off on his next career, whatever that may be. He's a guy with attitude. As I leave the governor's office, I know this will be my last visit there with him as the top dog. His eyes dart around the foyer as if to say, "Hey, it really doesn't matter where you hang your shingle." That big bear-hug arm lands on my shoulder, as Jesse says: "Harvey, I can't abandon my own freedom. In the end, you gotta know you have to live with yourself first."

Advice from a professional wrestler . . . a movie star . . . a radio personality, and . . . a former governor . . . and it's all the same person!

- **Things happen for a reason.** If you're tired, fed up, not feeling great about what you're doing—or you're fired— maybe that's telling you something. Nonstop frustration is usually a clue that you are spending your life doing something you are not cut out to do.

- **It's always better to fail on your own rather than have someone else fail you.** But if it happens, be like Jesse. Ask yourself, "What's next? . . . And it better be good."

- **When you feel like you're done, move on.** Staying in place past your prime doesn't do anyone any good. Least of all you.

- **Remember, security is a day-to-day thing.** There are no guarantees in life, but the better job you do of planning ahead, the easier it is to land on your feet.

MACKAY'S MORAL:

When you're pinned to the mat, the only place to look is up.

COLD TRUTHS ABOUT FIRING . . . AND BEING FIRED

- The real reason you are being fired is rarely the reason you are given.

- The best time to hire people is during a downturn when everyone else is firing them.

- When a smart boss fires someone, the first question they should ask is NOT: How do I feel about this person working for me? The first question they should ask IS: How would I feel about this person if he or she were working for my competitor?

- It's not the people you fire who make your life miserable . . . it's the people you don't fire who make your life miserable.

- The time to start worrying about what you'll do when you're fired is the day you get hired.

- The nicest, most loyal, and most submissive employees are often the easiest people to fire.

- When the domestic labor market is tightest and your job seems most secure is exactly when companies may try the hardest to move your job offshore to China or to India. Be prepared.

- The résumé that explains an unhappy firing situation clearly and honestly is not the one that potential employers find suspicious. The suspicious résumés are the ones with unexplained voids or breaks in a career.

- It doesn't matter who hired you yesterday. It only matters who can fire you today.

- The likeliest managers to get fired are often those who have the most trouble firing others.

- Maybe what you did wrong *got* you fired. It's only what you can do right that will get you hired again.

MACKAY'S MORAL:

The only way a fire can hurt you is if you don't know
what you're playing with.

TOM STEMBERG

Founder of Staples, Inc.

"You should always be looking for advice. But think about the agenda of the people who give you that advice."

Tom Stemberg had the Harvard B-school seal of approval. He was a distinguished George F. Baker scholar there. Tom went on to train in grocery retailing with Jewel's Star Market stores in Chicago in 1973, during the era when Don Perkins was the illustrious CEO of Jewel. Tom rose to become vice president of sales and merchandising. In 1980, he moved to another chain, Connecticut-based First National Supermarkets. There he held various management posts before he became CEO of First National's Edwards-Finast division. This division was a hot pricer—cutting costs and trading in volume.

In short order, Tom learned that Edwards-Finast was hotter than a pistol. "The chairman was shot," Tom recalls. "It was an unexplained murder, but there were alleged Mafia connections. For decades, the division had lost money. It was a very troubled company. A couple of guys in Cleveland had bought the company, and the business was very profitable in that market. However, in New England the company was struggling. The management didn't have sterling clean reputations. They had pleaded no contest to a price-fixing charge. My predecessor had been found guilty of price-fixing in both Cleveland and New England. On top of that, he was convicted of taking kickbacks from suppliers." Without a scent of it beforehand, Tom says he was selected to sanitize a pretty smelly situation. "I was Mr. Clean," he recalls, "brought in to wipe this entire mess up. We took the losses from a million dollars a month to breaking even my last month there. Then the rules of the game changed. My bosses had put out crazy forecasts to a very weak board of directors. When those numbers didn't come in, the guys I reported to put on tremendous pressure. I thought they were asking for things that couldn't be done. I got into an argument with them and that got me fired in January 1985."

What to do next? To protect his year's severance pay, Tom had to agree to a "non-compete" clause. This prevented him from working in specific industries, particularly grocery retailing. Unfortunately, this was the industry in which he had spent his entire career.

"After I got fired," Tom recalls, "I was approached by a man named Leo Kahn, who had just sold his supermarket chain for a hundred million bucks. He offered to back me in a business."

The first thing Tom and Leo attempted was to find a business to buy. No dice. They couldn't find an attractively priced one that didn't violate either his non-compete clause or one that was similarly tying up Leo. Tom was also looking for other jobs. Warehouse retailers were just beginning to spring up. "Before Price Club or Costco, European-owned U.S. Makro was really the forerunner of big-box grocery discounting," Tom recalls. "They had four stores in the States and they were looking for a CEO for their U.S. business. They wanted me to look at a store."

Enter NCAA basketball and destiny's next twist. To this day, Tom is a college basketball junkie. You'll find him there at the NCAA Final Four year after year. Naturally, he follows the Ivy League, too. In one weekend, Harvard played both Princeton and Penn. Harvard hadn't beaten both on the road in fifty years. Langhorne, Pennsylvania—the site of one of the four original U.S. Makro stores—is midway between the two schools. Tom figured this first contact with Makro would at least pay for the basketball outing. He was not in love with the store he saw. "This won't work in the U.S.," Tom concluded. "But Harvey, I didn't have a clear idea of what I would do next. I *was* amazed at the variety of office products that they were selling. When the idea registered, it was kind of a man bites dog."

Man biting dog is a familiar scene on an American Fourth of July. But, Destiny Step Three may have been the juiciest morsel on the landscape that year. That's when the next piece of the puzzle fell into place. Tom's ImageWriter ribbon for his Apple IIc computer went down on Friday morning of the July 4 weekend. He tried to find one at the local office-supply store. Nix. Closed for the holiday. Ditto for another office-supply store in West Hartford. He went to Businessland. Same story. At BJ's Wholesale Club, they had good prices, but no ribbon to fit his machine. Tom's realization was this: "If you are a small-business person, you are lucky to find what you need. But, if you find what you need, you're likely to be ripped off by the prices."

The office-products opportunity may have been nagging at Tom's mind, but Tom was still thinking grocery was his destiny. Then he paid a visit to his old mentor at the Harvard Business School, Professor Walt Salmon. Salmon asked Tom, "Do you believe in your heart of hearts that you can outexecute the top grocery chains in New England like Stop & Shop or Shaw's?" When he thought about it, Tom agreed that wasn't in the cards. Instead of trying to do that, the prof recommended Tom find some retail business that was growing faster than grocery was . . . and was underserved by efficient distribution. The answer jumped out: It was the office superstore!

At this point, Tom could sense himself zeroing in on a concept. But was his idea of what a customer would want reliable? Would most customers want what *he* wanted? There was a lawyer Tom knew in Hartford. This guy could squeeze blood out of a penny. His law firm had about forty people in it. One day, Tom asked him: "How much do you spend on office supplies per person?" The attorney thought about it and guessed maybe a couple of hundred dollars a year. The next day his admin assistant reported back to him that he was forking out a grand apiece for his people each year. Furthermore, he thought he was an expense-control hero because he got 10 percent off list. That's when Tom told him some companies were paying 60 percent off list, and the attorney started thinking: "Why shouldn't I be paying *half* of what I'm now paying?"

In a meeting with Leo, Tom mapped out what he had learned at Makro, and over the Fourth of July, and with the attorney. Leo thought an office-products superstore was a great idea and said that Tom and he should open one up. Tom was more cautious. "Leo, you're just an investor," he objected.

"To me, this is my life. I got fired once. I don't want to go through that again. What if we split the cost and get some research to underpin this?" Leo agreed. They hired a woman named Marcie Dew, who had been a teaching assistant to Walt Salmon at the Harvard Business School. For $20,000, the study was done. It said that retail office supplies were a $40-plus billion industry, growing in double digits, with huge margins in the distribution chain. It was really $100 billion at the end-user level. Tom and Leo pulled the switch and decided to start a business. They called it Staples.

"As we were writing our business plan," Tom recalls, "John Naisbitt's *Megatrends* came out. Naisbitt pinpointed all the factors we were relying on, such as corporate downsizing and more home offices. At the same time, all these new office appliances and IT technology that represented such a huge investment for the small-business person started to come out. These elements formed the backdrop as we started our business. The fact is we have made the distribution channel for office supplies for the small business so much more efficient."

Who were the doomsayers? The traditional retailers, of course. "You should always be looking for advice," Tom says. "You also have to think about the agenda of the people who might give you that advice. The chairman of United Stationers told us that what people really wanted was more service, not better prices." Staples remained committed to the value channel. According to Tom, "The Harvard Coop—the campus bookstore shopped by Harvard students and faculty—told suppliers that they'd be thrown out if they sold to Staples. That's illegal. Suppliers like McKesson, then in the business of selling office products, feared the consequences. We had to let the world know what was going on. We retaliated by running an ad with the punch line: 'Why would somebody as smart as the Harvard student pay $3.68 for 79-cent-a-dozen pens?' "

Staples today dominates office-supplies retailing in the United States. Their annual volume is $13 (will be over $14 in 2004) billion, done through 1,600 retail stores. Tom Stemberg has stepped aside as CEO of Staples and handed over the reins to Ron Sargent. Basketball junkie that he remains, Tom can look westward with pride to the Staples Center in L.A. that is now the home of both the Lakers and the Kings.

Did this all happen overnight? No chance. There were some mean bumps in the road along the way. Tom described two of the steepest to me: "It was the second day we were in business. We opened our first store—15,000 square feet—on May 1, 1986. We were pretty busy. Bain Capital Funding was backing us. And Bill Bain drove up in a Jaguar to buy office products from us. All of our friends came down. We probably did $8,000 on our first day. On the second day, we did a third of that amount. It got progressively worse. An outside researcher advised us to pay people in advance to shop our stores. The goal was to get immediate feedback on the experience. We sent twenty people twenty bucks each. The researcher called back all twenty and not a single one of them had shopped Staples. Nobody cared to show up. At that point, I was very worried. But,

Harvey, here's the amazing thing that happened: The few people who did show up saw that a box of copy paper was priced at $24 when they were used to paying $70. A dozen pads might have cost $12 elsewhere. At Staples, it cost $4. They were shocked by these prices. Word of mouth did it. The first shoppers told their friends. They in turn told the press."

Looming disaster on that second day of business was Despair #1. Explosive success triggered Despair #2. The second dark day was when the imitators emerged. "In 1987," Tom recalls, "there must have been thirty different office-products retailers. Every venture capitalist was touting an office product strategy. Kmart had one. Montgomery Ward had one. International Paper started one. Office Depot had quickly grown to a billion dollars, and we were at $300 million. Today we have surpassed them."

Did Tom foresee that he was creating the dominant brand in office-supplies retailing? "Not really, Harvey. Building a warehouse happened on purpose. We built a distribution center because you couldn't be efficient at the store level," Tom contends. "Back in 1988–89, everyone was distributing inefficiently directly to their stores. We chose to build an infrastructure. Our business began in the Northeast, which meant that our advertising, labor, and occupancy costs were much higher than the national norm. Advertising costs in the *Boston Globe* were a lot higher than the *Fort Lauderdale Sentinel.* As this competitive scenario played itself, three chains competed for the business in places like Dallas almost overnight. It was much easier for us to come from high-cost markets and to trim down, than for others to come from low-cost markets and learn how to work with much tighter controls. In the more challenging, high-barrier markets like Boston and New York, we had an edge. Today we have 145 stores in New York. Our closest competitor, Office Max, has thirty-five. We have forty-odd stores in Boston. Office Max has ten. This has led to huge competitive advantages in those franchise markets."

Success is sweet. Does it heal all the memories? Has Tom forgotten what it was like to be fired? Not in the least. "I have very strong views on letting people go, Harvey," Tom told me with plenty of conviction. "A person I worked with for many years is a woman named Jeanne Lewis. She once said to me, after we terminated an employee, 'Tom, if I ever get fired, no matter where I am working, I want to be fired by you.' From personal experience, I know what getting fired can take out of you. Firing people is no fun, but it can be unavoidable. My goal is always to convince the person that this isn't the right job for them. You want the individual to feel that they quit as much as you fired them . . . that you are helping them find a better situation. After you break the news, I always do my best afterward to help them. I'll never forget the people who helped me when I was down. Even if it's only a phone call. I'll always take the call of a person who is down, even if I can't help them with a job prospect."

Firing will be a constant career peril in future years, and Tom's advice to younger managers is preparation. "Build yourself up as an individual and as a manager," he recommends, "before you get to the point of possibly being fired. Then you have a broader portfolio to rely on. I was an experienced low-cost retailer who could apply that expertise to other industries. There will always be times and situations when things won't work out. If it ever gets to a point when you don't feel good about going to work in the morning and people around you no longer show appreciation for your contribution, you have to realize that job may not be for you. And it's time to move on. Not in a rash way, but after thoughtfully considering what makes sense."

Today, Staples looks like a lightning bolt of creativity. Was it really? As a youngster, Tom believed he would be an entrepreneur one day. He went into retailing because it was as close as a manager could come to running his own business. And he is about as methodical and brilliant a planner as you can imagine. But how about creative? "I went to the PDI assessment and executive development center in Minneapolis," Tom recalls. "They told me that I had two flat sides to work on. One was that I tended to be kind of brash. The second was that I had no creativity."

Tom's experiences have some unforgettable lessons:

- Think about frustrations you encounter in your own life as business opportunities. Tom is a good example. He was a trained retailer and found that no one was serving his needs as a customer. His frustration became the cornerstone for an entire new business.

- Take the calls of people who are down—they'll remember, especially if you happen to be in the same sinking boat some day.

- If you no longer feel appreciated at work, it's a good sign that your market worth in that job isn't appreciating either.

- Build your skills portfolio long before the day you may be fired.

MACKAY'S MORAL:

The next time someone accuses you of being plain vanilla, bore them to death with success.

You Don't Have to Be Bad to Be Blown Away

Several years ago, I was honored to be the guest speaker at the American Society of Association Executives. Recently I read a rather scholarly article in their publication *Association Management*, which is "the advocate for the non-profit sector." Their members include administrators who "manage leading trade, professional, and philanthropic associations." The article's title was "Why Good Executives GET FIRED." The authors, Glenn Tecker and Cate Bower, make some arresting points:

- "What is perceived to be, is." Sounds simple enough, but how often do we drive right past *that* billboard? You may be the most energetic and passionate guy or gal on the squad. However, if you're seen as sluggish and lukewarm, that's what you *are*. That's how you're branded, like it or not. One of the most common reasons good people end up in bad places is that they fail to merchandise themselves. Remember, nothing sells itself.

- "... [I]n the absence of information based on the truth, 'activists' and 'agitators'—well-meaning or not—develop assumptions that explain what they are seeing." What a mouthful! On the other hand, what a hunk of reality. Translation: If you don't create an identity for yourself, the world will make one for you. *There are no unexplained people.* Everybody—especially every busybody—is always analyzing other people's motives: "Marie is frustrated because she didn't get that promotion three years ago." "You can see that Tim is full of hidden anger the way he slams down his tray in the cafeteria." A friend of mine told me this story: He was a classical music nut. He was being quietly evaluated as the company representative to sit on the board of the city's symphony orchestra. The firm's chairman asked him what he thought about the legendary pianist Emil Gilels. The young vice president thought Gilels was a master and said so. "Especially in the Claudio Monteverdi piano sonatas?" the chairman asked. "Incomparable!" the young man answered, sensing the chairman's enthusiasm. Of course, the young man knew that Gilels never played a Monteverdi piano sonata, because Monteverdi never wrote one. The piano was invented more than a century after Monteverdi died. Unfortunately, the chairman knew this, too. He had baited a cunning trap. By being too nice and politically smooth, the young man was branded as a musical dunce by the chairman. Nothing was ever said, but the fellow was passed over for the orchestra board slot. He was also dismissed as an unreliable information source in general. His career in that corporation sputtered from that day forward. You are on camera 24/7.

- In many instances, leadership, Tecker and Bower say, isn't exactly sure "about what constitutes success." Especially in high-risk situations and business turnarounds, success isn't a target. It's a *moving* target. Let's say a company sets a 7 percent growth goal, and the industry suddenly starts growing at a pace of 9 percent. What was once stretchy can become slack overnight. Being recruited for a kamikaze mission to save a sinking ship? Make sure you get in writing exactly what you are supposed to do. If the goals change—and they often do—be certain that the changes are documented, too. And that any revised timing plan is realistic. There's no substitute for a time and action calendar.

Nowhere is the fuzzy picture of success more of a problem than in following the act of a strong leader. Jeffrey Sonnenfeld wrote a book about management succession called *The Hero's Farewell*. In it he quotes Ralph Waldo Emerson: "An institution is the lengthened shadow of the one man." People—especially successors to CEOs—are often recruited based on chemistry. "By golly, he or she is the spitting image of the old guy or the old gal!" In a year or two—and often earlier—the spitting image becomes a spitting contest. It's dangerous to act too much like the boss too soon.

Completely competent people are fired every day. They can be too honest. Too reserved. Too aggressive. Too timid. Sometimes even too competent for their own good. Staying hired is not a question of competence. It's a matter of meeting someone else's expectations. That said, is staying hired a good thing? That's altogether a different question.

MACKAY'S MORAL:

When you spend more time controlling other people's expectations than fulfilling your own, it may be time to move on.

JOE TORRE
Manager of the New York Yankees

"Tough times don't last. Tough people do."

"I think we're getting fired here," Joe told his wife, Ali, over the phone. Read the tea leaves: *This* dismissal looked terminal. Scratch one major league manager who chalked up fewer victories than losses. More than a thousand losses on his score sheet. Fifty-five years old. And this was the third team to can him as a dugout boss.

But not so fast. Who says being down at age fifty-five automatically means you're out?

Not this Joe. Here's a guy who as good as stole home plate from first base! The Yankees' Joe Torre is the most effective manager in baseball today. His Bronx Bombers have put away three World Series in the last six years. His career "save" outdoes anything the sharpest bullpen ace could hurl.

Let's start with that third firing first. While I'm talking with Joe, he downs a whole box of atomic Red Hots. His stomach has got to be lined with titanium. Comes from all those years as a catcher, only now he has developed a protector *inside* his gut instead of over it. In 1971, Joe was an MVP at third base with the same Cardinals who had just fired him in 1994. Out he went as manager during the year of the baseball players' strike. Maybe *because* of it more than any other one thing. You remember '94 . . . the year of no World Series.

When Whitey Herzog stepped down as manager in St. Louis, Joe was the first replacement to come to mind. Joe managed there for five years. Then a changing of the guard took place, and the Cards brought in a new president and a new general manager. "You're hanging by a thread, because you know you'll be fired . . . but not when," he told me. "I had way under a .500 record. The baseball strike was going on and management tried to do the player-replacement thing. The St. Louis front office wanted me to go about my job as though the regular players were never coming back. I told August Busch III, there was no way I could do that. I refused to lose my credibility with my players. During that conversation with August, I knew this job wouldn't last long."

Still, Joe was surprised *when* the roof finally caved in. "The front office knew I would be fired, but I had no hint of it," he said. "Wow! I had never been fired during the season before. It had always been afterward. It started on a Thursday night and I was in my clubhouse office. We were in the process of trading Todd Zeile to the Chicago Cubs. I had stayed there till nearly midnight. The trade was almost finished but not quite. I went home and they called me at 1:00 or 1:30 in the morning to tell me the deal was done and they were going to announce it at 1:00 p.m. the next day. The next morning I went to get a haircut. I was coming home and listening to the radio at 10:00 a.m. and learned that the Todd Zeile trade was public. I phoned Cardinal general manager Walt Jocketty to let him know I heard it on KMOX ahead of the release time. Jocketty then asked where I was and I told him at home. He said, 'I'll be right over.' I told my wife, Ali, 'I think we're getting fired.' " According to Joe, "Walt started to cry and said, 'We have to make a change.' I tried to cheer him up and told him not to worry about it. Getting fired was like a trip to the dentist: Just get it done." If it sounds like Joe was taking firing in stride by now . . . he wasn't. "The St. Louis firing was the toughest," he stresses to me.

St. Louis may have been the toughest. The New York Mets was the first. Still, it wasn't a totally new experience. As a player, Joe had been traded twice. He knew what it was like not to be wanted. He lasted five losing seasons as manager of the Mets until they dropped him in 1981. He had piled up a record to wince at of 286–420. "It was my first managing job," he reminisces. "You have a sense when something is going to happen. They changed ownership. Fred Wilpon and Nelson Doubleday came in. They brought in Frank Cashen from the Commissioner's Office as general manager. Even when Frank fired me, we still remained friends." Joe is not one to hold a grudge. Respect is a Torre trademark. It's also a great gateway to stay in the hiring network when you're bounced out of a job.

After they've been fired, plenty of people bite their nails. When will the axe fall *this* time? The most important ingredient a manager—any manager—brings to the table is motivation. It's tough to motivate if you're scared. Joe takes the opposite tack: Having been fired should just make you more realistic. "When you are in the role of trying to be a motivator and you get fired, it conditions you real well to do a job right," he says. "If you have done a job for four or five years, and you haven't won, then it's time for a change. In earlier managing jobs, people would wait for me to come home from a road trip, wondering if I would be signed to an extension. My answer to them: If I waste my time worrying about things like that, I'm really cheating the people who hired me to do a job. You only have control over what you are doing right now." Amen! Eighty to 90 percent of what we worry about never happens anyway.

During the World Series of the same year, Joe was hired as manager of the Braves. The Braves weren't in the Series, but you can bet they wanted to be there the next year. Joe firmly believes the key in managing is getting the *second* job. Think about it and it's no surprise: major league managing is a tightrope walk without a net. Only one team is the champ, and every other franchise will do what it can to claw its way to the top.

What's true for managers is, of course, even truer for players. Trading, demoting, and even selling players had a long tradition. Anything for an edge. In his classic *The Boys of Summer*, Roger Kahn tells how Brooklyn Dodger president Branch Rickey answered a press question: "Was his star home run hitter, Ralph Kiner, for sale? 'I don't want to sell Ralph, but if something overwhelming comes along, I am willing to be overwhelmed.'"

Few managers get to retire. Most are bounced out the door. The second job is "what helps you on your way," says Joe. Another advantage can be to get the second job fast. Then you don't have the chance to wallow in misery.

A fast shuffle to a new spot can have its downside, too. Ted Turner, founder of CNN and TBS (Turner Broadcasting System), owns the Braves. Joe liked Ted, but the deal just didn't seem to work out. From the start, it was destined not to. *How* and *why* you're hired should also sink in. You may think it's because of *who* you are. The reality may be you're a compromise. Joe was smart enough to see this pretty early when he joined Atlanta: "The Braves wanted to hire a Triple A manager, Eddie Haas," he remembers. "The Turner Broadcasting System president wanted someone with a little more recognition. My having played for sixteen years and managed in New York gave them that. From the first day, the general manager John Mullen said to me: You weren't our first choice, but let's make the best of it. Not the most ideal circumstances." Joe got the job in Atlanta because of what the Braves wanted. Joe lost the job because of what he felt was right. He's still proud of that today. "The most important thing in any job is to do it the way you feel it should be done, not the way other people think it should be done," he contends. "You might as well lose your job on your own merits as opposed to trying to do something to keep your job. I've never worked at a job because I was afraid to lose it. I got fired because I didn't get to do what I wanted to do."

What role did "TNT" Ted Turner play in all this? "Ted was in the middle. He was kind of a part-time owner because he had so many other things going on," according to Joe. "My wife and I enjoyed socializing with him. But all the people who had worked for him for years were on Ted's back to have him make the change that would send me on my way. Ted fired me personally, and it was awkward for him. When we saw each other after the split, he was sociable, even funny. I remember going over to the Owner's Box at Yankee Stadium in 1996 during the Yankees-Braves World Series. He and Jane Fonda were still together, and she was there. I told Ted I just wanted to say hello. He smiled, 'Well, if we can't win it, I hope you do.' Since there are only two teams on the field . . ."

This second managing job in Atlanta had lasted three years, until 1984. Joe thought he did pretty good—winning his division in the first year and coming in second for the last two. Good wasn't good enough. He was out, and the phone calls didn't come in so fast this time. Joe had no managing options and went to broadcast for the Angels for six years. "During that period I was interviewed a number of times for managing jobs, but I had only one serious offer," he recalls, "and that was from the Cardinals to manage in the AAA minors." While he was with the Angels' broadcast team, Joe developed an esteem for Angels owner Gene Autry and how he respected people in his organization.

Joe doesn't think the visibility of being a booth broadcaster helped him get hired by the Cardinals as a manager. "It gave me something to do," he admits. "It also gave me a chance to observe other managers—particularly Sparky Anderson. When you are doing your own job, you don't have a chance to do this. I realized managing is all about people and communications. Strategy is the other part of it, but it's 'people' strategy: You have to know when to change a pitcher. You have to know when you have to add people who will make the team go." Halfway through his broadcasting career, Joe was yearning to get back into managing. He may have been benched himself, but did he ever use his head! He studied other managers the way hitters study Barry Bonds.

After the Angels broadcasting booth came the return to managing in St. Louis and the land of the Clydesdales. As I said, that adventure lasted five years before Joe was treading in a pile of what Clydesdales leave behind them. "I've been fired three times," Joe reflects. "Getting fired is always a shot at your ego . . . none was a shocker at the time it happened. The general manager stops coming to the clubhouse. People don't return your calls. You can usually see it coming."

After the Cardinals, came the Yankees. With the Yankees came the glory!

The thing that impresses you about Joe and that titanium tummy is that he is steadily learning, win or lose. It makes him stronger for what comes next. Take his attitude toward the press. Reporters could make him go ballistic. "During spring training one year, we had an inter-squad game," he remembers with a bitter aftertaste. "They put the press clips from the New York papers on my desk daily. The next morning after the game, I read one writer who accused me of stacking the lineups in this inter-squad matchup. He said I was trying to make one pitcher look good and the other one look bad . . . playing one part of my team against the other. I got infuriated. Another example: When you're managing a winning team, and there's a disagreement in the clubhouse and players will fight . . . or argue . . . then it's 'inspiring competitiveness' . . . but if you are in last place, then it's 'tension.' I read the papers during the season, but not the Yankees game stories. I won't listen to talk radio either. I don't care what the media say. I have come to realize that a lot of this stuff didn't make sense and there was no reason for me to read it."

Joe still lives in a world of risk. Every manager or head coach does. Look at what happened to Jimmy Johnson in Dallas after two consecutive Super Bowl wins. I asked Joe about life with George Steinbrenner today. "A manager has to develop a trust with the front office," he answers, "but trust vanishes very quickly when—as my dad used to say—you don't 'decorate the mahogany.' You have to check the wind. George can tell you a lot of things, but if you don't win, he's not a very happy camper. It's important to have access to your owner. I didn't have that in Atlanta or in St. Louis. It was very tough to make a point. In New York, I do. It's not always wonderful fun, but you do have the chance to plead your case. My failures in the past were linked to the wrong philosophy. I remember picking up NFL head coach Bill Parcells' book on coaching and management. He wrote, 'If you believe in what you're doing, stick with it.' That has stayed with me. For a manager to do that, you have to create an atmosphere of trust with the players. I decided to do exactly that."

You can tell that Joe's managing philosophy has seeped into his personal life. Joe has been up front about his two failed marriages. He now has a very successful one with Ali. A divorce is a lot like being fired. Joe agreed both were big-time whacks at your ego. "Any time you have a failed marriage, you ask yourself what's wrong with me, what did I do wrong?"

He adds, "I really didn't like myself very much in my twenties. When I moved from the Braves to the Cardinals in 1969, I took stock, made some changes, and became more responsible. Like firings, divorces are tough. A line I once heard makes all kinds of sense to me: Tough times don't last. Tough people do. I say that to my players: 'It's a tough time right now. Don't look for a reason why it's happening. Just deal with it. Get through it, and you'll be better for it. I just try to use this attitude for every experience I have—personal and professional—and move on.' "

Joe Torre directed the Yankees to the World Series in his *first* season with the team—his *first* postseason appearance as a manager since 1982 (with Atlanta) and his *first* trip to the

World Series after thirty-one seasons as a player or manager. Torre and the Yankees won the World Series four times in his first five seasons as the club's manager. Torre is just one of three men to manage a team to as many as three consecutive World Series titles. Casey Stengel (five straight) and Joe McCarthy (four straight) are the others.

More than any prominent figure around today, Joe Torre has given "I've been fired" a good name. He's damn proud of it, too. "Before earning my first World Series," he tells me with plenty of emotion, "I tried to find ways to speak to young people about being successful, and yet I had nothing to show for it. I thought it was important that you do the best you can. If you do, then you're a success. When you lose, you don't say the other team is lucky or that you had a tough break. During those losing years for me, I learned to carry myself with my head held high. I told my guys how proud I was of them after they lost game seven of the World Series in Arizona in 2001 after three straight Series wins. You don't have to be on the winning team to be a winner."

I can vouch for that, because I was in the front row for all seven games. The final showdown in Arizona was a classic. And the dignity with which Joe and his Yankees accepted defeat is a marvel. Joe's a winner's winner.

MACKAY'S MORAL:

Keep your eye on the ball . . . and three strikes
doesn't spell out.

Don't Let Them Tag You Out

- In 1983, **Tony LaRussa** was named American League manager of the year after leading the Chicago White Sox to the A.L. West title. Less than three years later, LaRussa was unemployed after being fired by the White Sox at midseason. Less than a month later the Oakland Athletics hired him. In 1988, LaRussa led the Oakland A's to the first of three consecutive A.L. championships. Going into the 2004 season—his twenty-sixth as a major league manager—LaRussa is seventh on the all-time victories list for major league managers and sixth on the all-time list for games managed.

- In May of 2003—three years after being fired by the Cincinnati Reds—**Jack McKeon** became the oldest (seventy-two years old) ever hired to manage a major league team when he took over the floundering Florida Marlins. At the time, the Marlins were 19–29. Over the remaining four months, McKeon directed the Marlins to a 72–42 record. The Marlins reached the playoffs as a wild-card team and eventually went on to defeat the favored New York Yankees in the 2003 World Series.

- In his first nine seasons as a major league manager, Casey Stengel's teams never finished higher than fifth (in the eight-team National League). The Boston Braves dismissed Stengel during the 1943 season with the Braves thirteen games under .500. But in 1949, Stengel took over the New York Yankees and managed the Bronx Bombers to ten American League pennants in twelve seasons. The Yankees won the World Series seven times under Stengel. Stengel finished his Hall of Fame career by managing the expansion New York Mets for three seasons.

- Baltimore Orioles Brooks Robinson, called the greatest third baseman of all time, was sent back to the minors after a disappointing first year in the major leagues. He went on to set major league career records for games played, assists, double plays, chances, putouts, and fielding percentage. In 1970, he was the World Series MVP.

- Ty Cobb, regarded as the greatest player of his time, was fired as the Detroit Tigers player-manager following the 1926 season after it was discovered that he and Tris Speaker had apparently rigged a 1919 game. When he retired after twenty-four big-league seasons, Cobb held almost every major league batting and base-running record. Cobb won ten batting titles, led the league in runs scored five times, RBI four times, slugging percentage eight times, and on base percentage six times. His total of 4,191 hits and 892 stolen bases are the second and third highest totals ever.

- **Rogers Hornsby,** whom some consider the greatest hitter in National League history, was fired as manager of the Chicago Cubs in August 1932, despite his team being in first place. Hornsby bounced from team to team because his managers and club owners didn't like him.

AXE OR BE AXED

"The scientific name for an animal that doesn't either run from or fight its enemies is lunch," according to Michael Friedman.

Evolution happens at different rates of speed. Management—as we know it—didn't exist a century ago. Management is a blend of art and science. It has evolved very fast. Managers who don't evolve with it will fall victim to killer sharks with faster fins and sharper jaws. One of the things they rarely teach you in business school is how to fire people. No excuse for that! If you want to keep your job, you better know how to take other people out of theirs in an intelligent and effective way. If you can't or won't do what the company needs to survive, the company and its bosses become your enemies. And you could land on their menu.

Why? The handwriting is posted on the wall. This pink slip is anything but rosy, and it comes from the Bureau of Labor Statistics. "During the January 1999 through December 2001 period, 4.0 million workers were displaced from jobs they had held for at least three years." Restructurings, reorganizations . . . downsizings, outsizings. Call them what you will. They all mean: out on the street. Since the most recent recession didn't begin until March 2001, one can only imagine the carnage since then. One of the inescapable facts of life in business is this: If you don't know how to fire people, you increase the likelihood you yourself will be fired.

Heartless as this may sound, there's a reason. "At top levels," as Korn/Ferry senior client partner Tierney Remick explained, "you have to be able to make the tough decisions as well as the easy ones. The decisions must not only be intelligently made. They have to be clearly communicated. What gets some executives in trouble is conflict avoidance." If you don't restructure the accounting department or customer service, somebody else will. And you could well be written out of the script.

What's a manager to do? When a restructuring effort is necessary, be a leader. If possible, be an *initiator* before the roller-coaster ride starts. Communicate clearly why the restructuring needs to happen. "This includes what the outcome of the restructuring is designed to be, how the ultimate restructuring will enable improvements, and what the implications will be for the new skills needed," Tierney says. "Communicate why. When the cutbacks happen, individuals are more likely to feel they have been treated fairly. They may not agree, but at least they will understand why. Then administer the restructuring fairly, quickly, and humanely."

Many managers and even entire companies shirk communicating why. People don't like to give bad news. They want to get it over with and to avoid explaining it. That shortchanging may be the most inhumane part of an unpleasant situation. "The communication gives people something tangible to hang on to," Tierney explains. "It often increases their respect for the leadership."

Martha Rogers of the Peppers & Rogers Group has never

been fired in her adult career. That void, she says, has made her especially sensitive to the trauma that results when people lose their job. "Today we have 160 people," Martha says with pride. "Recently we sold the business to Carlson Marketing Group, and they have been wonderful partners. We kept our name and our people and our location."

"Martha, what was the recent recession like for your firm?"

"In the world of 2001-02, our company lost many competitors. We had to be very careful that we were not one of the casualties ourselves. If we shirked from making strong decisions, Harvey, *all* of our employees would have been out of a job. Many who left were highly qualified, solid performers. For business reasons, their positions couldn't continue. When we made the reduction, we put together the best severance and farewell packages we could. We had to look out for them in the best way we could. Not everyone left with the warmest feelings, but many did."

"You have actually had to implement a downsizing. What was it like for you on doomsday, the day of the cutback?"

"At the time, my colleague Don Peppers was based in Norwalk, Connecticut. I never had been officed there, but I flew over there on the day that we implemented the reduction. I wanted to be there if people wanted to throw rocks . . . cry . . . or ask questions. One executive sought me out during the day and said to me, 'Martha, this must be such a hard thing for you. Don't worry, it's the right thing to do.' I still had a job, and I knew I would have a job the next day. He had just learned he didn't, and he was reassuring me! In the first round of layoffs, we found every single one of them a job. In the second round, all but two. And those two decided to take a little break in their career. Since then, a couple of more people have been let go."

"Martha, being an employer is a very responsible role, isn't it?"

"Before the recent downturn, the firm had a company picnic

with several hundred people. The guests were our employees and their families. Don and I were off to the side, and we turned to each other. One of us said, this is a lot of mortgages and college funds, isn't it? We're responsible for these people's well-being."

"In good times, you feel a real nice rush, don't you?"

"You nailed it. But the reality in tougher times is a challenge. In addition to the official program, our partners also got together to do some things privately. I'm not trying to say we were wonderful, but in little ways we tried to behave humanely."

"Do we do a good enough job of preparing young people for the job jungle?"

"Harvey, that's a good question. We had hired some young people right out of school. They left school with lots of opportunities. Hardship hadn't been imagined by them. They felt entitled to what they had been given in life. When things went bad for everyone, they thought they only went bad for our firm. In some respects, they were less willing to deal with change than people who were twenty years older than them.

"I have two children—one thirteen and one nine. I would hate to see them experience adversity, but the realities will continue to be tougher. No matter how much is expected of you, Harvey, you must continue to deliver more in your job. Why? Because you are surrounded by people who will deliver enough, and the bar is always being raised. There's value in learning the adversity lesson early. Survival is one aspect. Empathy is another. You may one day be in a position to make somebody's life miserable or just not so great. Not so great is better. You can be humane about making somebody's life not so great."

MACKAY'S MORAL:

Hard knocks: Learn what they are and how to dish them out with a fair hand . . . or they'll be dishing out you.

Twenty-five Reliable Signs That . . . the Curtain May Be Coming Down on Your Career

1) *You're no longer invited to meetings you were always invited to.*

2) *One of your subordinates is now being invited to attend meetings that he was never invited to before . . . and you didn't do the inviting.*

3) *Your boss is seen having lunch or dinner at a restaurant with a manager from a competitor who is about on your career level.*

4) *You are relocated to a new office space, which is more distant from the power base of your department.*

5) *You are asked to accept a transfer to a remote area, where the prospect of achieving anything for the company is limited.*

6) *Your operational duties are cut back and you are given assignments that are less urgent or "more strategic" in nature.*

7) *Your reporting relationship is changed to a more junior manager.*

8) *Your reporting relationship is changed to a manager with a reputation for taking tough actions—especially difficult personnel decisions.*

9) *Your boss reduces the frequency or length of regular meetings with you.*

10) *Your regular performance review is postponed . . . or suddenly rescheduled and made urgent.*

11) *When you have one-on-one meetings with your boss, your statements—particularly ones that are controversial or emotional—are repeated back to you, as if your boss wants to note something for the record.*

12) *Your boss has a sudden interest in tracking the timing-and-action calendar for projects you have been given—so that your performance can be clearly documented.*

13) *Your boss sends you carefully worded written communication about performance shortfalls, when the same message would usually have been given to you orally.*

14) *Your boss steps in and makes difficult decisions on your behalf, especially ones that you have been postponing for some time.*

15) *For lunch or for after-hours socialization, your circle of peers in other departments suddenly and unexpectedly shrinks.*

16) *A committee is formed to restructure the company or your department, and you are not a member of it.*

17) *Your visibility with the press or as a spokesperson to industry groups is cut back.*

18) *Your prominence in photos in the internal house organ or other company publications is reduced.*

19) *Your boss has a sudden, unexplained interest in the names and numbers in your Rolodex or computer.*

20) *Someone in the human resources department meets with you to "tidy up" your personnel records.*

21) *You lose your status as a mentor or trainer for new managers coming into your department.*

22) *Your income is frozen with the argument that you have reached the peak in your compensation range.*

23) *You are no longer copied on important e-mails, memos, and reports—especially those that could be significant to competitors.*

24) *You are no longer recommended to attend personal training and development programs, especially those outside the company.*

25) *Your boss suddenly wants to meet with you away from the office for a chance to have a leisurely discussion.*

Judy Benaroche Johnson

President and CEO, Rx Worldwide Meetings

"I look at the bright side.
I've now got a character coated with Teflon."

"I was stunned. I had no warning. The human resources manager called me in. My boss was there with her. 'Your services are no longer required,' were his words. I burst into tears. In my opinion, it was done very poorly. I had a site inspection trip to look at a property for a client scheduled for the next weekend. They told me I wasn't going on that trip. They babysat me while I picked up my things, as if I was going to take something. It was a horrible feeling."

That's how Judy recalls the thunderbolt that nailed her. In August 1995, Judy was fired from Sunbelt Motivation and Travel. Bill Boyd, the owner of the corporate parent, had been a friend of hers, and Judy was honored when she was asked to move to Sunbelt as national sales manager. Boyd was taking over as the international president of Sunbelt at that time, and he had just been elected president of Meeting Professional International—the industry's trade association. He had turned over running the meeting planning division of Sunbelt to Judy's direct boss. "Although the work itself wasn't a great fit for me, it was a good, prestigious job that paid well," Judy says. "I called on different companies to sell incentive programs. These were travel incentive awards for more senior sales people as opposed to merchandising incentives."

The sunshine kept beaming down. "I had done really well," Judy says. "The year before, I had sold a million dollar piece of business and was the top winner of our company incentive program. I had just bought a car. I had recently bought a home. For years, I had been a single parent. My daughter was in college out of state—a sophomore at the University of Iowa in Iowa City."

Then came the clouds. First, Judy's sales "were slightly off. I had been counting on my sales trip for Cisco Systems to bring them back in line. That was the trip that was canceled. As Sunbelt saw it, I think they felt I wasn't going to produce anyway." At about the same time, a consolidation took place. Sunbelt had talked about merging with another company, because they didn't do any merchandise incentives at the time. "They thought it would be a nice complement to our business," Judy says. "We were strong in travel incentives and travel generally. I didn't expect there to be much of an overlap. But they kept the salespeople from that company. Several of them had contracts, and I didn't. I was told I was a casualty of the merger, but I was the only person to be let go. I left Sunbelt in the same position I had started with them three years earlier." From Sunbelt to sunset.

"When I left the office, I went home and felt an immediate sense of shame," Judy recalls. The emotion of the moment hasn't left her one bit: "Harvey, I had never been let go from a job before. This happened pre-9/11. The economy was strong. While I wouldn't wish it on anyone, it's a little more plausible today to have been let go. The only severance I received was two weeks' pay. How would I tell my family and especially my daughter? I had to call her and tell her that it was pretty certain we wouldn't be able to let her finish out the school year. Over the next couple of weeks, I started making plans. I knew that I had to sell my house. I wanted out of Dallas, and I planned to move to Chicago. I didn't know how I could face anyone in my industry."

I asked Judy if she ever thought of calling an attorney. She said that was out of the question. "Because our industry is so small," Judy says, "the thought of litigating never crossed my mind. Since Bill Boyd has so much power in the industry, I was afraid to do anything. What grounds would I have had? I had no contract. On the other hand, Texas is an 'at will,' 'right to work' state. They can't enforce a non-compete. I also knew I needed to reach out in this small industry for another job. I was scared to death of damaging my network for future job possibilities. I had never been down that street."

In those weeks after being ushered out of Sunbelt, Judy rebuilt contacts within the industry and turned to her network. She says people were extremely supportive. They invited her out to lunch or dinner to give her a hearing and to see what they could do. One of Sunbelt's biggest competitors is Maritz Performance Systems. A friend of a friend got Judy an interview with them, because they did indeed have an opening in Dallas. The interview was in the lobby of a hotel in Dallas. "My shoulders were slumped," Judy recalls. "The Maritz interviewer went through my résumé and asked me if I did this or that. I kind of shrugged and said, 'Sure, I guess so.' Because of the shame I felt, it was one of the worst interviews of my whole life."

Judy's efforts to find a job fizzled. She felt lost. Again she thought about moving to Chicago, unable to decide if she wanted to stay in Dallas. Her network of friends kept her going and her spirits up. Looking at the employment pages, Judy saw an ad for a program called Recreating Your Future. "Honest to God, I don't know what made me call. They were having an open house. During that visit I was just overtaken by the spirit and enthusiasm of the person who was conducting the orientation. It spoke to me. This was a twelve-week course. At the end came the zinger. She said the tuition was $3,000. In my book, $3 million would have been no different." Then this woman, Lou

Smith, explained that if Judy took a test and passed it, the state of Texas would pay for the program because they classify it as retraining. The people who showed up for the test came from all walks of life: dental hygiene, real estate, and auto mechanics, you name it. Judy passed, and Texas paid.

The program—since discontinued—began in October 1995. The first class assignment was to write a letter to your former employer on your feelings about being let go. Throughout the next two weeks, one course activity would be to read these letters to the class. Because she needed to travel out of town, Judy had to read her letter the first day. Twenty-five people surrounded her in a circle. When Judy wrote the letter, she thought it was nothing. "I got it out of my system when I wrote it. Reading it to that group was a different story. After two lines, I broke down and cried in front of all these people. How angry and sad I was!"

Over the twelve weeks, this program helped Judy recognize just how low her attitude had sunk. "Then they built you back up and set you on your feet. It meant everything for me. The class had a really varied makeup. Some, like me, had lost really good jobs. Some wanted to do something they had never done before. A third group didn't have a clue—like a forty-year-old woman with no dance lessons who wanted to become a ballerina. Lou Smith was the woman who had started this school. She is very spiritual and unusually gifted at helping people stage a recovery from a setback." Judy started selling her strengths again. She began measuring her progress in life once more. Judy says the experience was the most amazing thing to have happened in her life.

Again, the network entered in. A friend of Judy's told her that another friend, Ellen Harden, was relocating her company to Dallas. "From the first interview," Judy says, "Ellen and I adored each other. Full-time, the salary would be less than half of what I had made at Sunbelt. Still, I agreed to work part-time in December while I was still in the retraining program. Despite how much I liked and admired Ellen, I thought that this was the most unprofessional, rinky-dink company I had ever seen. Ellen allowed me to make changes and introduce systems."

At the time, Ellen had only one client: Merck. "What would happen, I asked myself, if we ever lost that client? She let me start diversifying the company. Together, we grew. I joined Ellen full-time when I finished school. Because the compensation was so much lower, it felt a little like I was buying time until I could get a 'real' job.

"When school was over," Judy says, "I started seeing the man whom I subsequently married. I had been single for seventeen years. Things really started moving along for me. The more involved I got with Ellen and her business, the more I enjoyed this company. The money wasn't there, but it was so exciting! Early on, she promoted me from meeting manager to director of meetings. This allowed me to really grow as a manager. I was constantly saying to myself, 'Okay, I'll stay another week.' After a while, I stopped looking." The personal growth factor was a huge element in Ellen's retaining Judy.

Then things got rocky. Not for Judy. For her boss, Ellen. Early in 1999, the two went on an out-of-town program together. Ellen commented she wasn't feeling well and said that she would go to the doctor on Monday. Then came the results: the doctors found a tumor in Ellen's heart. "The next day she was in the operating room," Judy recalls. "When they opened her up, they learned it wasn't a little tumor, but a big one. It was a one-in-a-million situation. The tumor immediately metastasized to both of her lungs. They didn't expect her to live, but she survived and spent five months in the hospital. She never really came back to work from the day she told me that she didn't feel good. In 1999, I was made president of the firm.

"Ellen wanted me to have the business. When she got sick, she told everybody that she wanted me to have the company. Her daughter in California knew that her mother wanted me to have it. Ellen never finalized her will before she died. Her daughter ended up getting nothing. She is still in litigation with her stepfather, and the case is going to a jury trial. I waged a yearlong court battle to have the company extracted from the rest of her estate. We succeeded in convincing the court. My husband, Michael, a partner in the business, and I ended up buying the company in August 2002. These were hard times for the company. The principal reason it wasn't sold on the open market was that it wasn't cash-flowing after 9/11. It suffered the plight of so many travel-related businesses." Through hard work and a real belief in the company, Judy and Michael pulled the firm through the post-9/11 crash and into the black.

Today the company, formerly known as Eharden and Associates, has had its name changed to Rx Worldwide Meetings, Inc. They gross over $3 million in sales and specialize in investigator and pharmaceutical meetings, product launches, and sales events. You can visit their website at *www.rx-worldwide.net*. Their successes have continued, but so have their challenges. Rx Worldwide's lease was up, and Judy really wanted to buy an office building to house the firm. All the banks turned her down, but she finally got a loan from the Small Business Administration and landed a building. Judy says philosophically, "We've been here a month and been robbed twice. But look at the bright side: It didn't faze me. My mom says I've now got a character that's coated with Teflon."

Judy's lessons:

- Judy wasn't happy at Sunbelt, but she felt that she couldn't walk away from the job because of the money she was making. Ultimately, the money walked away from her.

- Judy went to Sunbelt because of Bill Boyd's prestigious reputation in the industry. But she didn't directly work for Boyd, and she says she "knew from the first day that she wouldn't fit in." Although she reports that she has a good professional relationship with Bill Boyd today, the issues were between her and her immediate supervisor. People may think that a company hires them, but they really go to work for a boss. Unless there's a restructuring, it's almost always the immediate boss who makes the firing decision.

- Judy never dreamed she would run a company of such size today. If the cards hadn't fallen the right way, this might never have worked out. As Judy puts it, "God did for me what I wouldn't do for myself."

- Getting fired may eventually be the best thing to happen to you, but it's no ticket to a smooth ride. What you get is the chance to play with a new set of more complex problems.

MACKAY'S MORAL:

Confidence isn't a game. Find the tools to command it, if you want to be a player.

DOWN AND UP #2

- **Lance Armstrong** was fired from the French team Cofidis in 1997, after he began treatment for testicular cancer. They even refused to pay the rest of his salary and medical bills. And the rest—shall we say—is history.

- **Regis Philbin** and his *Who Wants to Be a Millionaire* show were dropped by ABC because of overuse . . . and then brought back for a "sweeps month" stint with a higher payout. Firing isn't new to Philbin, though. He was let go from one of his first TV jobs on *The Joey Bishop Show* in 1969 when Johnny Carson and *The Tonight Show* ruled late-night television.

- **Katie Couric** was "fired" from doing on-air work by CNN after the network's president said he never wanted to see her face on a TV screen again. Now the on-air host of *Today* has a record $60 million, four-year contract.

- **Paula Zahn** was fired in September 2001 by Fox News, which accused her of breaching her contract. The next day she signed with rival news network CNN.

- **Don "I-Man" Imus** was fired in 1977 from WNBC. He was beset by drug and alcohol problems. *Imus in the Morning* is today considered one of the most influential shows in radio.

- **Bob Woodward** was let go from the *Washington Post* and told to get more experience. He did and returned to the *Post* with Carl Bernstein, becoming two of the most recognized journalists, winning most major journalism awards, including the Pulitzer Prize. They coauthored two bestsellers, *All the President's Men* (1974) and *The Final Days* (1976). The first book was made into a movie in 1976 and set box office records. As we go to print, his latest blockbuster book, *Plan of Attack,* is number one on the *New York Times* bestseller list.

- **Joan Rivers** has been fired many times. Fox fired her in 1986 when she launched *The Late Show.* In 1994, Tribune Entertainment cut *The Joan Rivers Show,* and her subsequent Broadway show closed. She faced financial catastrophe. In 1997, she wrote the bestseller *Bouncing Back: I've Survived Everything and You Can Too!*

THE BEST THINGS IN LIFE MAY BE FREE . . . BUT NOT HIDDEN

Are you prepared if you get a pink slip? Do the hiring decision makers at your competitors know you exist? You might have just the vital statistics another company needs, but what good is it unless the right people know?

The best things in your life may be out there waiting for you . . . but not if Mr. or Ms. Wonderful can't find you.

Catbirds have many interesting ways to get noticed. Slate gray and dark-headed, they walk along porch railings eyeing occupants of deck chairs. Then they hop up to gardeners as they are weeding and sing for minutes at a stretch from tops of small trees—sitting, as the saying goes, in the "catbird seat." Catbirds can meow like a cat from the shrubbery. They can even throw their voices around like a ventriloquist and mimic scores of other birds. Ornithologists explain this behavior as part of the breeding and survival process. The better they are at getting noticed, the greater chance catbirds have of finding a mate and producing offspring: their form of survival of the fittest.

What can you learn from the catbird about raising your visibility after you've been fired?

- **Go to trade conventions.** Concentrate on meeting the top players among your principal competitors. Do your homework—à la the Mackay 66: a sixty-six-question profile that I write about in *Swim with the Sharks Without Being Eaten Alive*. (You can obtain a free copy of the profile at *www.mackay.com*.) Learn about the personal interests of key attendees. Now you have at the ready a couple minutes of dazzling small talk. When you can rap with the VIPs about their hometowns and the schools they attended, they'll be saying to themselves, "Who is this caped crusader?"

- **Get involved in industry associations.** They're perfect cover for being in contact with just about anyone in your industry. Even if you're an adversary, bombing positions that your competitors hold near and dear, you'll be remembered for tenacity and dedication. More than once I've gone into a bargaining session and lost big-time, yet I ended up with tremendous admiration and respect for the lawyer on the other side. The next time I was facing a tough negotiation, I hired that person.

- **Do community work where it can do the community— and you—the most good.** If you want to be visible to other companies, you have to go where the ducks are. Nonprofits are constantly on the lookout for volunteer help from all directions. If you're fired, you might pick a nonprofit that is being backed to the hilt by another company in your industry. Try being a doormat and doing a thankless task. It could open the very door you need. Whatever your initial motivation, I guarantee you'll get hooked on volunteering. Rule of the golden thumb: The great organizations, which contribute to the community, recruit great volunteers.

- **Become the name on every Rolodex or personal computer in town.** Trade journals are salivating for articles by industry writers. The spread of e-publications all over the web makes the press even hungrier. Business writers, reporters, securities analysts, and academic types are always in need of pithy remarks and reliable industry statistics. That's you. Establish yourself as an industry expert. The best way to prove that you're *not* is to stay safe and secure, hidden in your own little corner of your own little nest, your only public appearances coming on your way to and from the parking lot.

- **Don't accidentally go into hiding.** If you're a married woman, make sure your name is listed in the phone book separately from your husband's, or at least with your initial. Recruiters aren't happy about having to call you at the office to discuss your next career move. Even if you're the only specially skilled person in the Western Hemisphere who can dip her finger into a pot of envelope glue and tell that it's done cooking, no one is going to plow through twenty-three pages of Andersons set in six-point type in the local phone directory to find out which one you're married to. And male or female, if you move or are relocated, make sure that the important industry people in your old area know your new home address and phone number. In fact, letting people know your whereabouts is a good excuse for a mailing or phone call to those you need to stay in front of.

You should do all of these things if you're out of a job, likely to be ousted, or sitting pretty. In fact, the time to start doing them well is when you're sitting in the lap of success. More people have been hired by being in the right place at the right time than for any other single reason. But you can't take advantage of that unless the person doing the hiring knows where you are.

MACKAY'S MORAL:

They can't hire you if they don't know who you are.

LARRY KING

Award-Winning Host of CNN's *Larry King Live*

*"You didn't create the day. Why not say that
everything that happens to me today is a gift."*

Not many of us think of Larry King as a print journalist. For
most, the King is that ubiquitous interviewer, the star of CNN,
who talks to everyone from presidential hopefuls to Hollywood
megastars to a besieged Martha Stewart and beyond. Still, early
in his career in the 1970s, Larry wrote a column for the *Miami
Herald*. And he got fired from it.

Before he was about to interview a Hollywood diva one day
on the *Larry King Live*'s pulsating set, Larry and I talked about
the trials of being fired. I asked him if the *Herald*'s managing
editor Larry Jinks sent him any signals before letting him go.

"No, he just called one day and said they were dropping the
column," Larry said as he snapped his ever-present suspenders.
"My boss felt that I was writing about too many friends. These
were people I knew and mingled with. That's how I found out
things about them that benefited the column. He thought that I
mingled too much with the people I wrote about. I wore many
hats doing both radio and television and doing the column. At
the time, I was probably the best-known media personality in

Miami. Jinks eased me out when he became editor." I could sense in Larry King's voice that he felt there was no doubt about the parity of the person who fired him and the individual who had hired him. The famous John S. Knight, one of the great publishers in American history, had brought Larry to the *Herald*. "I had been doing columns for the *Miami Beach Sun*," Larry recalls. "When Walter Winchell dropped his column, the *Miami Herald* needed to fill a hole on the entertainment pages. That's when John S. Knight asked me to come over to the *Miami Herald*."

What an interesting twist, I thought to myself. "Can you get fired for being too nice, Larry?"

"Harvey, it wasn't about being too nice. It was about writing on people who were also friends of mine," Larry said with impressive sincerity. "The *Herald* felt it was kind of like self-promoting. The *Herald* is very strict. Like the *New York Times*. If I went to lunch with someone, I had to pay for it, and I had to submit the expenses back to the paper. They can't have the potential subject of a column pay for the meal. You can't let anyone take you to lunch. Many papers have those kinds of rules. I couldn't separate the two, because I was having lunch or dinner with a friend. It was very difficult for me when they dropped me, but I don't blame them. I never carry a grudge."

Remembering what I had read about check overdrafts and personal bankruptcy, I commented to Larry, "Life for you was pretty tough then. Did it just compound the pressure for you?"

"Sure," Larry said as he downed a folic acid with a swig of decaf.

"Whom did you turn to for emotional support?"

"Charlie Bookbinder, who owned Pumpernik's Delicatessen, was a great friend. He gave me my big start by having me do interviews at the restaurant. He was always there for me. I also had a lot of built-in things."

"Such as what?" I probed.

"I've always had a survival streak. I come up off the floor.

Knocked down—get up. I never accept that I'm out. It's like boxing. I might be knocked down in a round, but I've never thought I'd lose the fight. I've always felt confident. Even when I was just doing local radio and TV, I always thought that something national would happen. However, I didn't know that there would be a CNN and even an international role."

"You've had the greatest comeback from being flat on the canvas of anybody I've ever seen," I said, nodding my head with considerable awe. "How devastating was the personal bankruptcy?"

"It was pretty devastating, but I had started my national, coast-to-coast radio talk show on Mutual Broadcasting. We were the first such daily talk show. I had come up from Miami, and we had a national all-night show. I was making an average amount of money. I had started a local television show in Washington. When I went over things with my lawyers, they decided I would never get even," Larry said with pointed realism.

"So, bankruptcy may be a plausible and necessary measure?" I asked him.

"Personal bankruptcy was the way out. I determined in my heart that I would pay everybody off. Eventually, I did," Larry answered with pride.

"Your network of friends and your loyalty to them is legendary. You've had five different wives, for example, but the same best man for each of the weddings. Even if these guys couldn't have had a direct impact on your career, they must have been a real lifesaver in keeping your attitude up. Larry, tell me about your network of friends and your loyalties."

"My best friends are the kids I grew up with," Larry said. "Every morning, I have breakfast with two of them. I live in L.A. now. When Herbie Cohen comes into town, we're always together. We talk almost every day on the phone. The number-one trait I value in people is loyalty. These guys—who like me the most and are the closest to me—do not like me for what I do, but for what I am."

"What exactly is the difference?"

"I lead an extraordinary life in that I can't believe sometimes that I will interview Bill Clinton . . . and a half hour later, I'm at the Palm with Tommy Lasorda talking about the teams in the playoffs," Larry explains. "I have the kind of life where I can go to Marvin Davis' house for dinner on Saturday night with Sidney Poitier and Sidney Sheldon . . . and be at the track at Santa Anita the next afternoon with guys who are inveterate bettors. I wear so many hats."

"Not only do you have plenty of hats. Most of them seem more like crowns than caps."

"Look, I'm seventy years old, and I have three grown kids and two little kids . . . and a wife who has a twenty-two-year-old stepson. I still can't believe I have a house in Beverly Hills. It was just written up in *Architectural Digest*."

"You're afraid to go to sleep, aren't you?" I asked. "You're like me. You might miss something."

"I don't like sleeping," Larry confessed. "When I get up in the morning, I'm alert immediately. My wife, Shawn, lolls around in bed. I'll watch my son. In daytime, I like breakfast. I like lunch. I like dinner. I like different things. I love sports. Sometimes I worry that I've got nothing to worry about. There's a wonderful movie—*Broadcast News*—where William Hurt says to the comic Albert Brooks, 'What do you say to people when every dream in your life has come true?' Albert Brooks replies, 'You shut up.' That sums up my life."

"So, all in all, being fired was a turning point that opened up a new path for you?"

"I also have bounce-back qualities, Harvey. Sometimes getting fired is a break. You can look at firing two ways. Firing can be a terrible tragedy. Or you can say: I don't have to go there tomorrow, so I can make other moves. I can look at other avenues and can fight back . . . and have the time to fight back. Someone once told me that it isn't the tragedy of life; it's how you react to the tragedy. You know, the half-empty glass . . ."

"This comes through in your interviews. I know of no one

who has the gift of appreciating the talents and strengths of others as well as you do, Larry."

"I remember once talking to this Indian wise man Swami Kanji Chinmayananda, a brilliant man, who was silent for twenty years in his life," Larry waxed philosophical. "He taught me, and I will never forget this: 'If you are friendly, all good things come to you.' If you get up in the morning and open your eyes, realize that it's totally a gift you had nothing to do with. That you *got* today is something you had nothing to do with. You didn't create the day. Why not say that everything that happens to me today is a gift? So what if it's raining? Would you rather not see the rain? You're lucky you're alive. If you sit down and order toast at the restaurant and it's burned, the best way to get good toast is to be nice to the waitress . . . the best way to get more bad toast is to be angry. What happens if you come home and your house burned down? You have a tremendous opportunity to build a new house. My wife is a strong religious believer. She believes when you die you go somewhere. I don't believe that. She handles death much better than I do. It doesn't destroy her. I'm afraid of death. I don't want to die because I don't know that there is anything there. I am a classic agnostic."

"Of all the guys you've interviewed, does anyone come to mind as classics who got fired?"

"Clint Eastwood and Burt Reynolds were fired—I think by Universal—the same day or same year. Both were told that they had no future in acting. Sylvester Stallone was thrown out of drama class at the University of Miami and told he had no ability. A nightclub owner in New York told Danny Kaye that the one thing he will never be is an entertainer. You'll find many rejections in show business. They are rejected and then take advantage of a break."

"So, you can't wait around for luck?" I asked.

" 'Luck is the residue of design,' " Larry answered, quoting legendary Brooklyn Dodgers general manager Branch Rickey. "Most of us don't really know the meaning of rejection. You know what true rejection is? It's what the director told the actor to whom he was about to give a pink slip: 'Charlie, *before* they made you, they broke the mold."

"In television, it seems almost de rigueur to have been fired, doesn't it, Larry? Even wildly successful figures like Regis Philbin have tasted the axe at one point or another, haven't they?"

"As you know, Regis is a fellow New Yorker, and he has been a frequent guest on my show. He got fired when he was the announcer on the Joey Bishop TV show. He also lost a show in San Diego once. Everybody in broadcasting has been fired. It's the nature of the game. Firing is rejection: How do you deal with rejection?"

"If that's so, Larry, how do you increase your odds of survival in broadcasting and fields like it?"

"That grand old man of television's early days Arthur Godfrey once told me, 'The whole secret of the broadcasting business is that there's no secret. Just be yourself. If you'll be accepted, you'll be accepted for being yourself. If you try to be someone else, you'll never know.' Jackie Gleason held the same view and helped me on the tube. He appeared on my shows. He did promos. He promoted my career a great deal. The great ones were always themselves. If you are truly yourself, you'll not only be accepted, your chances are much higher of being original, too. When I got a Peabody Award, broadcasting's equivalent of the Pulitzer, Alistair Cooke was the speaker that day. There were about twenty Peabody winners in the audience. Alistair Cooke said, 'The problem in television is that everyone is a copycat. If someone is successful, others imitate them. Only 1 percent of the people in television are original. All the rest are copycats. The 1 percent is in this room.' "

"You've had some heavy-hitter businesspeople on your show, too. What was the best advice you ever heard on firing from a business executive?"

Larry thought for a second and then said: "There was a guy

who was with American Express and then headed up Avis Rent-a-Car. His name is Robert Townsend. He believed the following: When you decide to fire someone, let them go that day. He then pledged to pay them until they got a job. The funny thing was that these people got jobs pretty quick."

"One of the reasons that people can't imagine Larry King getting fired is that you keep getting better. How do you do it?"

"I've never lost my enthusiasm. I've never had an agenda. I've never gone on the air with the intent to harm or to hurt other persons. I'm just there to learn. And I have never gotten jaded. I still like what I do. I like some shows better than others. I don't like it when I have to do a show on a subject that I'm sort of bored with, but I understand that producers need the public to watch something. When that light goes on, something pops in me that is unexplainable. I can be tired. Something could have gone wrong. That hour is my refuge. It has to do with control. I control that hour. It's my hour. Not many people in their lives get a chance to control things. They think: I can't control my kids, my spouse. In that hour, I ask the questions. I go to the phones. That's hard to come down from."

MACKAY'S MORAL:

Want to beat your odds for survival?
Know yourself to be yourself.

ONLY IN AMERICA . . .

You were just fired. End of sentence. But wait. Where exactly were you fired? Thank your lucky Stars and Stripes you were fired in America. The land with the quickest rebound path from underdog to top dog. The land of nonstop opportunity!

It was in America that reporters once rushed up to Yogi Berra—the New York Yankee legend and America's number-one philosopher.

"Yogi, Yogi, did you hear the news?" they cry.

"What's that?" Yogi asks.

"Dublin has just elected its first Jewish mayor," they tell him.

"Only in America!" he beams with pride.

LESLEY VISSER

Sports Broadcaster

"Don't retreat. Advance in another direction."

"Lesley, let's do this like we're on the sidelines. I'm you, and I'm gonna stick this mike in your face. But, of course, I'll never, ever be as good as you."

"Go for it, Harvey."

"So, you were ejected. Did you see that call coming? Any inkling that a flag was about to be thrown?"

"Zero. Blindsided. I got the telephone call the day they announced the change in June 2000. It was from John Filippelli. He's a good man who runs the YES Network today for George Steinbrenner. John said, 'Lesley, I have some terrible news to tell you. . . .' I was being dropped from the staff of *Monday Night Football*. Don Ohlmeyer was coming back to run the show and would be announcing some changes that day. I was stunned. At the time, John was executive producer and Howard Katz was president of ABC Sports. To this day I don't blame John or Howard for this. Howard was great to me at ABC. Maybe I should blame them, but I don't."

"Do a replay for me. What in that instant kept you going, Lesley?"

"First, I have been around winners all my life. I've been covering sports for thirty years. My career started at the age of twenty with the *Boston Globe* following the NFL in 1974. I was the first female beat writer to cover the NFL. Will McDonough—the late, great writer from the *Globe*—taught me that champions can take a punch. I once asked Billie Jean King at Wimbledon: 'What kind of pressure are you under in the final match?' She looked at me and said: 'Pressure is a privilege.' " (For more background, see the Billie Jean King chapter.)

"How did your fans weigh in?"

"Within five hours, I had 400 messages. One was from Pat Riley, who left me a voice-mail, saying: 'In every adversity, there is a seed of equivalent benefit. It's up to you.' My removal was staggering to me because I had loved *Monday Night Football*. And it was very public: The next morning the front page of *USA Today*—above the Kuwaiti oil prices—announced 'ABC's Don Ohlmeyer Takes Lesley Visser Off *Monday Night Football*.' "

"So, you were out of the game, Lesley, but I bet you were already starting to regroup."

"I've been around great rebounders all my life. That's one of the blessings of sports, Harvey. I remembered a quote from Douglas MacArthur: 'We are not retreating . . . we are advancing in another direction.' I'm not going to be on *Monday Night Football*. So, where do I advance?"

"And with whom? Because you were cut from the team, weren't you?"

"No, that's not true. I was cut from the *Monday Night Football* squad. ABC wanted to keep me. The ABC folks called me and asked: 'What else can we give you? Do you want to work on *World News Tonight*? Do you want to host *Wide World of Sports*?' "

"Your head must have been spinning. It would be like John Elway getting sacked. As soon as he gets up, the Broncos are offering to renew his contract . . . but as a tight end. What did you do?"

"Two girlfriends of mine were in Paris. They said: 'You've gotta get out of town. Otherwise you'll be answering calls from every radio station. Get on a plane and come over here!' I did exactly that. CBS president Leslie Moonves just happened to be in first class on the same plane. He walked over to me and said: 'You are not staying at ABC . . . you're coming back to CBS!' I had been with *The NFL on CBS* from 1984 to 1992. That's exactly how my next job arrived. I was truly 'Touched by an Angel.' "

"That's a million to one! I bet you were on cloud nine for seven hours. You didn't need an airplane. You could have just flapped your arms at 30,000 feet."

Time and again, in a firing the given reason is almost never the real reason. Lesley would be too gracious ever to say it. I'm not sure she's ever wasted a moment thinking about it because she's such a forward-looking person. But I have talked to a lot of people in the sports world, and the verdict is clear. It was ageism that got her cut from the *Monday Night Football* squad. ABC wanted a younger face. When they had such a beautiful one, I wonder why. More importantly, ABC would have retained the competence and experience that Lesley offered. The duo that succeeded Lesley looked like they had never held a network microphone at a live football game, let alone talked into one. It's no surprise that neither Ohlmeyer nor his two sideline sidekicks didn't last long.

When I asked Lesley if she thought of her ABC days as a lemon without lemonade, she countered: "I loved the time I spent at ABC. I was there for eight years and never had a bad day. They made me the first woman on *Monday Night Football*. My work was consistent through my entire time there. Dropping me wasn't done for professional reasons. I was acknowledged as the best at what I did. When I left *Monday Night Football*, NFL Commissioner Paul Tagliabue sent me an engraved crystal from Tiffany that read: 'Thank you for all you did for Monday Night Football.' I reported from the World Series. I covered the Triple Crown. I did World Figure Skating with Dick Button and Peggy Fleming. It was a fantastic experience."

"And tennis, you've done a lot of tennis, haven't you? I've been to thirty Wimbledons, and I must have spotted you there at least a dozen times."

"I've covered fifteen Wimbledons. When I started, we used to have to send our copy by Western Union. The Brits still called us the Colonials. One of the great moments of my life was when Bud Collins was inducted into the Tennis Hall of Fame and he asked me to be his presenter. It was an honor."

It's hard to think of the youthful-looking Lesley Visser as a pioneer, but that's exactly what she was. "It was an absolute frontier when I started," she recalls, "and I have been on the front line for three decades. There were no provisions for equality in the NFL back then. Since I was the first woman to cover the NFL, I would have to wait in the parking lot for the athletes. There was no provision for locker room access back then. There were no ladies' rooms in the press boxes. So I had to pray I could make it back from the public restroom in time or I'd miss a field goal."

The capper though is what happened in Three Rivers Stadium in 1976. "I was out there with my pad and pen waiting for Pittsburgh quarterback Terry Bradshaw," says Lesley. "Terry came out and I went up to him and asked him a question. He took the pen, signed an autograph on my notebook, and walked away. We're best of friends now, but back then I actually had to explain to him that I was a reporter."

Lesley knows in-your-face humiliation few of us have seen. Her ability to handle it has been a powerful part of her comeback skill set. "No one prepares you for that," she contends. "When I speak at colleges, I say the one thing you can't prepare for is humiliation. You can study. You can be the smartest. You can graduate number one, but somewhere along the way there will be times in your career and your life that you are going to be caught off guard. I never forget the Nora Ephron line: 'That which does not kill you makes you funnier.' *Now* the Bradshaw story is funny. When it happened, it wasn't. It's how you handle the hurdle."

Lesley tells young women: "If you want to survive in sports broadcasting, you need four elements: knowledge, passion, stamina, and a sense of humor. I'm not saying it's easy to have these four traits, but you need them to play at the highest level. The lack of passion is a special problem. There are too many fraudulent men and women—but especially women—in this field. If you really don't love sports . . . if you don't want to see Carmello Anthony or Serena Williams or Michael Vick, then don't pretend. To me, sports are not a vanity project. Sadly, that's how many young women view it. You have to love sports because that's where your passion takes you. It's not about being famous. The passion becomes your career. There are two kinds of women who cover sports. There are women who love and know sports and they end up on TV, and then there are women who just want to be on TV and they end up in sports."

Lesley dismisses the latter as "karaoke reporters." "They are like Milli Vanilli. They don't have independent thoughts. It's whatever the producer says to them in their earpiece. They are like the movie *Broadcast News*. People ask me what do you think of this type and my answer is: Nothing shocks me! After all, I'm a Red Sox fan. Lifelong, by the way. As you might imagine, many young women send me letters or tapes. In a flash, I can spot the ones who won't succeed. They are the ones who ask 'How much money can I expect to make?' or 'Can I get on *Entertainment Tonight*?' I know they aren't going to make it!"

"Why have you lasted for thirty years while you see so many others cycle through?"

"I think there are two reasons why: my legitimacy and my authenticity."

"Did your background in print journalism strengthen you for broadcasting?"

"There isn't one way to get there, but for me it's central to *my* success. I'm still a writer at heart who works in TV. Hopefully you hear that distinction on the air. I never speak clichés. I don't let athletes say clichés to me. I don't use them in pieces. I am a writer. The central blessing in my life was being at the *Boston Globe*. We were 'Murderers' Row': Bud Collins on tennis, Will McDonough on football, Peter Gammons on baseball, and Bob Ryan on basketball. John Powers won a Pulitzer."

"Your colleague Boomer Esiason says you are 'unbelievably prepared.' Is total preparation key to duking it out in a job like yours?"

"There can be simultaneous truths—you have to have the ability and the ability to deliver it. To be the best at anything you must be enormously prepared. I once asked the great TV commentator Charles Kuralt what the secret of TV is. He said it's like the duck on the pond—he appears placid on the surface, but he's paddling furiously underneath. In any job on camera, you know when someone isn't prepared. They are fighting for the right words, not knowledgeable . . . not clever . . . not funny. So it's a combination: being absolutely prepared and being able to think on your feet. When I went from print to TV, I was just speaking on deadline instead of writing on deadline. The skills translated."

"When you returned to CBS in 2000, Lesley, did you define new objectives for yourself?"

"David Rockefeller said, 'Part of the challenge for twenty-first-century man is knowing what you *don't* want to do.' I was asked to host the *CBS Early Show* for a week. I was curious to find out: Do I want to do this? I really have great admiration for the people who do that job, but it didn't work for me. I could tell after one day, I just did not care about the Canadian autoworkers, God bless 'em. I cared if Michigan beat Notre Dame."

"How will the sports broadcasting world be different in the next ten or twenty years?"

"I really hope there is more diversity and less screaming. Harvey, you yourself write about instant gratification in our world. It leads to a lot of ill-considered noise. What I would like to see are . . . okay this is selfish . . . more women, but also more African Americans, more Asian Americans, and more Native Americans. I'd like to see the volume turned down, more thought and vocabulary."

"You've had other setbacks as well, like breaking your hip while jogging in Central Park in 1993. Was rebounding from that like coming back from the hits you've taken as a reporter?"

"Not really. In 1974, there was no greater adversity than being the first woman in print journalism to cover the NFL. It was both a great blessing and a huge trial. But the *Boston Globe* was such a powerful organization. They said, 'We're going to hire a woman and give her significant responsibility. We believe in her, and we will fight for her.' I faced adversity from day one. Shattering my hip was a different kind of adversity. But once again, I was blessed. How lucky am I that a young man found me in Central Park, recognized me, and insisted that the ambulance take me to Lennox Hill, a great orthopedic hospital. God, I could have fallen down in a back alley in Bombay, but I didn't. I got hurt in the backyard of the greatest medical community in the world. I'm also blessed with optimism, and some great folks helped fuel it. I remember when I was in the hospital, coach Bill Parcells was one of a number who called me regularly. These were individuals I really respected. Sports are filled with these kind of people who face adversity all the time. Athletes, coaches, players. As a small child who loved the Boston Celtics, I learned another enduring philosophy from coach Red Auerbach, who said, "It's not who starts . . . it's who finishes.""

"Red Sox, Celtics. Did you do play-by-play for the Little League in Bean Town?"

"On Halloween, Harvey, all the other girls put on Mary Poppins costumes. I would dress up as the Celtics guard Sam Jones."

"This next item I call 'woman bites dog.' CBS will actually loan you to NBC to cover the Athens Olympics this summer. That's some tribute to your professionalism. You're so good, you're nondenominational."

"I'm really flattered that Dick Ebersol and David Neal would ask me. I am going to work the Opening Ceremonies at the Olympics for the network I am *not* with! I believe the reason I am being allowed to do it—and God bless him for it—Sean McManus is the president of CBS Sports. His father is the legendary Jim McKay, who is always referred to as 'Mr. Olympics.' [For those wondering about the last names, Jim's birth name is also McManus, but he changed it to McKay.] So Sean knows what the Olympics mean. One of the great privileges of my life was to work with Jim McKay at ABC. So that is why Sean said to me, 'Just don't get too comfortable over there.' It will be fabulous to be working in Athens."

"What advice would you give young people—especially young women—about facing and overcoming setbacks?"

"Well, I would say remember what Pat Riley said. 'It's up to you if you will interpret a setback as an opportunity.' And, remember MacArthur, too. 'You have to look at it as an advance in another direction, not as a retreat.' You need to know inside yourself that you are not a fraud. If you pass that test, then a few other traits will help you to rebound from setbacks: self-esteem, talent, curiosity, persistence, and optimism. That's what lets you handle rejection and move beyond it."

Let's not forget credibility and authority. One of my favorite quotes about Lesley comes from Dennis Miller. He calls his ideal woman, "Julia Child in the kitchen, Traci Lords in the bedroom, and Lesley Visser during a game."

Here's how to stay on *your* game. . . .

- Never retreat. Advance in another direction.

- Remember, opportunity promises both gain and pain. Only you can decide which wins out.

- Fight humiliation with humor.

- Frauds never reach the finish line.

- Just because we call them "mentors" doesn't mean they have to be men. The most successful people count men *and* women among their role models.

MACKAY'S MORAL:

It's only a man's world if you're satisfied with
waiting in the parking lot.

IF YOU ARE UNDER THIRTY, THE LIKELIHOOD THAT YOU WILL BE FIRED IN THE NEXT TWENTY YEARS IS 90 PERCENT

For statisticians, a probability greater than 89 percent is not a likelihood. It's a certainty. It's not a question of *if* you'll be fired, it's a question of *when*. The 90 percent figure isn't my number. It's the estimate I got when I recently asked a leading human resources executive. People graduating from college today—U.S. government statisticians say—are likely to have ten to twelve different employers in the future. Additionally, they will likely make three to four career changes. If you are under thirty, it is almost certain that one—and probably several—of these job and career changes will *not* be of your own choosing.

Face facts:

- **Are you on pins and needles that your company *may* go out of business? Wrong! Your present company is *likely*** to go out of business. And it doesn't much matter which company. In fact, it will be the exception if your company *doesn't* go out of business. Of the 500 companies on the prestigious Standard & Poor's list in 1957, only seventy-four were still on the list in 1998. Fast-forward to the year 2020, and do you know what will happen? According to Richard Foster and Sarah Kaplan in their book *Creative Destruction,* more than 375 of the S&P 500 companies will be firms we don't know today. Today's young people will ride a merry-go-round for their meal ticket. 'But I work with the esteemed so-and-so,' you might protest. Just remember that the so-and-sos of the last twenty years include Enron, Sinclair Oil, Montgomery Ward, Dean Witter, and Swissair. By the year 2030, the only folks with ten years' seniority will be at CBS on the staff of *60 Minutes*. When you're on that merry-go-round pony, watch out! Instead of grabbing the brass ring, you're more likely to be nailed by a brass knuckle.

- **Restructuring, like dieting, is a way of life.** Even if your company doesn't go out of business, it will be on staffing diets for the rest of its life. Look at every large company around, and you'll see that restructuring isn't exceptional. It's perpetual. When systems can do what people did, people go. When firms merge, bodies fly.

- **A diamond may be forever, a job is not.** Peter Drucker—who is in his mid-nineties—is the dean of management experts. His life and career have been a model of things to come. Drucker has been a securities analyst, a journalist, a professor, a consultant, an administrator, and a best-selling author. Six careers and still going strong! Drucker keeps tabs on his students. Do you know what he found? "Practically all of them will start working for big companies," he writes. "Then they go to work for another big company. Four years later, they go to work for a medium-sized company." Why? In part they start out at big companies like GE to get job security. But after three years they realize there ain't no job security anymore, not even at GE. They're still young and still not very high up. But next they work with a joint-venture partner that is much smaller. They get more exposure, more know-how, more bullets on their résumés. By then, they may not be even thirty! But they are enhancing their hirability by seizing an opportunity to learn. The truth is, it's not just that big companies don't offer job security anymore. It's that there isn't much security for companies themselves. Who says so? Standard & Poor's does!

- **Fat chance is no chance.** "I'm so healthy and athletic, I'll be lucky and I'll never get cancer." I felt that way, too, but it happened to me. Luckily, I'm a twelve-year prostate cancer survivor. . . . "I'm so skilled, I'll never be replaced." Talk to those gifted artisans at tool and die shops whose metalworking capabilities mean nothing today and who have lost their jobs to computer-literate equipment operators. . . . "I'm so good, they couldn't afford to fire me." Don't forget about the people whose skills and accomplishments were so stratospheric that their success intimidated their bosses into firing them. Will you dodge the speeding bullet? Just like at the dog track, my money is on the bunny.

The question is not *if* you're going to be fired, the question is *how* you will handle it. The worst time to learn about mixing up a pitcher of lemonade is when life deals you a lemon.

Over the years, I have come to know thousands of executives all over the world. They have shared their personal stories with me. Every successful executive I have ever met has mastered the art of rebounding from a setback, often a firing. Those managers who go through the trauma of a firing and **can't** rebound are the ones who go on to drift through a series of dead-end jobs. They become resigned and defeated. They are convinced they can't master their destiny. Those who battle back gain even more remarkable confidence that they can lick anything life throws their way.

MANNIE JACKSON
Owner and CEO of the Harlem Globetrotters

"I had all the trappings.
What mattered to me was being underutilized."

"Like every young executive, I made a run for the CEO job at
Honeywell. I didn't get it. I was being paid very well as their executive vice president in charge of mergers and acquisitions.
Most people would say, 'Mannie, just sit back and enjoy it.' My
office in the executive wing was elegant and I had all the trappings. Despite that, you know what stared me in the face every
morning when I came to work? The fact that I knew I was being
underutilized."

Mannie Jackson is a driven guy. Mannie was the first
African American to own a major league professional sports
team. He was the first African American captain of the University of Illinois basketball team and was both All Big Ten and
All-American. Then he played with the Harlem Globetrotters
for three years. After that came his meteoric business career. It
began as manager of educational development with General
Motors. Then he became director of labor relations for GM's
Cadillac Division. Next, he moved to Minneapolis-based Honeywell as vice president of human resources, then VP of market-

ing. In 1983, he was named president and general manager of Honeywell's telecommunications business, which he grew over a seven- to eight-year period into a profitable and significant operation. When that division was shut down for strategic reasons, he became a corporate executive vice president and chief of marketing and administration.

To this day, Mannie describes his departure from Honeywell as amicable.

It was a case of just being swept to the side. Banish any illusion that Mannie would let his golden career be ground into dust. Of all the executives I have known, Mannie epitomizes preparation-plus. He didn't leave Honeywell until the early 1990s. But back in 1986, he became a founder and board member of the Executive Leadership Council, a newly formed business and civic organization. The council, of which Mannie eventually became president, gave African American executives a network and a leadership forum. Through Mannie, it also gave Honeywell access to increasingly influential minority executives at the highest levels of other companies. "Part of my value to Honeywell was the access I had to a huge network, including the banks," Mannie recalls. "I became their relationship person for all the business units. This was guerrilla marketing. And it gave me access to a large number of contacts, which we mined with determination.

"When you leave a company, always do your best to maintain good relationships," Mannie believes. "You have to take a longer view of your career and relationship building. I never languish on the negatives. It was disappointing to me, but it was a good departure. Perhaps I wouldn't have been chairman or CEO of Honeywell, but I was certainly a confidant of top management and a high-level decision maker and influencer of policy and direction. I understood the company and had served in leadership roles in virtually every business unit of the company."

Mannie had also created a private investment group before

leaving Honeywell. "I had several investments in businesses that were generating cash flow," Mannie says. "I was also making investments in building teams of people in these businesses around the country before I struck out on my own." Talk about digging your well before you're thirsty!

Mannie insisted on having a clear focus for his business. "I developed a skill in repairing businesses that had been thrown into the garbage can. None were flourishing," as Mannie puts it. "They were often in declining markets. Harvey, I learned I just had a knack for acquiring and repairing postpeak businesses." The underutilized person is often the best judge of the underutilized business.

Reenter the Harlem Globetrotters—surely a sentimental attachment. After all, Mannie had been a standout player for the team in the 1960s. The Globetrotters were founded in 1927 in Chicago by entrepreneur Abe Saperstein. One has to remember that the Globetrotters were the only game in town for black players until 1950, the first year that the NBA allowed integrated teams. "Abe Saperstein was an important guy for me," Mannie recalls. "I observed him carefully and the way he did things. He was a world-class promoter and a great salesman. He also had great relationships with people."

Saperstein died in 1966, and the team was sold for less than $4 million. In the years afterward, the team passed through new owners more times than a Meadowlark Lemon hand around. They included a group of Chicago investors, then Metromedia, and finally International Broadcasting Corporation, which made the team an exhibition attraction alongside shows like the Ice Capades. International Broadcasting fired off an air ball in 1991 when it filed for Chapter 11. That paved the way for Mannie to put together an ownership deal that was sealed in 1993.

At GM, Cadillac, and Honeywell, Mannie learned plenty about brand management. He quickly put it to work in reviving an organization that had stood at the edge of bankruptcy. By 1996, the Globetrotters had tripled their revenues and were performing for Nelson Mandela and a liberated South Africa in Pretoria. Columbia Pictures bought the team's movie rights, and Disney bought options to make a musical out of the Globetrotters story. In the year 2000, Mannie took the team to St. Peter's Square in Rome for an audience of 50,000 with Pope John Paul II, as he was inducted as an honorary Globetrotter. (The Pope's jersey number is 75.)

Mannie built a string of sponsorship and endorsement programs with marquee consumer brands like Wheaties, Sprint, Northwest Airlines, Denny's Restaurants, Reebok, Disney, and Burger King. He was able to utilize their channels of distribution and their networks of people. "The money was crucial," Mannie says, "but in retrospect, aligning the Globetrotters with prestigious brands may have been even more important."

In 2002, the all-important Q-ratings of sports teams showed that the Globetrotters "maintained their position as the most liked and most recognized sports team in the world." When compared with 1,742 sports personalities, the Globetrotters ranked second only to Michael Jordan and ahead of Tiger Woods. Another great milestone was reached in 2002: The Globetrotters were inducted into the Naismith Basketball Hall of Fame.

When you think of the Globetrotters, you think of fun, but Mannie cautioned me about that image. "Abe Saperstein wanted his black ballplayers to be recognized as solid global citizens and great athletes," Mannie contends. "Abe didn't see his players as clowns and just showmen." In fact, that concern about being taken seriously may have caused Mannie to overreact earlier in his career. "Images of being seen as a dumb jock or not being taken seriously because of race really affected me, Harvey," Mannie recalls. "It made me try to be so profoundly serious that I'm sure I was a pain in the butt to others. I tightened up. Someone who knew me at the University of Illinois said I was not the guy he remembered from a few years ago. 'You are too hard on yourself. Lighten up.' I was trying to be someone else. I was no longer lighthearted. I tried to come across like the picture of a classic executive you would see in the *Wall Street Journal*. Eventually, I did lighten up. I decided to approach life the same way I would approach an athletic contest: building teams, being forthright, looking forward, being honest, and being positive. Along with that comes the energy that you get from just being loose."

Mannie's earliest lessons in guiding himself came from working with Coach Joe Lucco at Edwardsville High School in Illinois. "Joe Lucco was the first person to embrace me as a person and respect me," Mannie recalls. "He ignored color. He taught me how to win by example. The importance of preparation: he really strengthened my grasp of it. He helped me deal with the skills in responding to setbacks. Coach Lucco showed me how to access that resource within myself." Back then, Mannie had a flair for being a flamboyant dresser. His fedora was the capper. Once the coach didn't like the way Mannie dressed, so he was sent home to change. When Mannie got back to the high school, the team bus had left. To make the game, Mannie had to take a taxi for $9, a fortune back in 1956. Lucco told him if Edwardsville won and Mannie scored at least thirty points, his cab fare would be paid for. You know what? It was.

How about when Mannie has to let people go himself? "When someone has to be terminated, I don't view it as a negative. And I don't personalize it. Many good people simply find themselves in the wrong situation. In recent years, I've served on six Fortune 500 corporate boards, and I judge a CEO on his or her track record of building teams. One of the most important things leaders have to do is to build teams around themselves. I know my goal is to build the best team I can around myself. I start assuming everyone wants to be a winner. The people who are going to hurt us are not the people we let go, but the people we keep. And you always have to ask: Do I have the people for a mile-high performance team? And are they being given the right leadership to do the job? It's making every experience an energizing and positive event."

By the way, does Mannie miss that gilded cage at Honeywell? Mannie puts it this way: "By walking out the door, Harvey, in the first fourteen months after leaving Honeywell, I made more money than I had earned in the entire twenty-five years before. Both my net worth and—more importantly—my self-worth are at levels well beyond my wildest dreams. For many reasons, I have Honeywell to thank."

Mannie Jackson's dunking stakes are a lot bigger than $9 cab fares these days.

- Your company may give you the boot, but don't boot the networks that company has opened for you.

- If you think you are going to be an entrepreneur, get your feet wet *before* somebody sets you out in the rain.

- The odds are best for entrepreneurs if (1) they know the business they are getting into, and (2) the business is undervalued, not overvalued.

- If you're performing subpar, or if someone on your team is, don't ask if they are doing the wrong thing. Ask first if they are in the right place.

MACKAY'S MORAL:

When you're undervalued, even the Ritz can be the pits.

FOULING OUT IS NOT FOREVER

- Most experts agree that **Michael Jordan** is the greatest basketball player of all time. But Jordan's basketball legend developed slowly. He was cut from his high school basketball team his sophomore year. He eventually made the team and led it to the state championship. The first glimpse of his talent came in 1982, when, as a freshman at North Carolina, he made the game's winning shot against Georgetown, lifting the Tar Heels to the national championship. Jordan went on to play on six NBA championship teams and was named to the All-NBA first team ten times.

- One college coach wasn't interested in **George Mikan**, who was cut from his high school basketball team, because he was too awkward and wore glasses. But after arriving at DePaul University, he blossomed into the nation's premier college basketball player. He earned All-America honors three times and turned professional. In his first seven seasons with the Minneapolis Lakers, he led the team to six league championships. In 1950, Mikan was voted the "Greatest Player in the First Half-Century" by the Associated Press. Mikan was named to the Naismith Basketball Hall of Fame in 1959.

- **Isiah Thomas,** a member of the NBA Hall of Fame, was fired as head coach of the Indiana Pacers at the end of the 2003 season by Larry Bird. Thomas was one of a record eleven eastern conference head coaches fired within a two-year period. Thomas went on to become president of the New York Knicks and promptly fired the Knicks head coach Don Chaney and replaced him with **Lenny Wilkins,** who had been fired a year earlier by the Toronto Raptors.

- **Bobby Knight,** a three-time winner of the NCAA men's basketball championship, was fired by Indiana University in 2002. Six months later he was hired as the men's head basketball coach at Texas Tech.

- **Spud Webb,** the 5' 7" NBA phenom, was released by the Detroit Pistons before he ever got a chance to try out. The Atlanta Hawks gave him a chance and he went on to play twelve years and won the 1986 NBA slam dunk championship.

Susan
Clark-Johnson

CEO and Publisher of the *Arizona Republic*

"Be ready for the challenge before you're ready for the job."

"Sheriff's deputies and National Guard lined up on the street across from the administration building where I worked. I was in the public information office of the University of New York's Buffalo campus. Kids were picketing in a peaceful protest rally against the Vietnam War. Suddenly the confrontation turned ugly. The sheriff's people started lobbing tear gas canisters into the crowd of picketers, and things flared into a melee. I was stunned because there was no reason for this to take place. Turning to the fellow for whom I worked, I said, 'This is outrageous! I can't believe this is happening.' He looked me straight in the eye and said, 'You are never allowed to have an opinion.' I was out of a job the next day," recalls Susan Clark-Johnson.

It was 1970, the time of Kent State and the Vietnam War. Sue had already started her career as a journalist with the *Evening Press*—the Gannett newspaper in Binghamton, New York. She had moved to Buffalo when her husband relocated to begin his commitment with the National Guard. She found that there weren't any jobs in journalism there, so she took a post in the university's public information office. "Freedom of speech is fundamental in an academic environment. It's impossible to imagine it being deprived. I was raised in a family where there were plenty of discussions. The words my boss uttered were at direct odds with one of my core beliefs," Sue says.

To suggest that Sue has free speech and journalism in her blood is an understatement. Sue's parents were divorced before she was six. She lived with her father much of the time while she was growing up. He was a freelance writer. Newspaper editors around the country were her babysitters. At age ten she got a typewriter, not a doll, as a Christmas present from her father. "I learned to think on that typewriter at a very young age. When I was fourteen, I became a stringer for a twice-weekly paper—the *Patent Trader* in Westchester County—at 20 cents an inch. I wrote a l-o-t of inches," Sue remembers with pride.

Graduating from college in 1967, Sue went to work at the *Evening Press*. "In those days, papers had a women's and society section, not a features department. I was twenty years old and one of eleven women in the women's department. One day the women's editor just disappeared," Sue says. Management asked Sue if she would pull things together until they found a new editor. After they didn't in six months, she went in to her boss and noted she had held things together reasonably well. She said she wanted to be the women's editor. They agreed. During her stay in Binghamton, Sue moved the section away from the conventional cherry cobbler recipes and bridal shower reports toward truly newsworthy features.

"After my abrupt departure from the university," Sue explains, "I was unemployed for three or four months. Gannett had an opening in Buffalo that fall and they hired me. Since my husband was in law school at the time, I was our sole support. But, it was important for me to do something I truly wanted to do. When I left the university, I asked myself a question: Is this what I am cut out to do?" If working in the information office meant Sue was not entitled to have an opinion, she was obviously not cut out for that job. Certainly not holding down a job working for a boss with such absurd beliefs.

Anybody who has been fired, Sue believes, needs to wrestle with this question: If this is not what I am cut out to do, what exactly *am* I cut out for?

Sue first became a publisher of a Gannett paper at the age of thirty. That meant she had caught the eye of Gannett's publishing legend Al Neuharth.

Neuharth, since retired from the Gannett organization, was the maverick genius behind the inception of *USA Today*. He numbers among the most *aggressive* optimists I have ever met. One of his great all time quotes is, "Don't just learn something from every experience, learn something positive." I remember being invited as an observer to a management retreat held in a Minnesota hunting lodge. The meeting took place on the tail of *USA Today*'s launch in September 1982. The managers I was observing were the senior executives of a large newspaper publishing organization. They were some of the brightest people in the state. Thirteen of these fifteen press industry gurus predicted that the journalistic community would be writing *USA Today*'s obituary in no time. Neuharth proved them dead wrong.

Early in her career as a publisher, Al Neuharth said to Sue: "You're not ready for the job but you are ready for the challenge. Trust me, there are no free rides. You may be the only one of two women today, but if you don't make it, I'll fire you." Sue regards those words as "the most motivating thing ever said to me. While he had a smile on his face and while he didn't say it viciously or vindictively, I knew that he meant it. Al Neuharth is an unbelievable visionary who knew how to raise expectations and build a results culture."

Those are expectations Sue has mastered meeting. She has been publisher and CEO of the *Arizona Republic* since the year 2000. Her paper is now ranked number thirteen in U.S. circulation. Sue is also senior group president of Gannett's Pacific Newspaper Group and has oversight responsibility for twenty-three newspapers throughout the West, including Hawaii and Guam.

Sue has been a good deal more than a publisher. She is one of the savviest *managers* of publishers in the newspaper industry today. I asked her to recount two of the most memorable cases of firings she was involved with. There are few executives more accomplished at letting people go. However, Sue is also a person who takes this responsibility with great seriousness and personal dedication. "Regardless of our feelings," she says, "we have to focus on what's needed and, at the same time, be open enough to work with the differences in people. All that while staying within policy and consistent with our practices. It's a tough balancing act. And one's feelings are woven integrally into the entire process. Personally I dread having those conversations more than anything else I do. I don't sleep well the night before. I role-play the encounter endlessly. When it's done, I feel completely drained. If it gets to the point where I don't agonize over it, then I probably shouldn't be doing this anymore."

In two cases Sue recounted, "Employees were terminated because their performances were subpar, but the root cause, in my mind, was because they weren't a good 'fit' with the position or the specific work environment. There were the customary ongoing performance reviews and discussions pinpointing concerns and recommending remedial actions. In both cases, I was straightforward in assessment during review periods. In both cases, it was very difficult. I would like to think I tried to meet them on their own terms, but you have to accept a certain reality. We can't control the behavior of others, but we can be flexible and have empathy when warranted.

"In the first case the employee took responsibility for his behavior," Sue explains. "He worked hard to meet me halfway. While devastated that he had, in his view, 'failed,' his behavior allowed me to work with him, to work together to create as positive an outcome as possible for him and for the organization. His severance included counseling with a top-notch placement firm. That counseling led him to ultimately agree that the role he had been in just wasn't right for him and that perhaps the industry wasn't a good fit either. In the second, the employee refused to acknowledge there was a problem. She fought, lied, threatened, and tried to intimidate. I had to be very firm and steadfast. She never did accept responsibility for poor performance."

Sue credits much of her success to a willingness to take risks. Harkening back to that fateful day on the Buffalo campus, she still embraces much of that idealism and optimism. "Ours was an exploratory generation," Sue believes. "We thought all things were possible."

That idealism permeates another focal point of Sue's life: a crusade against discrimination. Sue has won a fistful of awards for her unflinching campaign against racism and bigotry. Sue believes definite progress has been made. Tougher laws, for example, have gone a long way toward reducing the unfair firings that were so commonplace for women and minorities. But Sue also says that disadvantaged people facing employment discrimination still need to do a better job of knowing their rights.

While an idealist at heart, Sue is also a pragmatist. When I asked her about the most important things she has done to level the job playing field in her own organization, she was quick to answer, "I encourage women to take up golf, especially those who interact with customers. I didn't play golf, and I felt it was a disadvantage since so much business is transacted on the golf course."

Amen. At Mackay Envelope Company, we have done much the same: recommending lessons to the golfing uninitiated, especially women. It's amazing how many work-driven thank-goodness-it's-Monday cultures know the special place that golf still occupies as a competitive edge.

- If you have strong beliefs, tread lightly around compromising jobs. You're not likely to last long.

- If you don't want to be cut, don't do a job you're not cut out for.

- Everyone avoids the task of letting people go. It's the exceptional manager who studies and masters a difficult and thankless skill to do it well for all parties concerned.

- Know the game within the game. If you want to win at the game of business, it doesn't hurt to master the game of golf.

MACKAY'S MORAL:

You can be ready for the challenge before you're ready for the job, but always be prepared. It's easy to tumble from a tightrope.

SUICIDE BY POISON PEN

If you're going to finish yourself off, a poison pen sounds like a pretty dumb thing to use. Hard to believe how many people do just that. They get fired from a job, boil inside, and then go ballistic. They write the explosive letter of a lifetime. They don't just say every vicious thing they wanted to say to their boss. They say every vicious thing they wanted to say to the world for the last twenty years. Am I telling you not to pick up that pen? Not necessarily. Ventilation is often good for the soul. When you're airing your soul, though, it's a good idea to keep the window closed. Go ahead and write that letter, but heaven help you if you actually send it.

- **Your former employer will be very careful about what they send you in writing.** Be just as smart and cautious as they are in what you send to them. Plenty of people fool themselves. They try to make the letter sound like it's coming from an attorney. If it sounds like a legal letter, that's how your old boss is likely to read it. If you're not an attorney, the former firm may conclude you have just retained a dumb lawyer. If you *are* considering suing your former employer, never send anything not blessed by your actual legal advisor.

- **The most moving letter in the world won't get you rehired.** Do companies reverse firing decisions? Nearly never. You can use all the persuasive tools on your gun belt. Reason slicker than Einstein. Be a hotter passion pistol than Christina Aguilera. Call for more righteous reckoning than a revival preacher on the stump. Appeals won't work.

- **Get ready to play the next hand.** You may say that you'll never darken someone else's door for a favor again. You may be completely convinced that you can live without Old Witherspoon's goodwill. Chances are you're wrong. They made their decision. Only time will tell if they were right. Staying cool and calm means you won't endanger either your networks, your references, or possible future consulting arrangements. Don't grovel. But don't throw gravel in people's faces either. Going off half-cocked and behaving inappropriately is a pretty good way to prove your ex-boss was right.

- **Be mysterious.** Often the most powerful edge you have is to keep your former employer guessing—that is, until you may need a reference or a connection. They're asking themselves: What will she do next? Whom will she work for? Your former employer is rarely your enemy. Then again, these people aren't exactly your pals either.

I just saw a "rage letter" from an employee who was permanently downloaded from a technology firm. In it, she says:

- Talking with her boss was "a waste of precious oxygen."

- Her boss's brain was overtaxed even for a "techno-moron" because even "binary" thinking was too complex for him.

- The guy spent his days "shiftlessly looking for fault in others."

- As a reprisal, the list of "passwords to every account on the system" could easily be published.

- The expected letter of recommendation for the departing employee should be spell-checked because she was tired of correcting her boss's mistakes.

- Her boss was "sad proof of the Dilbert Principle."

- And, much more. The kind of much, I must say, that would whet the appetite of a tabloid sleaze-squeezer.

Few people have the credentials and industry clout of a Lee Iacocca. When they're axed, not many folks can tell their boss where to get off and still stay balanced on the seesaw.

If getting fired can be the best thing that ever happened to you, then there is such a thing as a perfect firing. There are perfect divorces. Perfect cancer operations. Perfect crash landings. Do you want the chance to make your firing the best thing that ever happened to you? Then—for your own good—don't let your emotions screw it up!

MACKAY'S MORAL:

He who burns bridges better be a darn good swimmer.

MICHAEL ALTSHULER

President and CEO, Mem-Cards Corporation

"You can either call someone and have a pity party or find someone who can straighten out your thinking."

"I pinned the president of the company against the wall and screamed 'Give me back my attaché case!' " remembers Michael Altshuler. This was twenty-six years ago and he was then a salesman for an office-products distributor in Atlantic City, New Jersey. It was a cold, crisp morning when the crap hit the fan. Mike is not particularly proud of this moment in his history. In fact, it took the Seabrook precinct of the New Jersey State Police to pry him free of his grip on the president of his company, but Mike was furious.

Michael is a strapping guy. The kind of guy you definitely want on your side. He'll tell you he lacks the talent and conviction that go into being a professional athlete. I'm not so sure. At forty-seven, Michael still has the makings of an NFL linebacker. Post-handshake, my wrist swears it's so. Today, Michael is the founder and CEO of Mem-Cards, a revolutionary company that takes a book's best ideas and puts them on cards. Mem-Cards today represents a stellar list of self-improvement and professional sales authors like Zig Ziglar, Brian Tracy, Dr.

Tony Alessandra, and Ken Blanchard. Michael is also an accomplished motivational speaker and professional sales trainer. It was our common membership in the National Speakers Association that drew us together.

But back to that January morning in Jersey. Events started at 7:00 a.m. The president of the company called Michael up at home to tell him that there was a big deal brewing in Cumberland County. The president asked Michael if he could show up for an 8:00 a.m. meeting on that Monday morning. Michael was in the shower before he even said yes. He tooled down to his office and quickly made his way inside to his tiny cubicle. What he saw there startled him. Squeezed into this bread box of a room, he found the president of his company, the vice president, and the corporate service manager, all up from the home office in Atlantic City. It didn't faze him. Michael was still thinking that the deal that had baited him was for real. The corporate service manager was the biggest guy of the group physically. He walked up to Michael and grabbed his attaché case as soon as he set it down. The president said, "Mike, we have to let you go. We're firing you."

His former employer was selling Savin copiers, when Savin launched the first Japanese challenge to a market then dominated by Xerox. And Michael was their point man in the copier business. He was breaking records and being written up in national newsletters. Michael was celebrated as the copier stud. He was the company's number-one salesman at the age of twenty-one—working twelve to fourteen hours a day and making his company a boatload of money. Never in the history of the company did they have a salesman who produced like he did. As a result, his employer opened a new branch in Cumberland County, which required him to move. This was all farmland at the time, a huge geographical area but no major industries. Hicksville. He didn't care. Despite the unpromising territory, Michael sold a record thirty machines in just ninety days, all to individual accounts!

So how did Michael end up getting sacked? Part of the reason was the speed with which his career had moved in the first place. After a year and a half, Michael had dropped out of college in Tampa. He was living with his father just outside of Atlantic City and working in the shoe department of a department store. Michael had always been a bit of a hustler. He was confident, but rough around the edges. Increasingly, he knew that it would be important for him to land a professional sales job and start a real career. He finally got the job he had hoped and prayed for.

Then came his first clash with authority: dress standards. Michael was used to showing up for work in a cardigan and chinos. Michael's boss had an issue with how he dressed. As much as he wanted the professional selling job, Michael wasn't going to give in. He was ready to chuck it all and quit. Seeing that his son had a bit of an attitude problem, Michael's dad—a career life insurance salesman—took him out for a memorable dinner at his favorite seafood restaurant. "Would you like lobster or a hot dog, son?" his dad asked him. Michael couldn't believe what his dad was saying. He had always ordered lobster when dining at this restaurant with his dad. Plus, Michael had just come back from college, where he ate his lifetime quota of hot dogs. Confused over his dad's question, he quickly asked for an explanation. "You better learn something," his father emphasized: "If you're going to quit and blame others, you will spend the rest of your life eating hot dogs. If you want to chow down on lobster, you will have to become accountable for your own actions." Michael got the message and rewired his attitude. He got the suits. He got the ties. He dressed for success. And he broke records.

Then the second shoe dropped. After he got his new territory and moved into a cramped one-bedroom efficiency in the New Jersey wilderness, Michael started to reflect on how he was being paid. He took a look in some professional journals and saw what the going rates were for copier salesmen. Although he was producing at the top of the charts, he was being paid at bottom scale. Michael called around to some other copier firms. Sure enough, what he suspected was true. He was being way undercompensated for the job he was doing. Here's where Michael admits he blundered. Tucked away on his desktop and crumpled up in his wastepaper basket, he left his notes on what he had learned. A co-worker happened upon this data. The temptation was all too great to shave a few inches off the copier stud's stature. "That person let headquarters know about my research," Michael contends. Headquarters plausibly concluded that Michael was about to bolt the company for greener pastures and probably take his accounts with him. To this day, Michael insists: "I had no intention of leaving. I just wanted to clarify the relationship and get paid fairly for my sales results." I believe that's actually what he intended.

When Michael asked why he was being fired, they said they knew he was looking at competitors. "They were afraid I would take those customers and convert them over. I was perceived as a competitive threat who would steal the accounts. I was bewildered, then I felt betrayed. How could they do this to me? When they took my attaché case, the sense of betrayal turned to fury. This was my personal property." The state police showed up. The three corporate execs told their side. Michael told his, which was that these were his commission claim vouchers and records. The police said it was a civil matter. They took the attaché case and sealed it with tape. They put it into evidence and said the matter would have to be decided in civil court. It was just like a TV crime scene. A year and a half later, Michael won in court and got the attaché case back. "The legal system vindicated me," Michael says. And he is proud of the trail of success that has marked his career ever since.

On the day he was fired, the first person Michael called after the fiasco in his cubicle was his father. "You can either call someone and have a pity party or find someone who can straighten out your thinking," Michael recollects. "I believe that there are two types of people in the world—encouragers and discouragers. People who will pull you up or those who will push you down. I was fortunate to have parents who were both encouragers. My mom was loving, nurturing, and supportive. My dad was a 'my way or the highway' type of guy, and most of the time he was right. He was a self-employed life insurance salesman all his life. His advice was simple. 'Now you have the chance to be self-employed. We'll go out and get you started on your own as a broker in the copier business.' "

Remember what the great motivator Napoleon Hill said: "Every adversity, every failure and every heartache carries with it *the seed of an equivalent or a greater benefit.*" Michael converted anger into determination. He wasn't fired, he was fired up!

His dad helped him set up appointments with a number of companies. Michael ended up structuring a brokering agreement with a company called Stewart Industries in Haddonfield, New Jersey. He moved into another apartment in Lindenwald, New Jersey, and started buying copiers at 10 percent over their cost. At the time, he let Stewart Industries do all the service and provide supplies. He had yet to learn that this was the most profitable part of the business. He ended up selling so much equipment that the trade-ins and new machines were filling up his apartment, from the living room to the kitchen. And then the copiers started invading his bedroom. That was where he drew the line. He got a tiny office and a secretary and hired a service manager. The office was so small that the service department was in the bathroom, and they actually had to excuse themselves with the service manager to use the facilities.

Michael started selling Savin copiers in Atlantic City that he would buy through Stewart Industries. He was not an authorized dealer, meaning that he didn't have a factory-trained technician. What he was doing was not illegal, it just meant that he was not an official dealer for Savin. Michael ended up competing with his former employer for the copier business at Bally's Casino in Atlantic City and beat his old firm out on a bid for $24,000 worth of equipment in their own backyard.

That was the turning point. At twenty-four, Michael switched affiliations to another line. He became the youngest authorized copier dealer ever for Sharp Electronics. Finally, he could offer factory-trained technicians and parts. And he could enjoy superior pricing advantages. He started replacing the Savin copiers with Sharps. There were just three or four casinos in Atlantic City then. Now there are twelve. Donald Trump became his largest customer, doing millions of dollars in business with him.

To recognize his father's contribution, Michael decided to name his new company Adrian-Lewis, Inc. The name was a combination of his father's and his own middle name. He remembers driving up to his father's home in a bright blue van, sporting the company name. His father beamed. Adrian-Lewis became known as the King of Copiers throughout the industry. Even though he lived to be only fifty-four, Michael's dad could see that hot-dog days were a thing of the past. "He knew that I had made it and would always make it."

Michael became a millionaire before he was thirty. He traveled around the world and lived his dream. A Mercedes and a Jaguar stood in the driveway in front of his mansion. His firm's major accounts included not only world-class casinos, but also hospitals, large law firms, and banks. Michael ended up owning the copier business in Atlantic City, even though Adrian-Lewis' headquarters remained in Folsom, New Jersey, about forty-five minutes from Atlantic City. He sold his company in 1995 for over $3 million to Alco Standard Corporation, which is now IKON Office Solutions and a major player in the high-end office-solutions industry. Had he not been fired for investigating compensation data from competitors, Michael believes, these breakthroughs would never have happened. How much did staring down his former employer have to do with his determination to succeed? How much did it matter being in their face? It didn't hurt, he admits. "The best boss I ever worked for was the one in the mirror," Michael believes. "That person won't fire you. I believe everything happens for a reason. It built my character and fueled my fire."

Back when he still had his own company, Michael took on a challenge of a different sort. At the age of thirty-six, a member of his staff encouraged him to try out for the *American Gladiators* TV show in Hollywood. After months of chasing the dream, he became one of twenty-two contestants to make it onto the show. That was from a group of over 10,000 men who tried out. Michael decided to donate his portion of the purse to a homeless shelter in Atlantic City.

When he sold his business, Michael moved to Florida with his pride and joy, his son Kyle, to pursue yet another dream. Michael became a motivational speaker and professional sales trainer. But even that wasn't enough for Michael. He wanted to make an even greater impact on the world but realized he couldn't do it alone. So, with his right-hand aide, A. J. Ripin, by his side, Mem-Cards was born. Michael saw there was no shortage of good ideas, strategies, and tactics available in today's sales and business books, just a shortage of people taking action. "We're not in the information age," Michael believes, "we're in the information-overload age. Today, less is more. It's all about execution, and what distinguishes the top 20 percent of performers from the remaining 80 percent is action and the ability to keep their eye on the ball. People go to seminars or read a self-help book, but the effect doesn't last and life just pulls you back into its grip." Mem-Cards changes that cycle, Michael believes. They get people to take action. Mem-Cards are like a cross between flash cards and CliffsNotes* for personal and professional development books. They are a book's best ideas and insights extracted and presented on pocket-sized cards. Michael now works with over 150 leading authors in packaging their ideas and helping people take action on those ideas to create long-term change in their lives both personally and pro-

*CliffsNotes is a trademark of Wiley Publishing.

fessionally. He projects over $100 million in sales over the next three years. Why not?

What makes the Michael Altshulers of the world rebound is stretch. They don't just bounce back enough to get on their feet. They rebound to a level beyond. And they just keep bounding higher and higher.

MACKAY'S MORAL:

If you want to feed the tiger within, hot dogs don't cut it.

THE VERGER

Some time ago, the renowned cosmetics executive Leonard Lauder—himself a graduate of the prestigious Wharton School of Finance—mentioned a story to me that W. Somerset Maugham published in 1936, during the height of the Great Depression. I finally found a dusty copy in a used bookstore.

The story is called "The Verger," and it first appeared in book form in an anthology called *The Cosmopolitans*. In this tale, Mr. Foreman—a wealthy tycoon—is asked: "And you mean to say that you've built up this important business and amassed a fortune of thirty thousand pounds without being able to read or write? Good God, man, what would you be now if you had been able to?"

The man answers: "I can tell you that, sir," said Mr. Foreman, a little smile on his still aristocratic features. "I'd be verger of St. Peter's, Neville Square."

A verger is somewhat like a janitor who takes care of the inside of a church. Only church mice are poorer than vergers.

Back in the 1930s, a fortune of 30,000 British pounds would have made Foreman look like Bill Gates.

The moral of the story is *not* that it pays to be illiterate. The moral of the story is that it pays *not* to let certain skills trap you into dead-end situations.

- How many brilliant engineers have been fired as the heads of electrical, contracting, and machinery companies because they thought the artistry of their blueprints was more important than the details of balance sheets?

- How many scholars stumble through a lifetime of poverty because they master the *Britannica* A to Z, but never learn the laws of action or success?

- How many times are exciting and profitable risks avoided by following a timid, low-key course of behavior?

- How many brilliant ideas go by the wayside because the geniuses behind them never stopped to learn people skills?

Sometimes people who get fired rush back to school to "get educated." They are convinced that a lack of formal education and a tidy degree contributed to their downfall. Sometimes, maybe.

Still, it doesn't hurt to remember that:

- Directing legend Stanley Kubrick audited some classes at City College in New York, but never got his degree. Instead, he learned about photography doing freelance shutterbugging for *Look* magazine while hustling chess games for money in Greenwich Village.

- Advertising genius David Ogilvy was expelled from Oxford, and spent seventeen years as an itinerant journeyman—learning about service and selling as a Parisian chef, a door-to-door salesman, and an associate to the famous survey taker, Dr. George Gallup.

- Wal-Mart founder Sam Walton abandoned his plans to attend the Wharton School of Finance after the University of Missouri and joined the JC Penney Training Program instead.

- Bill Gates, the driving force behind Microsoft, is a college dropout—from Harvard, no less!

The list of high-school dropouts includes Pierce Brosnan, Peter Jennings, Sean Connery, Sir Richard Branson (founder of Virgin Atlantic Airways), and Sir Peter Ustinov.

I constantly preach: If you think education is expensive, try ignorance. Amen! But it's a lack of **relevant** education and experience that does the damage.

MACKAY'S MORAL:

Education may get you out of the gutter, but it's only **relevant** knowledge that can lift you off the sidewalk.

JOACHIM DE POSADA
International Motivational Speaker and Moderator

"Security is superstition."

Use life to train the trainer. That's what Joachim de Posada did. He took the hard knocks life dealt him to become a master teacher in the school of *avoiding* hard knocks. Part of the training? Getting fired by two of the biggest companies in the world. For a lesser person, these experiences would have left tire tracks. Today Joachim is well on his way to becoming the Earl Nightingale of Hispanic America, a memorable motivational speaker.

Joachim de Posada received his degree in psychology in Puerto Rico in 1973. Afterward, he opened a practice with a partner. The two gave psychological counseling and helped people deal with problems like phobias, fears, and personality disorders. The pair also did talks on self-improvement, self-esteem, goal setting, and the use of self-hypnosis to help people achieve what they wanted in life. Joachim also had a television program in San Juan at the time.

One day, after one of his talks in 1974, an audience member approached Joachim and asked, "Professor, do you know how to sell?" Joachim said he really didn't, outside of selling ideas. The questioner persisted and suggested that Joachim should mix in some sales principles with the motivational sales message. If he did, he would be hired to speak to this person's company. How many people? When he heard the number "500," Joachim's attention was riveted.

Next day Joachim called his broker at Merrill Lynch and asked for the names of the three best companies in sales in the whole world. Her answer: IBM, Xerox, and Procter & Gamble. He decided to make a pilgrimage to the three to learn what he could about sales. Xerox in Puerto Rico was his first call. Recognized from his TV show by Xerox managers, Joachim explained that he was hunting down information on selling. The Xerox general manager told him that IBM and Procter & Gamble actually used Xerox's selling principles. Hey, what a break: one-stop shopping! Joachim then made Xerox an offer. He would come in for one month and do motivational seminars for their people. This included team building and hypnotizing the tech reps to give them more energy. In this pure barter exchange, Xerox would in turn teach Joachim as much as possible about sales.

Xerox made a counteroffer. They would send Joachim to Xerox University for a whole month to learn everything about sales. He would get this $25,000 program for free. Then he would come to work for Xerox as a sales representative, getting paid a very good salary. He would also help them with team building, motivation, etc. The hitch: He had to make a commitment for at least one year. Joachim was on a search for wisdom. Xerox had a nose for talent. They turned the tables and recruited him.

Joachim went to Xerox U on the mainland. On his return, he started selling. In no time, he says, "I was making tons of money! Much more than any psychologist in the entirety of Puerto Rico. I was the third best salesman in all of Xerox, and I got to eat lunch with the chairman of the board, David Kearns. I was showered with bonuses and even a medal."

Meteoric success then double-crossed Joachim as it often does managers on the rise. He was promoted to the wrong job. New management decided Joachim was perfectly suited to become sales planning manager. No human interaction. A lonely desk jockey job jammed with as much paperwork as you could feed through a photocopier. In six months, Joachim quit Xerox and moved to Miami. There he was rehired by Xerox as a sales representative. At the same time, he maintained a psychological practice on the side. (He had actually done this as well in San Juan.) Selling in Miami was much more competitive than it had been in Puerto Rico. He threw in the towel. In a few months, Joachim resigned from Xerox once again and dedicated himself solely to his psychology practice.

Out of the blue, Joachim got a call from Xerox in 1979. They offered him a position as sales training manager in their Learning Systems Division in Stamford, Connecticut. This was the dream job he had always hoped for with Xerox! Not planning, but training and motivation work, with plenty of human interaction. He was the first person—and maybe the only person ever—to have been hired by Xerox *three separate times*!

His sales class members gave him presents when they graduated. Joachim thought he was a big hit. One year into the job, Joachim started having problems. As the personnel manager put it when they met for lunch, "Joachim, you are very bright, very enthusiastic, energetic, and a risk taker. But, in this New England culture you are perceived as a maverick. You are too different, you stand out too much. You don't blend in." Joachim was shocked, but he figured that he could trust Xerox to look out for him. When the curtain on the next act rose, he says he probably should have seen the handwriting on the back of the set. "Xerox brought in a low-key, New England type. I trained him and showed him the ropes. When that was done, the personnel manager called me in and said that my position was being eliminated and I was terminated. The newcomer took my position. Harvey, I was devastated. I thought it was the end of the world. My self-esteem hit rock bottom. I felt like a failure—worthless and betrayed." Even psychologists know the sting of defeat. Joachim felt that he had let his family down—moving up north, working fourteen-hour days, and being rejected because he was "different."

After he picked himself up from the floor, Joachim said, "I looked in the mirror and said to myself that I could succeed without Xerox. They may have had the right to fire me, but they could never take away my knowledge, experiences, accomplishments, and self-confidence. I knew people, the psychology of human beings, and I knew *HOW TO SELL.*"

Being fired from Xerox increased Joachim's sense of responsibility to himself. It showed him how important it was to be able to rely on family and friends in facing a setback. It focused him on the actions that he needed to take to regain his footing. Being fired made him determined always to have a Plan B and not to put all his eggs in one basket. The experience reinforced an important conviction about security in life: *there isn't any.* As Helen Keller put it, "Security is mostly a superstition. It does not exist in nature. . . . Life is either a daring adventure or nothing."

"No matter whom you work for," Joachim says today, "no matter what position you hold. You are and will never be 100 percent secure. Be prepared for anything."

After he left Xerox, Joachim embarked on a career as a consultant.

He did fairly well. One of his clients was Cargill Investor Services, which is based in Chicago and is a subsidiary of the Twin Cities company Cargill—the massive grain brokerage and food giant—which is one of the largest privately held businesses in the world. After a consulting engagement doing sales training for Cargill in 1983, the company hired him for a permanent job, but *not* as a sales trainer. Cargill felt that his knowledge of psychology would be a formidable asset.

"Cargill trades futures in important commodities," Joachim

explains. "These markets go up and down based on the psychology of the people, on perception. It was nonetheless a completely new career. I got a commodities trading advisor license. That meant passing one of the most difficult tests I have ever had to take. But I persevered and passed it. Then I was promoted to vice president of Cargill Investor Services for Latin America—one of only three Hispanic officers in a 55,000 employee company."

Cargill had a particular first task for Joachim in mind. For years, he says, they had been trying to persuade the vice president of a Swiss bank to move their largest customer's commodity account to Cargill. Cargill believed Joachim's skills as a psychologist, coupled with his Xerox experience, would be able to dislodge this account. This was one Swiss Alp of an account! It was $3 billion a year. At one point, it was the largest speculative account in the world. Joachim studied the prospect. He spent months scrutinizing their transactions, with whom and how they did deals, and their mind-set. He learned everything he could about their decision makers, their likes and dislikes, and how they made decisions. "When I was finally ready, I took a trip to the Bahamas—a favored tax haven for many big European and American banks. There I met with the bank's decision maker," Joachim says.

Things didn't go exactly as planned. Joachim dug in to his sales pitch, using every last crumb of information he had extracted. Suddenly the banker looked at the left lapel on Joachim's suit. He saw a Rotary pin. Then he asked Joachim: "Are you a Rotarian?"

"Yes, sir, I have been one for nine years," Joachim answered.

The banker stood up, came to his side of the table, grabbed his hand, hugged him, and said, "I am a Rotarian, too. I do business with Rotarians. We are men of principle. Let's get the papers signed." Joachim got the business. It was a major victory for Cargill and netted a hefty year-end bonus of $20,000 for Joachim. Should he have forgotten about doing all that homework? No way! Should he have seized the moment when the Rotarian connection landed in his lap? You bet! It's those little details that can prove to be the decisive tipping point.

For eight years, Joachim battled it out in commodity market trenches. He practiced his unique blend of rigorous research and a knack for interpersonal and persuasion skills. Few businesses demand more in guts and raw nerves than commodities. (But, don't forget, as Helen Keller said, "Security is superstition.") Cargill Investor Services restructured and decided to consolidate its operations. "It only kept offices where major futures exchanges operate," Joachim remembers with some sadness. "So my office was closed, and everyone was let go. It is ironic that I had just won the Manager of the Year Award and was flown to Chicago to be wined and dined when suddenly the decision was made to close the Miami office. I interviewed for another job within the company—that of worldwide quality-control czar based in Minneapolis. I didn't land the post. Then they offered me a sales position in the Corn Syrup Division in Memphis, Tennessee. I really didn't want that job. I decided I was going to be in management or I wouldn't stay. The result: I got fired again."

Joachim ended up with a good severance and will have an attractive pension at the age of sixty-five. The Xerox experience had steeled him to this second dismissal. He had learned to love Cargill. He had thrived on the heady experience of lunching with the likes of Cargill CEO Whitney MacMillan and visiting the elegant Cargill headquarters in Minnetonka.

This second defeat forced Joachim to sit down and make an important decision. Instead of helping a Xerox or a Cargill attain their dreams, he would pursue his own. Back in his youth, at the age of eighteen, he heard the motivational speaker Earl Nightingale on the radio for the first time. Joachim said to himself, "I want to be like that man. I want to do what that man does." He set out to become the Earl Nightingale of Latin America or the Hispanic USA.

Today Joachim has a daily motivational capsule on WOSO, the number-one commercial English radio station in San Juan. He writes a weekly column in the *San Juan Star* in the Business Monday section. He lectures and does workshops and seminars for Fortune 500 companies all over the world. He works with sports teams in the Olympics and in all sorts of competitions. Joachim has advised the Los Angeles Lakers and the Milwaukee Bucks. He has been on CNN several times and appeared on other television programs watched by millions.

Joachim has just published his own book in English and Spanish—*How to Survive Among Piranhas: Motivation to Succeed.* Has Joachim arrived at his dream? No, but he is inching closer to it. Joachim has had plenty of determination and a little bit of luck. Some people have tasted even more good fortune than Joachim has had. "My cousin has it a little bit better than me and I am very proud of him," Joachim reflects. "He is the catcher for the New York Yankees and has signed a $51 million contract. Yes, he has it a little bit better than me . . . but I get to help and influence thousands of people, so I wouldn't trade what I do for what he does."

Joachim's life is a classic in how a true trainer got trained by life itself:

- He wove his career in and out of the corporate jungle at the highest levels and with fierce determination.

- He always had a professional skill he could fall back on when there wasn't an opening in the big business world.

- He wasn't afraid to change professions . . . or to use his professional skill of psychology in fresh ways—first in selling and then in the commodities business.

- He understands that what happens to you today is the reliable result of your thinking yesterday.

- Today he is applying his experiences to build a reservoir of knowledge and wisdom, which he can impart to others.

MACKAY'S MORAL:

Think like the shrink: The psychology of firing is anything but the psychology of failure.

DON'T LET REJECTION SCARE YOU

Anytime you feel like quitting throughout your career, perhaps you'll remember this story of one of our people:

- He failed in business in '32.

- He ran as a state legislator and lost in '32.

- He tried business again in '33 and failed again.

- His sweetheart died in '35.

- He had a nervous breakdown in '41.

- He was defeated for the nomination to Congress in '43, defeated again for Congress in '48, defeated when he ran for the Senate in '55, and defeated for vice presidency of the United States in '56.

- He ran again for Senate in '58 and lost.

This man never quit. He kept trying till the last. In 1860, this man, Abraham Lincoln, was elected president of the United States.

MICHAEL BLOOMBERG

Mayor of New York City

"How bad a day can it be when you are looking at the right side of the grass?"

In 1981, Michael Bloomberg and sixty-two other partners at the investment firm of Salomon Brothers were summoned to a conference center in Tarrytown, New York. The firm's Executive Committee huddled this crème de la crème of Wall Street traders and administrators into a conference room and delivered a message: This firm is being merged into another company. You're all fired. Each and every one of you.

One of the partners stood up and asked, "What happens if we don't vote for the merger?" The top guys answered, "What do you mean: If our plan doesn't get enough votes? . . . The deal is done!" As they say, the railroad track had already run right through this town.

Bloomberg had clocked six-day weeks and twelve-hour days for fifteen years. Now Salomon Brothers had merged into Phibro Corporation and was recharting its strategic course. Bloomberg had given his heart to Salomon. They returned it skewered on a spear. Was he anguished? He could hardly keep his glee in check. After all, taped to the spear was a check for

$10 million! It wasn't really severance money. It was his share of the proceeds when the company was sold. "Here's $10 million; you're history," they said. Ten million bucks is 10 million bucks, no matter what you call it. Bloomberg was thirty-nine at the time. He could have stayed history and pounded the beach of Costa del Sol for the rest of his life. Instead, he *made* history. He founded Bloomberg L.P. and became a billionaire. What's Bloomberg L.P., you ask? It's the number-one financial information empire in the world, and it feeds data nonstop to 126 countries over television channels, radio networks, magazines, newspapers, and 180,000 computer monitors used by financial professionals; it generates more than $3 billion in revenues each year. So what does Michael Bloomberg do for an encore? In November 2001, he was elected mayor of New York City—arguably the single most important elected job in the United States after president.

In the fall of 2003, I stopped by to chat with Mayor Bloomberg at New York's City Hall in Lower Manhattan. Entering the building brought to mind another experience I had: crossing Checkpoint Charlie on the Berlin Wall during the Cold War. Except it was like going from west to east: guards, security detectors, screening . . . all on the side of the *good* guys. All in the aftermath of 9/11. What causes a guy like Bloomberg to bounce back and do more? Even if it means being a public servant hunkered down in a bunker? "If I didn't do my part, then I'm no better than those I accuse of living mediocre, hypocritical, or selfish lives." That's the makeup of Michael Bloomberg. But let's track back to that fateful date in 1981 when Hizzonor got canned, or, as he himself remembers, "The day they kicked me out on my ass."

Michael Bloomberg is the closest thing to an oracle for buttoning down the financial scoop. Mr. Antenna! Did he see the Salomon buyout coming? He's dead honest. He did not. But that didn't faze him for an instant. When Salomon senior partners John Gutfreund and Henry Kaufman told him he was out,

Bloomberg replied, " 'Fine, it's time anyway.' They had some-body coming in that afternoon," he recalls, "to talk about ready-ing yourself to go on to your life after Salomon. . . . I said, 'There's no reason for me to go to that. Do you mind if I don't waste my time?' "

When the axe whacked him, did Michael Bloomberg stroll down memory lane and recall all those great deals he was a part of at Salomon? "I got into the car for the twenty-five-minute drive back to Manhattan," he remembers. "I think I was proba-bly a little bit upset. Nobody likes being pushed out. But, you know, you can't feel sorry for yourself. When you see that hap-pening, you have to say," the mayor clapped his hands together like a cannon shot that ricocheted off his office walls, "STOP IT RIGHT THERE!—that instant say—No, I'm not going down that path even in my mind. . . . Let's get on with it. . . . Here's where you are today. What do you do next?"

This was Wall Street at the height of the go-go eighties. Rock and roll. Mayor Bloomberg himself described it as life on a "roller coaster."

I asked, "In a high-risk job, don't you need to be prepared to be fired every day?"

Those famous brown eyes gleamed back at me, as the mayor fired off his next morsel of wisdom. "As you move up the ladder, you're not paid for what you have done in the past. You get paid for what you are going to do in the future. You *should* be forced to work harder and to make tougher decisions. You also get paid more for your preferred status. I always thought you should take less vacation, come in earlier, and stay later the higher up you go. You should have the more unpleasant jobs, not the easy ones. **You should grunt longer!** You should have *less* security."

"So there's a big difference between protecting the Big Boss's life and protecting his career," I thought to myself. The mayor proceeded to compare life in business with life in govern-ment. "In government, I think everybody's got the exact reverse thinking," he said, with no little passion. "We always protect the leader. The president has the ultimate security. Well, the president should have the least career security. The president is working for everybody else."

"When an incumbent is voted out of office, it's like being fired by the voters, isn't it?" I asked.

"I hope to never find out!" the mayor shot back.

"But you're not the type to shy away from a challenge either. You're wrestling with a grizzly bear when you reform the public-education system, and that doesn't make for a smooth ride in the opinion polls," I pressed on.

"Most people in government have aspirations to go on to higher office," the mayor reflected. "I started here at what I consider to be the top. Others might say no, no, I want to go for being a senator . . . a governor . . . or even president. I have no interest in any of that. I've got a better job than any legislator . . . or the governor . . . or the president, for that matter. I know I am much more suited for this job than any of those other ones, and I don't have any interest," he answered. I thought to myself: "Here's a guy who knows how to start at the top . . . and work his way UP. More isn't better. Being the best at what you do *is*."

"But, what about tomorrow? What if the sun suddenly sets on Gracie Mansion?" I asked, referring to the mayor's official residence.

"My Plan B is better than the other guy's Plan A," he answered. "If I had to leave office tomorrow, I could look you in the eye. I could look my kids in the eye and say I've done as good a job as I could. I've made the right decisions. I've been scrupulously honest. As Ed Koch once said, 'If the voters reject me . . . somebody else will get a better job, but they won't get a better mayor.' There's something to be said for that. I now know exactly where my next career is going to be."

"Where's that?" I asked, wide-eyed with curiosity.

"It's going to be heading the Bloomberg Foundation." It all fit. The mayor has great credentials for running nongovernment public institutions, too. He did a gangbusters job as president of the board of trustees at Johns Hopkins until he left that volunteer post in May of 2002.

I turned the conversation back to resilience and to what allowed him to bounce back from the Salomon experience so fast. Mayor Bloomberg readily acknowledged that he is "tougher than many others." I asked him if this was a matter of good genes or hard knocks, and he answered: "I don't know. My mom is about to be ninety-five. She took a fall about three months ago and broke her pelvis. There is no operation available to repair the damage. She has had a walker and a nurse. In two weeks, she got rid of the walker and she's already going up and down the stairs again. Suck it up and get on with it! There is always somebody worse off. You know the old story . . . I cried because I had no shoes until I saw a man who had no feet. I think that attitude is imperative. My father probably had it, but that is so many years ago now that I don't remember. Just get on with it. Remember, you're alive. If a loved one dies, it's very tragic. But I don't think that the person lost to you would want you to spend the rest of your life crying. I've never had a lot of sympathy for people or a situation where someone is always crying. How bad a day can it be when you are looking at the right side of the grass?"

"As mayor, aren't you often called on to commiserate with people when life kicks them in the stomach?"

"Harvey, there are two sides to it, and the big difference is always attitude. I just came back from the site of a fire uptown, a church with a supermarket under it. The church will be back in business in a couple of days. The supermarket will be open again soon, too. It was just three weeks since it opened, and the two owners had sunk their whole life savings into the store and lost everything. Will they recover? You know, I suppose so. One of the guys said that he strived for the sake of his young kids. But he didn't moan about losing the market. He was happy the kids were okay and nobody was hurt. The fire was tragic. I'm sympathetic, but we've gotten to the point in society where we pick up the paper every day, and everybody deserves our sympathy. The next step is always to peg somebody with the blame for what went wrong. Someone is always expected to. A member of the City Council saw a quote in the paper that read, 'Somebody did this, and somebody has to pay!' It was about the massive power blackout in the U.S. in August 2003. C'mon."

"Back to your firing at Salomon," I persisted. "Wasn't there *any* emotion that stuck with you?"

He thought for a moment and said, "I do remember who called me afterward. I remember the exact list. One's dead, but the others are still alive. If any one of them ends up in trouble, I'll call them. If you see them on the way up, you should see them on the way down. Whenever someone gets fired or has some real problems, I always call to tell them my thoughts are with them. Maybe I can't help that they are going to jail. I may have to say, 'You shouldn't have committed that murder, but my thoughts are with you.' You say it because that's what people need. I never call when someone gets a promotion. They'll never remember anyway.

"People remember two things in life—who helped you on the way up . . . and who kicked you on the way down when the sun wasn't shining."

My own memories drift back to the day of my father's funeral in the Twin Cities. Michael Bloomberg is right about being there at the dark moments. I can still recall every face at the cemetery.

The mood was heavy, and I wanted to lighten it. Recalling a story I had heard once, I asked him, "Weren't you almost fired at Salomon once when you were just starting out . . . and screwed up the pencils?"

He broke out laughing. "I was supposed to give a Salomon partner by the name of Ira Lectman a certain kind of sharpened pencils at the beginning of each trading day, and I intentionally gave him the wrong kind and I had also purposely broken them—I guess I was trying to ease the tension in the place and express myself. So he pushed me around the corner and said,

'Good thinking, 'cause this is your last job here. You're headed to the Equity Desk.' "

"A real lemons to lemonade story. Nearly getting fired made your career at Salomon."

"Stocks . . . equities is just where I wanted to go. The rest is history," the mayor said with some satisfaction.

"So, can you be a maverick in today's society and not pay for it with your job?" I wondered aloud.

"Some places you can and some places you can't," Mayor Bloomberg answered thoughtfully. "It's a high-risk/high-reward gambit. Everybody says they want original thinkers, but nobody really does. In one of our companies, we had a guy who always asked that question about being a maverick. He wears that hat, and he always will. He's an exception. People say they want tough input, but it really hurts when you get it. It's embarrassing and difficult. I don't have a good answer . . . which is a good reason to keep asking the question."

Mayor Bloomberg thanks John Gutfreund for having hired him at Salomon . . . and for having fired him, too. In both cases, he says that Gutfreund's "timing was impeccable." Would people generally benefit from being nudged out earlier? "I think you do few people a favor by keeping them on when you are afraid to make a decision about them or don't want to face that they are floundering. They continue to flounder and you are just wasting a period of their life. They could get on with it! If you want to pay them, pay them . . . but don't have them sit around. Perhaps, you conclude: I'm afraid to face firing you next January. Okay, I'll pay you severance for a year. What's the difference between a year and two months' salary? Let people get on with their life. You are not doing anybody any good by letting them stay there. It's no cheaper. Quite the contrary, the person's salary isn't the real problem. The real problem is that he or she is occupying a desk and doing nothing."

"Do you ever have it nailed! It's not the people you fire who make your life miserable . . . It's the people you *don't*. Tell me, did

Salomon help you to learn how to fire other people—as I am sure you have done in both your business and public careers?" I asked.

"Salomon was a scrupulously honest place, very truthful," he responded. "They treated people very fairly and had a clear merit system that encouraged a great work ethic. Everything was pretty much out in the open. That included the climate when people were fired."

"But tell me about the particulars. How do you actually fire somebody?"

"You should always look them in the eye and they should never be shocked," he said in a measured, serious way. "It's never been easy for me to fire anyone, either in business or in government. But it's always easier to do it when they know it's coming. They need warnings, whether the warnings are formal or not. They should not be surprised that they are not doing a good job. If they are shocked, then the manager hasn't done his or her job."

Still, that's not to say changing jobs is always easy, especially if your career is at a later stage. "Adversity is the courage to bounce back," the mayor firmly believes. "But that can be hard at times. People cannot go from big companies to small companies easily. As you get older, you get more support systems, and you are often not able to do things yourself, especially if you are used to delegating." Sometimes, however, people will build unnecessary boxes about what they *think* they can do. When people change jobs, Mayor Bloomberg says, don't duck into a world just because the scenery is comfortable for you: "It's fascinating what happens to so many smart people in the military when they retire. They tend to go to work for the defense industries and not go out and be in the public sector or other fields," he stresses. "I think they could do it. Today's armed forces have very well-educated people. They have enormous responsibilities, but when they get out, they are reluctant to go out and face the broader world. If they try to get over that hesitation, most of them will do very well."

Many people turn to a mentor when they are fired to rekindle conviction in themselves. Michael Bloomberg was one of those who didn't. "If I would have called my mother in Aspen," he reflects, "she would have told me to get on with it. I certainly told her the day that it happened, but I already knew what she would have said to me, if I had asked her for advice. My then wife was supportive. The kids were supportive. Not financially, of course. I was young and had plenty of money. I didn't have to worry about where the next paycheck was coming from. I remember buying my wife a sable jacket just after it happened. To me, it was a way of saying, 'No sweat. We can still eat. We're still players.' "

When did Michael Bloomberg first have a vision for the Bloomberg media empire? "I actually thought about it that day I got fired on the way back to Manhattan. I started thinking, 'What are you gonna do?' I probably had much too big an ego to go out looking for a job. And nobody called to offer me one. If another investment house like Goldman Sachs would have called me, I probably would have just taken it, partly to say to Salomon, 'Stick it . . . shove it . . . you guys made a mistake.' Thank God, I got fired! Even more, thank God, Goldman *didn't* call. So, Harvey, I ended up doing something else."

MACKAY'S MORAL:

Every event in life always has two sides.
Energize yourself by picking the proactive one!

Turning Firing Upside Down

James Whitaker, the first American to reach the summit of Mount Everest, said: "You don't really conquer such a mountain. You conquer yourself."

Whitaker was a relentless trainer. He tried to anticipate every challenge, emotional and physical. Obstacles came at him right and left: avalanches, dehydration, hypothermia, oxygen shortage at 29,000 feet, and the fatigue it caused. "You overcome the sickness and everything else—your pain, aches, fears—to reach the summit." To reach their destination, achievers like Whitaker focus on the road rather than the bumps in it:

- **Lost the job of a lifetime?** Were you right for it in the first place? How much time would you have wasted trying to make something work that should never have been?

- **Failed in a flash?** Experts say that the entrepreneurs who suffer the most and who achieve the least are the ones whose businesses die slow deaths. Better to get it over with in a hurry and move on than to agonize for years trying to squeeze life out of a weak idea.

- **Been beaten up?** The first golf balls were smooth. An avid-but-broke golfer couldn't afford new ones. He picked up nicked balls he found littered on the course. The funny thing was he kept beating his well-heeled friends with their shiny new balls. Today's golf balls have 432 dimples. These "rough spots" enhance the ball's distance and accuracy. The rough spots in our life sharpen our performance.

- **Stewing in your worries?** Did you know that the English word "worry" originates from an Anglo-Saxon term meaning to "strangle or choke"? It's not adversity that cripples us: It's worrying about what *could* happen. A day of worry is more exhausting than a day of work. Back in 1948, Dale Carnegie titled one of his classics *How to Stop Worrying and Start Living.* As a kid, this masterpiece had as much influence on me as any book I have ever read.

- **Short on know-how?** Lesson one: The person who knows "how" will always have a job. Lesson two: The person who knows "why" will always be the boss.

MACKAY'S MORAL:

Some people rebound from a firing setback because they are destined to. Most people rebound because they are determined to.

MARK VICTOR HANSEN

Coauthor of Bestselling *Chicken Soup for the Soul* Books

"You only do a miracle in a team. Everyone has teams."

Buckminster ("Bucky") Fuller was one of the wildest minds of the twentieth century—of any century, for that matter. Fuller was the genius behind the geodesic dome—huge space-frame hemispheres like the U.S. pavilion at the Montreal Expo of 1967. Expelled twice from Harvard, Fuller ultimately became the chief mechanical engineer in the U.S. War Department for World War II. His mind dabbled in darn near everything: from plans for a worldwide electric grid to the virtues of trimming your sleep time down to ninety minutes a night. There is even a chemical molecule named after him called the buckyball. To say that Bucky's wisdom bounced off the wall like a Super Ball is an understatement. He also had a gift for the well-turned phrase. Such as, "You can never learn less, you can only learn more." Or: "There is nothing in a caterpillar that tells you it's going to be a butterfly."

When Mark Victor Hansen entered his freshman year at Southern Illinois University, he was a dedicated party animal. But in a couple of years, the caterpillar decided to shed its lampshade and beer kegs to become nearly a straight-A butterfly. An inspiration for him was the presence of Bucky on the faculty at Carbondale. "My kinda boy!" remembers Mark. "I had never seen an *aura* before and this guy had one roughly three-by-six feet. He was over the top in learning. Bucky was operating on a whole different plane of existence from anything I had ever seen before. The forty different books he wrote lined his office shelves. He would ask questions like: 'How do you make the world work for 100 percent of humanity?' or hand out such assignments as 'Go and compute the size of the global electrical network.' In graduate school, I became one of his seven research assistants. I may not have been the smartest, but I was probably the most streetwise. If you tagged along with Bucky, you hung out with the who's who of the planet—from Nobel Prize winners to U.S. presidents."

Then came the Big Bang! In the spring of 1970, in the wake of the Kent State shootings and the general brouhaha over the Vietnam War, students ransacked SIU's Wheeler Hall. The National Guard had rolled in and tear gas wafted across the campus. The university closed down in mid-May until the beginning of the summer quarter. Bucky summoned his magnificent seven to his office digs, known as the Energy Orbit. One by one, they filed in. One by one, they exited sobbing, but were sworn not to tell the others why. Mark was the last to go in. "Bucky walked over to a shelf, pulled off a copy of his *No More Second-Hand God,* and stared me in the eye. 'I expect you to go out and do what you can to make everyone better off.' I was rocked and asked, 'What do you mean, Bucky?' He looked at me and said, 'I'll be clear. You're getting fired. The funding for all of us in this particular program is finished. You can't charge the work of the universe to any one individual or institution.' I never wanted to leave. I wanted to stay and be a university professor, but I was out the door . . . and sobbing, too."

Lesson learned? Buckminster Fuller articulated it: Don't think you can depend on some institution to fund your vision of the world. If you do, you're fogging up your glasses with the heat of your own passion. "I wanted to be able to pull off the kinds of things he did," Mark says. "I had tried to be Bucky Fuller instead of Mark Victor Hansen. I hadn't yet learned who I was supposed to be. Bucky didn't want me to be another Bucky. Nonetheless, it spurred me on to be at the top of my game some day." Not knowing yet what that game was, Mark ventured out as a dome developer. A "Bucky-for-bucks" if you will.

Mark started building geodesic domes. He did one for the Wall Street Racquet Club. Then an aviary. Next a botanical garden. A couple of homes. The domes were being constructed out of polyvinyl chloride (PVC). In three years, his little company was doing $2 million in sales. "I'm dining at the Top of the Sixes," recalls Mark. "I'm meeting the mayor. I thought, 'Holy-smoly, man, I'm in business. I am s-o-m-e-b-o-d-y.' My PVC was ordered out of Monsanto. The raw ingredient: oil. Then came the oil embargo of 1974. I was consuming $40,000 of PVC a month. All of a sudden, I couldn't get any more of the stuff. I was just a little user, and they shut me off."

Things started rolling downhill like a bucky-snowball out of hell. Mark had personally guaranteed all his loans. In short order, he was drained of cash. His family wouldn't even lend him any more money for food. He camped out in the hallway of a friend's apartment and lived there for half a year. When he heard his name paged on a commercial flight one day, he was sweating bullets, fearful that his creditors had found him. "I didn't have the $300 to hire a bankruptcy attorney," Mark remembers, shaking his head. "It was humiliating. I had to check a book out of the library to learn how to go bankrupt myself." This was firing number two, as his creditors kissed him off.

What gave him hope? A motivational audiotape by Cavett Roberts, the founder of the National Speakers Association. Roberts became one of Mark's first mentors. "The tape fell into my lap," Mark says. "Today, I would call that Synchro-Destiny. I listened to this tape 287 times. I checked each playing off on the plastic case like little notches on a gun. The lesson I learned: *I* created this bankruptcy."

Life bumped forward. Mark became more solvent . . . and a motivational speaker himself. He wrote several books. And, he teamed up with a like-minded colleague named Jack Canfield, who had already sold 70,000 copies of one of his book titles. The pair talked about creating a book together.

"Jack and I decided to do this book one day in 1989 after he delivered a great talk in Beverly Hills," Mark remembers. "A book of heart-touching, soul-penetrating stories. We thought we could do it in three months, Harvey. We discovered what you and others had told us—it would take us three years of 24/7. We discovered a formula called *Chicken Soup for the Soul*. We saw that the soul of America was desperately in pain. We were determined to comfort it."

A noble notion. What did it get Mark and Jack? Rejection notices from thirty-three publishers. Their agent concluded that "a book of soppy stories would never sell." Firing number three: their agent fired them, but the two persevered. They got turned down by 134 more publishers at a book fair.

The publishers in New York didn't get it. Finally, a little publisher in Florida did. Mark recollects: "The guy at HCI—Health Communications—Gary Seidler called up to report, 'Man, I cried all over my silk shirt. I think this will sell, but you guys gotta buy 20,000 copies at $6 each.' That's a vanity press. Still, all we needed was the distribution, and only an established publisher could give us that. If I had the distribution, I could take this rocket ship to the moon."

Where did they get such unflagging confidence? "We got a standing ovation at the end of our talks," Mark explains. "We got immediate feedback. We would deliver our motivational messages, but people would come up afterward wanting to know where they could find the stories. We interviewed the 101 bestselling authors in America. We wanted to learn from their successes and their mistakes. We interviewed Dr. M. Scott

Peck, the guy who wrote *The Road Less Traveled*. He opened a big door of awareness when he said, 'Let me tell you boys you can make $40 million in twelve years, but you got to do it yourselves. You have to do just one thing. You have to do a media appearance every day for the rest of your life. You can tape twenty in one day and be done for the month.' We did just what he said and have never stopped." How true that is: All the money in the world can't sell a bad book. But many great books never see the light of day because of poor promotion.

The rest is chicken soup à la king. By 1998, the pair had sold 28 million copies of the various Chicken Soup books: . . . *for the Teenage Soul*, . . . *for the Pet-Lover's Soul*, . . . *for the*, etc. If there's a soul in it, there's a chicken soup for it. In 2004, Mark estimated they had sold 100 million books—more than a billion dollars in retail value. The rate of sale, he says, had become 15 million books or better each year. Chicken soup is sloshing all over the planet. Jack Canfield just came back from India where the chicken soup craze is taking off, too. (Wise for the two not to have picked *Beef Soup for the Soul*, or the idea would have been dead in the Ganges.) Several years ago, *Time* magazine suggested another version for the series: *Chicken Soup for the Souls of 33 Publishers Who Really, Really Screwed Up*.

By Mark's reckoning, "We are now the worldwide bestseller of books. The bottom line is that we figured out how to sell books and we're not done yet. I predict we'll have sold a billion books by 2020 A.D. Our mission statement is real clear: Change the world one story at a time. We aim to create miraculous transformations. Our books cause you to have God bumps, goose bumps, chili bumps. I just talked to 10,000 Marine recruiters in Nashville. They invited us to help them figure out how to get more good people. 'We don't cry,' they said afterward, 'but you make our eyeballs sweat.' "

What is behind this incredible demand? Talk with Mark and you see shades of Buckminster Fuller. First, stories, he says, work all over the world. It doesn't matter if you're a Christian, a Jew, a Buddhist, a whatever. It's one common world. There is a built-in demand for the product. But that's not enough: What makes the concept tick now is the timing. "Everybody's got to rewrite their story," Mark insists. "We're at the most transformative time in history. We're going into the real electric information age, which is different from the industrial age, the earlier information age, and any other age we've had. We're still at the cocoon stage. We're going into a high-flying butterfly stage. This stage demands new lessons told in new ways. We are helping people look at stories in a new way. People are unhappy with being caterpillar drones. They want to soar." I check my perpetual calendar and say to myself, "This guy has got it." It was thirty-four years ago, in 1970, when all of us first started to learn what a computer does, that another soaring phenomenon took flight: a simple, little book titled *Jonathan Livingston Seagull* by Richard Bach. The lead weight that prevents soaring so often is rejection. If you can overcome the rejection of firing, it is within your reach to make getting fired the best thing that ever happened to you.

"Mark, firing is rejection. You have told other people how to beat rejection a 100 million times. For time 100 million and one: Just how do you do it?"

"When I give a talk, Harvey, I'll ask: How many of you have ever been rejected by anyone, anytime, anyplace, and for any reason? All their hands shoot up. Then I ask: How would you like one *clean* four-letter word to handle all rejection? They all raise their hands again. Then I tell them the word is n-e-x-t . . . next. Whenever someone says no to you, you have to say next. Eleanor Roosevelt laid it out, 'Nobody can make you feel inferior without your permission.' Let's shake off rejection like our kids do. Little kids are rejection-proof."

Becoming that childlike requires great genius. Picasso said, "Every child is an artist. The problem is how to remain an artist once he grows up." Mark believes staying simple often takes a miracle. "You only do a miracle in a team," he believes. "Everyone has teams. Businesses do—from teams in the factory up to the board of directors. Gifted athletes have teams of specialized managers, trainers, and marketers that help them. People in rejection need teams. When I was bankrupt, my friends had vanished. I could barely afford to eat, let alone to pay for specialists. So I created a virtual support team. It consisted of Walt Disney, John F. Kennedy, Andrew Carnegie, Mark Twain, and Abraham Lincoln. It cost me absolutely nothing. Every evening I would have a one-hour mastermind meeting and try to imagine how these giants—all of whom I respected beyond belief—would look at my situation. I would have a session in my head and ask them to help me sculpt a future that would be worthy of me."

Mastering the fear of rejection is tied to risk taking. A lot of people—include me in—regard Mark as the Guru of Prudent Risk Taking. What drives Mark to take risks? "You have two doors going forward in life," he answered me. "One is opportunity and the other is security. If you go for security, you lose both. It's time to stop tiptoeing around the pool and to jump into the deep end, headfirst. Risk is always there, but it is pretty minimal if you have a team that will help you rebound. You gotta have at least one mentor that you're the mentee to. I have had forty-four great mentors, including Bucky. Some are still around. They keep you straight. They help you do what Rudyard Kipling advised: 'Keep your head while others are losing theirs.' "

"Mark," I ask, "ladle out some chicken soup about how to get a job when you don't have one. What's the recipe?"

"To get a job," he believes, "you have to focus on goals. What are your goals? To find out, the tool to use is a journal. A page a day. What you recognize, you energize. You have to journal *every* day. But get it right. It's not just one full-time job you're journaling about. What are the multiple streams of income you will create in your lifetime? The first thing that pops up is the obstacles—all the cobwebs in the way of getting to the goals. Forget the resistance, think through the cobwebs. Write down: In ten years, what would I do, if I could do anything? If I had universal support, endless money, and total love. When you lose your job, it's the best time ever to figure this out. You can practice zero-base thinking. You're working with a clean slate. Get off the I-hate-him-because-he-fired-me bit. What is my ideal lot in life? What is my true calling? Once you've thought that out, you can probably compress the time you need from ten years into one year . . . or even one month . . . and sometimes one day.

"You know, Harvey," Mark summed up, "people let the hunger for security cripple them. You have to constantly ask the question: What is the one skill that will double, triple, quadruple or hundredfold my income? You'll find messages that God wants you to hundredfold one way or another in thirty-eight of the sixty-six chapters of the Old Testament. We underestimate what we can do. But the only way to get those results is to continually reskill yourself."

Who could have predicted that getting fired actually builds your skills?

Experts believe in history. It's up to *you* to believe in the idea that can change history . . . and change the experts.

- If you want a happy ending, rewrite your success story before somebody else does it for you.

- If you don't like rejection and you're doing your job, don't give people permission to make you feel inferior.

- Go for security instead of opportunity and you will lose both.

MACKAY'S MORAL:

The path to the richest chicken soup is through your noodle.

MISTAKES

"Learn from the mistakes of others. You can't live long enough to make them all yourself."
—ELEANOR ROOSEVELT

BILLIE JEAN KING

Winner of Thirty-nine Women's Tennis
Grand-Slam Titles

"Pressure is a privilege."

Billie Jean King played her first sanctioned tennis tournament in southern California. She was twelve, and she had played tennis for only a few months. Actually her game of choice was basketball. Her brother Randy Moffitt—Billie Jean's birth name is Moffitt, too—was a relief pitcher for the San Francisco Giants. Billie Jean didn't waft her way up through the country club route. She gutted out the game on parks-and-recreation asphalt courts. At her first tournament, Billie Jean played a whale of a match, losing in the third set 9–7. (Tiebreaks were a thing of the distant future.)

There were a few things she didn't quite have down yet. She didn't know that you play the best of three sets. She didn't know that balls that landed on the line—liners—were in. Worst of all, she didn't know that girls had to appear in a sanctioned tournament wearing a tennis skirt or a tennis dress. For that reason, you won't find a picture of Billie Jean among the participants in that contest. The czar of the Southern California Tennis Association—Perry T. Jones—was an old-school stickler for the rules. Billie Jean's mother had sewn her a pair of white shorts and dressed her daughter as clean as a whistle. No skirt, no slot in the photo—so ruled Jones. Billie Jean was told to stand aside while the shutter clicked.

What mark did that experience make on Billie Jean? "The experience hurt my mother, and that upset me. It also made me more determined than ever to do things, Harvey. By the time I was twelve, I realized how I wanted to change tennis, women's sports, and society."

And what about the crew of girls she played with? "We had one of the best girls' teams in the history of junior tennis. Players like Karen Hantze-Susman, who ended up being Wimbledon champion in 1962." But the tennis association head Perry Jones always gave money to the boys—not the girls—to travel back East. As a result, the girls' team became stronger, more united, and more determined to win.

This is classic Billie Jean King in the making. The Billie Jean King whose liberating impact on women's professional sports stands besides Babe Didriksen Zaharias in the generation before. The Billie Jean King who became the first woman in any sport to earn more than $100,000 a year. The Billie Jean King who nailed twenty titles at Wimbledon. The Billie Jean King who founded the Women's Tennis Association, Women's Sports Foundation, and cofounded World TeamTennis. We aren't talking woman. We are talking Superwoman.

Or are we? This is the "Clark Kent" King who has vision of 20/10 and played every set of her career wearing glasses. Without glasses she cannot see well from a distance, but with her glasses she sees much better than average. "Everyone said I would never be a champion wearing glasses, Harvey," she tells me. "You know what: God gave me bad eyesight but great reflexes." This is the Billie Jean King with "railroad tracks" on her two knees—from six operations, three per knee. This is the Billie Jean King with debilitating sinus-chest breathing problems. When you carry that kind of baggage, you learn to struggle against deficits and setbacks at an early age. And all this in an era before speedy recuperations, systematic weight programs, and scientific trainers.

We are talking Superwoman because we are talking super attitude. Billie Jean has copyrighted the motto "Pressure is a privilege." She owns it. I asked her what that powerful motto meant to her.

"Young people dream about being in the ninth inning," she reflects, "with two outs, a three-two count, and whacking a game-winning grand slam home run in the seventh game of the World Series. Everybody dreams about these moments. When I took up tennis, I read every tennis history book. I love history. You dream about having the moment when you are playing at Centre Court at Wimbledon. Or winning for Fed Cup (international team play for women). You are one of the few people in the world who has that opportunity and it's real. Face it. These are the fun challenges. Very few professional athletes win a professional tournament, even if they make a lot of money. It's a privilege to be a professional athlete and to have match points. It's very hard to finish in sports. In business, it's hard to actually make a deal. Let's face it; people have a hard time finishing. So, when you have the chance to finish as a winner, that's a gift."

The privilege of championship pressure is one thing. An athlete who has a lifestyle out of the norm is under pressure of a different sort. Not necessarily on the court, but in economically crucial areas like commercial sponsorships. Any time a sponsor says good-bye, it's like being fired. And whether the reason is personal, professional, or political, it still hurts.

"It's a lot better now," Billie Jean believes, "but it has not been easy. People fear the unknown. I don't understand why some people think a person would choose to be gay. Life is much more difficult if you are. But you have to be true to yourself. Yes, I've lost personal endorsements. And they have been costly. No one likes rejection, but you must be truthful to who you are as a human being.

"My generation started women's professional tennis," Billie Jean says. "I thought I would finally get my retirement money through endorsements. That didn't work out. I haven't had much time off. Because the wages we earned back then were so small, any hit in the pocket book was huge. I didn't retire as an active player until I was forty. I continued to play because I needed more money. You can sit and cry or feel lucky. When you go through adversity, you have a chance to come back stronger."

Another favorite saying of Billie Jean's is, "Champions adjust." She says, "It's true in sports, it's true in business, and it is definitely true in life. In tennis I adjusted on the court, and I am doing the same thing today. That has helped me make the transition from the tennis court to the business world. It's also true when a new baby comes into a family. You adjust."

Refusing to let herself get bogged down in what others think allowed Billie Jean to become the champion she is. Throughout her career she has made the tough decisions and accepted the consequences. And guess what? Billie Jean is still successfully in the game while scores of others have hung up their rackets and dropped out.

Making decisions is just one of the characteristics Billie Jean listed as the skills of a leader. Others include . . .

- Willingness to listen and hear

- Clarity of purpose/vision

- The ability to separate personal matters from business

With skills like these, and the discipline to go with it, Billie Jean has become, arguably, the single most influential leader in professional tennis. But she didn't get there by hogging the limelight. When I asked her why she stepped aside as captain of the Fed Cup team and is now the coach instead of captain-coach, she gave a surprising answer. . . .

"I could have been captain of the Fed Cup team this year, but I chose not to. I wanted Zina Garrison to have a chance as she has been coaching Fed Cup for the past five years. It's her turn. It is time to pass the baton. This is just right for me. I get to coach, but I don't have all the administrative work. I presented the idea that she and I should switch roles. I don't always want to be the leader. I like playing a supportive role a lot. I like both leadership and supportive roles. Sometimes it's fun *not* being the leader. We try to teach that in World TeamTennis."

"You have a much more flexible notion of being a champion than many people might," I observed. After all, how many CEOs would take a step back to let their second in command shine in the spotlight?

Billie Jean had her days at center stage and more than rose to the challenge. Flash back to September 1973, when more than 30,000 spectators assembled at the Houston Astrodome. An unprecedented 50 million viewers watched on their TV screens. Former male Wimbledon champion Bobby Riggs was hauled into the arena by a rickshaw with women doing the heavy lifting. Billie Jean King arrived on a velvet Egyptian litter borne by toga-clad football players. Riggs, fresh from defeating women's tennis champion Margaret Court that spring, had trained his sights on Billie Jean King. If he were going to be a male chauvinist pig, Riggs declared, he would be the numero uno among chauvinist pigs and beat what he called "the women's lib leader." At the time, Riggs was fifty-five, and Billie Jean twenty-nine.

"What was at stake in this match?" I asked Billie Jean.

"Social change," she instantly answered.

"Two hours on the court—and a victory in three straight sets—equals ten years marching," I added.

"You've got it, Harvey. I think my win really helped Title IX*

*Title IX of the Educational Amendments of 1972 is the landmark legislation that bans sex discrimination in schools, whether it is in academics or athletics.

to continue by helping to change the hearts and minds of people to match the legislation. It was passed June 23, 1972. If I lost to Bobby, I was very worried that would give people an excuse not to provide college athletic scholarships to girls, and women. Women's tennis was only in the third year of our professional tour, and we were really small. So it was an economic break-through. But socially, the milestone was even bigger.

"Men now in their forties are so sweet. They will come up to me and tell me how it changed their life when they saw that match. They might have been just ten or twelve back then. They say they would never have raised their daughters in the way they did if they hadn't seen that match. I call them the first genera-tion of *men* of the *women's* movement. They talk about their girls and boys in much the same way. It changed their whole lives. That's pretty potent."

"Did you know exactly *how* potent at the time you played the match? Did you realize you would change the lives of women and girls from that day forward? That dads and moms would alter the way they raised their kids?"

"I knew it was big," Billie Jean says thoughtfully. "There was super pressure for weeks and weeks like a heavyweight champi-onship boxing match. When a woman goes into a male arena, it's big news. Golfer Annika Sorenstam playing in the PGA Colonial is another recent example of the same."

But you take the risk: If you lose, it's just like getting fired . . . only in front of millions of spectators.

"Harvey," Billie Jean continues, "do you know that almost 90 percent of the sports media are controlled by men? Women's sports get 8.7 percent of the sports page. Dogs and horses get about the same. Men get the rest. When we enter a male arena like the men's PGA golf tour or me playing Bobby Riggs, that's when we finally get some media attention. It's not just sports. I did a casual survey of the *Chicago Tribune* a couple of years ago to compare images in the sports pages (including the ratio of male columnists to female columnists)—their smiling faces pasted next to each byline—and the ratio was about forty to one. If you're a little girl and see only male images, if you don't see your image, you don't get reinforcement. I relate to this. As a little girl, I felt very invisible trying to get into sports. I dreamed about being a pro. I wanted to change that. Two years ago women's sports passed the $1 billion sponsorship mark. Men are at $25 billion. Think about it.

"Harvey, did you know that Alice Marble was one of my role models? My parents would drive to Encino on weekends, and she would coach me. But did you know *this*? She played mixed doubles with Bobby Riggs. They both won the Triple Crown at Wimbledon in 1939 (singles, doubles, and mixed doubles), before the war started." Billie Jean King and Bobby Riggs, who passed away from prostate cancer in 1995, remained true friends for a quarter century after perhaps the most bitterly contested battle of sexes in the last century.

Having many role models is just one of the nuggets of advice that Billie Jean passes on to people rebounding from setbacks. Others include:

- **Have faith and believe in yourself.** Don't take things so personally. Make the hard decisions you need to make—even if some people disapprove—and move on.

- **Champion others.** Mentor someone.

- **Don't be afraid to ask for help.** "This was one of my weaknesses," she says. "I was embarrassed to ask, but I've since learned that people want to help."

- **Develop skills and try your best.** Girls often keep themselves poor. They think someone will take care of them. Make sure you understand how money works, and that you can earn a living for yourself.

- **Understand delayed gratification.** We live in a society of instant rewards. You must learn your craft and earn what you get. It takes a lot of work and sweat, but you have to be willing to pay the price.

- **It's okay to feel what you're feeling.** Don't deny it or it will stay with you. Nobody likes to feel hurt or terrified or embarrassed, but that's part of taking a risk. Ask yourself: How will you feel if you *don't* take a risk?

- **Know your history.** The more you know about history, the more you know about yourself, especially in the realm you choose.

MACKAY'S MORAL:

The best way to be somebody is to be yourself.

Down and Up #3

- **Walt Disney** was fired from a newspaper for lack of ideas.

- According to *Fortune Small Business,* **David Neeleman** was fired by Southwest Airlines with a non-compete clause so tough it nearly pushed him into starting up family dental clinics. Today the Jet Blue Airlines he founded is among the most successful and innovative new-wave carriers in the industry.

- **Rod Canion,** cofounder of Compaq in 1982, was dismissed in 1991 during an economic downswing. He used his healthy settlement to start a new business venture: Insource Technology.

- **Louis Rukeyser,** the host of PBS's *Wall Street Week* for thirty-two years, was unceremoniously fired because management felt his show wasn't in touch with younger investors. His show was quickly picked up by CNBC and became that network's most-watched program.

- **Steve Jobs,** who cofounded Apple Computer in his family's garage in 1976, was replaced by John Sculley, who was brought in from Pepsi. Jobs bought a majority stake in Pixar, a spin-off from LucasFilm, in 1986. Pixar won an Oscar for *Toy Story* in 1995. Jobs returned to Apple in 1996 when Apple bought NeXT.

- **Jeffrey Katzenberg** was fired as studio chief by Walt Disney Company in August 1994 and created Dreamworks, one of the most adventuresome cinema studios.

- **Mark Cuban** got a job in a computer store early in his career. He got fired because he yearned to sell and work on computers rather than sweep the floor of the store as the owner wanted. Today he is an Internet billionaire and owner of the Dallas Mavericks.

RON SHAW

President and CEO, Pilot Pen Corporation of America

*"No, you don't get it. This is not a stand-up routine.
I actually got fired today."*

Baron Marcel Bich was the founder of Société Bic. We know it as Bic, the French firm that pioneered the inexpensive ballpoint pen and pried the disposable-lighter market out from under Gillette. Marcel Bich was also a passionate yachtsman who competed for the America's Cup four times. King of the ballpoint pen business, the baron was something of an eccentric. When he jetted to America, with all of his vast wealth, he would never buy a first-class ticket. This was before the days of business class. Instead, he would buy two coach tickets so that he could curl up on the adjoining seat. He would bring a basket of French vittles with him because he refused to eat airline food. The baron would also never set his watch to American time. The Yanks had to work on French time during his visits—when they got to see him at all, that is. Like those imperious French aristocrats of yore, heaven help you if the baron—who passed away in 1994—decided to flick his Bic in your direction.

That's what—*mon Dieu!*—happened to Ron Shaw. Ron had been with Bic for thirteen years. He had a sterling career with the firm's U.S. subsidiary, rising to national sales manager. But he had never met the baron. America was already their biggest operation in 1974, and their U.S. sales were then $71 million. Then Bic bought a European hosiery manufacturer and came out with a line of pantyhose. It was called—hang on to your derrière—Fanny Hose. As U.S. national sales manager, Ron was in charge of the two cities designated as the test markets—Denver and Kansas City. Each month during 1974, Ron went to each of those cities and learned more about the ins and outs of pantyhose than he ever dreamed of knowing. The brand name was bad enough, but the product itself was substandard compared to what American consumers wanted and could get. Ron was a straight shooter. Through reports submitted to the U.S. Bic president, Ron proceeded to tell Paris the straight scoop on the hosiery line. Paris was not amused.

In the fall of 1974, picnic basket in hand, the baron flew to the States. Ron was to have his first face-to-face, but this was no picnic. Because the baron didn't change his watch, Ron was told to show up at 5:30 a.m. He actually showed up early at 5:00 a.m. and waited. And waited. At 3:00 in the afternoon, a secretary stopped by to say that the audience wouldn't happen that day. How about postponing the meeting until 5:30 the next morning? Ron showed up for his encore meeting. This time he was ushered in to meet with Baron Bich and Bob Adler, president of Bic USA.

"In fluent, though heavily accented English," Ron recalls, "Mr. Bich started asking me a lot of questions. They were structured like trick questions to try to trap me. For example, he threw a multiple-choice number at me: 'Are the most pantyhose sold in department stores, ladies' apparel shops, or drugstores?' The answer of course was none of the above. It was supermarkets. When I said so, he just smiled back and said, 'Oh, really?' Mr. Bich was a master intimidator. He looked at Bob Adler and said, 'This guy Ron Shaw really does know the market.' " The meeting took on a friendlier tone, but it was still something of a grilling. After all the years, the only thing Ron thought was: He finally got to meet Mr. Bich. It was the only meeting Ron ever had with him as a Bic employee.

The whole Bic company had a forced vacation over the December holidays each year. The first working day of the new year was on Friday, January 3, 1975. Ron was called into Bob Adler's office to meet with Bob and Jack Paige, vice president of marketing, Ron's immediate boss. They explained the baron's son Bruno was coming to the States and would be taking over Ron's job. The baron wanted Bruno to learn the business, and he was to start as U.S. national sales manager. Ron's Bic days were over. He was forced out and there was no other position available for him.

Bob Adler and Jack Paige were caught between a rock and a hard place. The orders out of the French headquarters were crystal clear. The situation was particularly hard for Jack. Even though Ron and Jack were very different types of people and came from totally different backgrounds, they had remarkably good chemistry with each other.

Ron was given a seven-month severance package, but he had a mortgage, two of his three kids in dental braces, car payments, and credit card debt. Ron was in the same boat as any typical thirty-six-year-old with a young family. He could see that sum vanishing in a flash. Ron didn't think the settlement was right in any case. At the age of thirty, he had become the youngest sales manager of any pen company in America. During his fourteen-year tenure, Bic's U.S. operations had grown from $1 million in sales to $71 million. But there was nothing Ron could do about the severance package either.

Fanny Hose? In five or six years, the brand landed on its keister! Bic is out of that business today. "I have no proof, but the truthful, honest reports I sent monthly on Fanny Hose," Ron reflects, "were not what Mr. Bich wanted to hear. I may have had the right facts, but I didn't have the right enthusiasm. These weren't personal opinions. They were cold, hard facts."

Bruno was the explanation, but not the actuality. As so often happens in firings, the reason given is not the real reason.

Most of all, Ron was just plain astonished at being fired for being honest about the business. "Not that Mr. Bich would have done this," Ron reflects, "but it would have gone down better if they told me I was being fired for stealing or fooling around with the boss's wife. Neither would have been true, but it would have felt more justified than just being shoved out the door." While Ron had met Marcel Bich just that one time several months earlier, he had known Bruno since the boss's son was a teenager. Ron liked Bruno and thought that he was extremely bright and competent. He has since risen to become chairman and CEO of Société Bic today. What happened wasn't Bruno's fault, Ron believed even back then.

On the day he was fired, Ron had committed to take his older son to a hockey game in downtown New Haven. His daughter had a sleepover for her girlfriends. "The day—time—and place: all of the details of the day I was fired are etched in my mind," Ron says, "like what you did on December 7, 1941, or September 11, 2001. When I came home from work, I couldn't say anything because all these kids were in the house. I can't remember if I ate dinner, but I'm sure I didn't eat much. I was scared to death with all of these obligations. Where in the world would money for tomorrow come from? Did I watch the hockey game? Not that I remember. I went through the motions of being a daddy. After we came home, I put my son to bed. All the sleepover kids were snoozing away. Then I told my wife."

You need to know something about Ron Shaw. Not only is he a fantastic executive, he was also a stand-up comedian before he got into the pen business. He took being a comedian very seriously and would spend all his waking hours polishing his act. He would add new material and purge numbers that didn't work. Ron first met Larry King working as a comedian in Florida because his agent told him that he had to show up and do this guy's program. Larry was hosting a nighttime radio interview program out of a window in Pumpernik's Deli at the time. "I showed up for the appearance—with misgivings, I might add. If Larry King is doing a radio show out of a deli window in Miami, I figured this guy had absolutely no future in broadcasting," Ron remembers with a laugh.

Ron was good enough to be the opening act for Dean Martin and Liberace at the Fountainbleu Hotel in Miami Beach. Famed toastmaster Georgie Jessel was backstage and passed on a memorable piece of advice to Ron. "If you're going to make a living in this business, kid, don't fall in love before you become a star," Jessel said. It was advice Ron didn't follow. He fell in love. So he left comedy and became a salesman so that he could support his wife and young family. First, he sold life insurance. That didn't last. "I couldn't deal with death as a constant element, day in and day out," Ron says. "Selling life insurance is figuring out a hundred different ways to say 'God forbid!' " Then came the Bic opening and his fourteen-year career with that firm.

The comedian in Ron never really vanished. He would always be asked to be the entertaining emcee at sales conferences. And he would inevitably find a humorous way to break the ice when a meeting became tense. He was constantly polishing up routines that he could use. Now we return to January 3, 1975. When Ron closed the bedroom door and told his wife, Phyllis, that he had been fired, she looked up at him with a twinkle in her eye. "Not bad," her look seemed to say, "now, what's the punch line, Ron?" Ron was flabbergasted. "No, you don't get it. This is not a stand-up routine. I actually got fired today. Out of the blue. Wham!"

Ron and Phyllis thought that things like this only happen in the movies. Ron had to spend a few minutes convincing Phyllis that it was real. Then something wonderful happened. Ron says that Phyllis has a lot of natural humor and is invincibly positive. "Her reaction was astonishing," Ron recalls. " 'What a great opportunity!' she said. 'You can go into business for yourself. That's what you have been always telling the kids to do!'

She doesn't drink or smoke anything. I would have sworn to you that she was chemically high on something, the way she went on about the possibilities on our doorstep. I asked her, What are we supposed to do for money? 'We don't need such a big house. An apartment will work just fine,' she reassured me. She was totally committed to help me get into my own business. That didn't happen, but what an emotional cushion!"

Ron went to work finding a job with the same dead seriousness that he had earlier pursued during his career as a comic. He first went up and interviewed for the job of VP of sales for Sylvania Flashcubes. That didn't work, and Ron still chuckles with relief today. "When was the last time you saw a flashcube, Harvey?" Because Ron was so widely known in business circles as the "man with the mike" at events, a number of firms contacted him. But he could also tell that many of the calls he got were curiosity driven and not serious contacts. "I had the chance to sit with the top guys," Ron remembers. "But, you know the old story: You can't get a job if there is no opening. People really wanted the inside dish on 'How could it be that they let him go?' "

Fortunately, some lucky breaks came his way. Since Bic was publicly held at that time, they had to issue an announcement that Ron was leaving "to pursue other career interests." It was covered in the *Wall Street Journal* and the *New York Times*. The Japanese pen company Pilot was a fledgling operation in the United States at the time. They spotted that Ron was available. Another friend of Ron's had met someone from Elta Industries, representing Pilot in the States, some fourteen months earlier. They encouraged Ron to interview with Pilot. He was scooped up quickly, although he was apprehensive about joining what was then such a small company. "When I was fired," Ron says, "Bic was the number-one pen company in America. Whatever the measure, Pilot was in last place. How could I go from being at the biggest to a job with the smallest disposable pen company?" Worse yet, Pilot was then based in a dingy old factory in Long Island City, New York. Ron had no interest in leaving Connecticut and raising his kids in New York. That wasn't all. People warned him that he would never become president of a Japanese-owned company.

Ron crafted a unique deal with his Japanese boss in the United States. If he could build the Pilot business from $1 million in revenues to $10 million, he could then move the company to Connecticut. For the first three years with Pilot, Ron commuted two hours and twenty minutes each way every day. He drove to the Bridgeport train station, took the train to Grand Central, connected to a subway for five stops, and then walked four blocks to the plant. "We reached $10 million in three years," Ron recalls proudly. "We were all set to move to Connecticut. It wasn't in the cards. Our outside accountant told Pilot that we couldn't move because we would forfeit our state tax loss credit of $360,000. So, I located a site in Port Chester, New York, one block from the Connecticut state line, and a developer built us a 20,000-square-foot site. It was still an hour-and-five-minute commute by car for five and a half years. The zinger: the outside accountant had screwed up. The state of Connecticut had a working agreement with the state of New York. Those credits would have been allowed. Today Pilot is based in Trumbull, Connecticut."

As Ron's mother would have put it, joining up with Pilot was *beshert*—Yiddish for "meant to be." "In 1975," Ron notes, "the yen/dollar exchange rate was 306. Today it's 105. Pilot was making all kinds of money on currency exchange, let alone having a helluva profit on the pens to begin with." Today, Pilot is the third largest and the fastest-growing writing instrument company in the United States. The Tokyo-based parent is a billion dollars big, and the United States is the key market. Ron is today the president and CEO of Pilot Pen Corporation of America. He was only the sixth American in history to be appointed to any board of directors of a publicly held company in Japan. In fact, that guy from the Miami deli window, Larry King, happened to be in Japan doing a series of programs when the news of Ron's election to the Pilot board broke in 1992. It led to Ron being on the Larry King show after a thirty-four-year hiatus! It took that long to get his act rebooked. Ron now serves on Larry's cardiac foundation board. The comic spirit? It never really evaporated. Ron appeared as a humorous spokesperson in Pilot's national television ad campaign for six years.

Ron is an infectiously upbeat guy. He'll tell you about his tattered volume of Napoleon Hill motivational wisdom that still occupies an honored place on his nightstand today. Ron struggled from a blue-collar, Jewish background to become a noteworthy success. He also has seen the changing realities of the office-supply business. Big-box retailers like Office Max, Staples, and Office Depot redefined the office-supply business and put 8,000 local office-supply stores out of business in short order. The number of outlets went from 13,000 to 5,000. Today Pilot uses sales reps to reach the smaller outfits. So, Pilot—like so many other firms—has restructured to a lean organization of just 260 in the United States. That has involved letting people go.

When you ask Ron what lessons he can share about firing, he turns uncommonly serious: "The most important is not to fire people on Friday. Before I left Bic, an unfortunate incident happened. While I was with Bic, a salesman in Florida was writing anti-Semitic letters to our headquarters. He knew that both Bob Adler and I were Jews, and he still signed his name to the letters. The regional manager—under my guidance—went to Florida on Friday. He met with the guy at his hotel room, and he let the guy go. The dismissed salesman ran from the hotel, got into his company car, and took off from the hotel. The regional manager called me. 'What do I do now?' he asked. 'You just fired him,' I said, 'The company car is technically stolen property. I guess we have to call the cops.' Apprehended, he surrendered everything, including the car. We thought that was the end of the matter. Two days later, on Sunday morning, he excused himself at church services, saying he was going to the men's room, and put a bullet through his head behind the church."

"That was one of the most horrible things I have ever had to live with," Ron still feels today. "You know what went through my mind? Had I not made that decision, two children would have a father and a woman would have a husband. But I snapped my finger, and I changed the destiny of an entire family. Look at the mess I created. Immediately, I felt guilty for the entire situation. I did not go to a psychiatrist, but it took me months to come to my senses and accept that I was looking at this the wrong way. This man was sick. Would he have written letters like that had he been in his right mind? From that day forward at Bic, no one got fired on a Friday, at least as long as I worked there. (Until, of course, *I* got fired on a Friday.) You go into a depression over that weekend. To begin the whole process by sitting and moping and feeling sorry for yourself on a Saturday and Sunday is just the wrong beginning. There is no financial security, and you are worried to death. Every bad thing you could think of runs through your head. At Pilot, Friday firings are a no-no."

Did Ron ever see the baron again? About a year after he joined Pilot, Ron and Bich happened to be on the same international flight together. The conversation was very friendly. The basket? *Oui!* The first-class seat: *Non! Non!*

MACKAY'S MORAL:

When you're planning your career, make sure there's no son of a Bich waiting in the wings.

WISDOM? YOU BET YOUR APHORISM

I've been told many times that I could have had a career in fortune cookies instead of envelopes. That's because I love to come up with those pithy little sayings—either mine or from others—fortunes, aphorisms, or as I call them, morals.

Turns out that my hero, Aesop, has a lot of fans out there—those morals are what people remember.

I hope these morals provide lessons for business and life. And may some of them end up on bulletin boards and refrigerators.

- Cream doesn't rise to the top . . . it works its way up.

- People who say that something is impossible should not interrupt those who are busy getting it done.

- There aren't any rules for success that work unless you do.

- When the elevator of life breaks down, your best bet is to take the stairs.

- The road to success is marked with many tempting parking places.

- If at first you don't succeed, you are like most people.

- Triumph is just *umph* added to try.

- The real opportunity for success lies within the person and not in the job.

- Falling down doesn't make you a failure, but staying down does.

- Success is doing what we like to do and making a living at it.

- There's no defeat except in no longer trying.

- If you don't climb the mountain, you can't see the view.

- He who doesn't hope to win has already lost.

- You can't get anywhere unless you start.

- There is no free tuition in the school of experience.

- Experience is a good teacher, but a hard one. She gives the test first and the lesson afterward.

- An obstacle is something you see when you take your eyes off the goal.

- The difference between failure and success is doing a thing nearly right and doing it exactly right.

- People stumble over pebbles, never over mountains.

- Success is putting your "knows" to the grindstone.

- The only place where success comes before work is in the dictionary.

- A successful person is usually an average person who took a chance.

- Past failure often furnishes the finest material from which to build future success.

- Success is to be measured not so much by the position one has reached in life as the obstacles one has overcome while trying to succeed.

- People have to saddle their dreams before they can ride them.

- A competitor is a person who follows you into a revolving door and still comes out ahead of you.

- People never fail at anything—they just give up.

MUHAMMAD ALI

Three-Time Heavyweight Boxing Champion
of the World

"Being stripped of my title made me a stronger person."

"Cassius Marcellus Clay," an induction officer read the name aloud. It was April 28, 1967, at the Armed Forces Examining Station in Houston, Texas. Muhammad Ali refused to step forward. After he was advised of the consequences of his action—up to five years in prison and a fine of $5,000—Ali was asked the question once again. Once more, Ali didn't budge. He was then asked to provide grounds for his refusal to respond to the draft in writing. Ali wrote down: "I refuse to be inducted into the armed forces of the United States because I claim to be exempt as a minister of the religion of Islam."

Ali's wife, Lonnie, has shown me into the Champ's office in their gorgeous home in Berrien Springs, Michigan. His staff is preparing to send off some autographed photos and a pair of boxing gloves that will be auctioned off for some good cause halfway around the world. "Vietnam—that seems like so long ago," I say to Ali. He smiles as he looks up. Beset by Parkinson's disease, he still has the composure that made him so steady in the ring. Over a span of years, I have had the opportunity to meet with Ali on a number of occasions one on one. I've also had the privilege to host him on my plane or in small groups away from the cameras, the kind of settings where I could chat with him about a turbulent and decisive moment in his career. In addition to talking with him for this book, I have sometimes relied on some of those earlier discussions. If there is one thing I have learned about Ali, it's that he is a rock. His beliefs are as steadfast over the years as those powerful legs that anchored him so well in the ring.

Every meeting with Ali is a milestone. My only regret is that I don't get to see him as often as I would want. He and I log about the same travel time each year. More than 200 days. That's not to say Ali always finds the skies friendly. "I fear Allah, thunderstorms, and bad plane rides," he concedes. There's the classic story about a flight attendant who tries to get Ali to buckle up before takeoff. "Superman don't need no safety belt!" Ali boasted. "Superman don't need no airplane," the attendant shot back with a grin.

Ali isn't just America's number-one hero. He's the Homeland's number-one Muslim, too—the mentor of millions. In the aftermath of the 9/11 disaster, Ali said: "I am a Muslim. I am an American. As an American Muslim, I want to express my deep sadness and anguish at the tremendous loss of life that occurred. . . . Islam is a religion of peace. Islam does not promote terrorism or the killing of people. I cannot sit by and let the world think that Islam is a killing religion." Ali has stayed on track with a personal philosophy on killing that crystallized decades ago. It started in Houston. And it all centered on Southeast Asia.

Vietnam became a catch-22 in modern American history. Muhammad Ali—the former Cassius Marcellus Clay—had no intention of being snagged in a morass where you couldn't find your way out, because the rules of the game were illogical. In a statement prepared for the Houston standoff, Ali wrote that the public had "the impression that I have only two alternatives in taking this stand—either I go to jail or go to the Army. There is another alternative and that alternative is justice. If justice prevails, if my constitutional rights are upheld, I will be forced to go neither to the Army nor to jail."

Did Ali feel desperate and alone at this moment of truth? Not the Champ. When I asked him how he felt, Ali said that he was *happy*. "I knew when I didn't step forward in the lineup, I would be convicted of draft evasion, Harvey. I was then told my title was being stripped. I wasn't angry. I was happy because I was showing them up. The army said, 'If you go to Vietnam, you won't have to fight or carry a gun; you could do exhibition bouts like Joe Louis did.' But I didn't care. As far as I was concerned, my going over there was still aiding and abetting the killing of innocent people—people who'd never done anything to me. I don't mind fighting in self-defense, but these people hadn't attacked me or my family or my country. We went over there seeking these people, they didn't come after us! I thought, 'There are people right here in America who don't respect me, who would lynch my relatives if they could. Why should I be fighting over in Vietnam? I should be fighting over here.' "

Muhammad Ali entered the American lexicon when he was still Cassius Clay and won the amateur heavyweight title in Rome during the 1960 Olympics. As a pro, he first won the heavyweight title in 1964, defeating Sonny Liston. That same year, he became a Black Muslim and changed his name to Muhammad Ali. The sect's founder, Elijah Muhammad, "taught his followers that white people were devils, but I never really practiced it," says Ali.

Ali gazes down at his fan mail, stack after stack of it. After a pause, I ask him when he first found the truth of Islam's message. "Harvey, I think that my eyes started to open to the truth of Islam when Malcolm X made his journey to Mecca and realized that there were Muslims of all colors." When Ali made his own hajj to Mecca he encountered blond-haired, blue-eyed Muslims from Turkey, Russia, and Albania. He became convinced that Islam "is the most misunderstood religion in the United States"—tainted by Hollywood caricatures of Moors "swinging big swords and cutting off people's heads. They didn't show people praying in a mosque or on hajj."

Ali's reasoning is what makes his case so compelling. He told me, "I never felt anger or outrage toward people. I was prepared to go to jail for my convictions. I knew Allah would protect me and my family would not go hungry. I never thought about getting even. I was only following the tenets of my religion and the war being fought in Vietnam was not a 'Holy War.' " It's amazing how centered and independent Ali was as he faced his situation: "During this time, Harvey, I was on my own. The government and religious leaders did not help me. I believed in my faith and prayed a lot."

Ali clearly saw the complexity of the road back for him. First, he had to resolve the pending prison sentence facing him. Second, if he surmounted that hurdle, he needed to again successfully defend his championship. Even before he had a chance to return to the ring, crowds bolstered Ali's morale: "I received a lot of letters from people on both sides. I didn't let it affect me one way or the other. What encouraged me were the number of people that would show up on college campuses to hear me talk. I never thought about the media or press being on my side. I knew they were waiting to see what would happen. I just know they always showed up when I made those campus speeches, to make a living." The crowds encouraged him, but Ali gave me an astonishing answer when I asked him if being trained as a fighter helped him to rebound. "Being trained as a boxer did nothing to equip me for setbacks. I believed in my faith. Life is full of setbacks. There could always be more setbacks. If you care enough about what you are doing, you keep on going and train harder. The most important thing I knew I had to do was to restore my stature and get a big fight. I knew I had to fight Frazier."

Ali never expected to be the subject of a Supreme Court ruling. Finally the Supreme Court quashed Ali's conviction in 1970. It was famed sportscaster Howard Cosell who called Ali to let him know that the Court had ruled in his favor. (Ali's jousting with Cosell was legendary, and he once offered $300 to the man who could bring him Cosell's toupee dead or alive.) His title was restored, but he lost it to Joe Frazier in 1971. He defeated Frazier in a rematch in 1974 and then won the title again by defeating George Foreman later in the same year. "As soon as I defended my title and won it back," Ali recalls, "I knew the world saw me as the undisputed champion. With the title came all the invitations and appearances of a champ." Ali was later to lose and regain the title a third time.

In retrospect, how does the entire saga look to Ali today? He is remarkably philosophical: "Having anything taken away from you that you earned, enjoyed, or deserved makes you feel bad. I was fortunate never to have a bad judge or referee, but I have seen it happen to others." Even Judge Ingraham, who initially sentenced Ali to five years in prison for refusing the draft, commented on Ali's politeness and dignity in the courtroom.

By the way, Ali did actually end up in jail during his struggle. It was in 1968 in Florida for a stretch of ten days. The charge had nothing to do with his draft charge. It was for driving a motor vehicle without a valid license. Ali recalls: "Jail is a bad place. . . . A man's got to be real serious about what he believes to say he'll do that for five years, but I was ready to go if I had to go."

Ali's advice to others who lose their job and standing: "If a person was fired because they did something wrong, they should take the punishment and forget it. If a person was innocent and they were treated unjustly, they should fight it. People are easily frightened to take a stand because they fear the consequences. There are a lot of people who have taken stands and have been punished unjustly. The public doesn't know about it, because they are not famous. Being stripped of my title made me a stronger person. Harvey, these events made me who I am today. It wouldn't have been the same if I had stayed Cassius Clay and went into the service."

What I know is this: This is the same man of conviction whom the United States chose to light the Olympic Torch in 1996. Our entire family—nine strong—was gathered there in Atlanta to savor that moment. This is the champion that Bill Clinton chose to be seated next to when Clinton was successfully renominated to the presidency.

"Still, the Vietnam ordeal was one hair-raising contest for you," I said to the Champ.

He leaned back and smiled. Then he said with a knowing look and measured wisdom, "Nelson Mandela went through more than me."

MACKAY'S MORAL:

Ali fears "Allah, thunderstorms, and bad plane rides,"
yet he flies 200 days a year. Face fear to whip it.

THE CATHEDRAL

Two bricklayers were working on a building. A sidewalk superintendent paused to ask precisely what they were building.

The more stolid bricklayer replied: "I don't know and I don't care. All I do is slap this crummy mortar on these crummy bricks and pile them up in a crummy line."

But the second and more imaginative bricklayer enthused: "I'm helping to build a great cathedral with a beautiful spire that will point straight up to heaven."

So the second man was *fired* because they were building a garage.

MACKAY'S MORAL:

Too little vision and too much vision . . .
Both can cause a career collision.

MARTHA ROGERS

Founding Partner, Peppers & Rogers Group

"The best way to learn something is to try and teach it."

Sunday school isn't always a picnic. For sure, it didn't turn out to be one for Martha Rogers. Martha is one of the leading academic and business "teachers" commanding a lectern today. Guess what? She got herself fired from her first teaching job. Interesting? You bet it is. Because being interesting was what got her fired.

Not long ago, Martha was named by the influential *Business 2.0* magazine as one of the nineteen most important business gurus of the past century. She and Don Peppers are the founding partners in the customer-strategy consulting dynamo known as the Peppers & Rogers Group. Don and Martha pioneered the "one-to-one marketing" concept that has led to a series of bestselling books on building the value of the customer base and one of the hottest consulting shops in the country. Martha has won celebrated teaching awards. In 1999, she became an adjunct professor at the Fuqua School of Business at Duke University. Peppers & Rogers is a 120-person consultancy that was recently acquired by Carlson Marketing Group but still retains its own independent identity as a firm.

When Martha was seventeen and still in high school, her northwest Florida Presbyterian church's leaders asked if she would be willing to teach a Sunday school class. Martha agreed and was assigned a fifth-grade class. The church was fairly large and so was the group of fifth-graders. The first day she taught, she followed the curriculum exactly. The kids were d-y-i-n-g of boredom. As any parent knows, fifth-graders are just at the age when they start to be cool, and this ordeal was as uncool as you could get.

Over the next week, Martha wrestled with the problem. Give the curriculum its due, she thought, and be sure to cover the assigned basics, but she better get some sizzle into this show or nobody will be taking home any of the messages. This was the South. Gridiron land. If you have been in the South on a Sunday morning in late fall, you know that it's one continuous postgame show. Who beat whom in the college games on Saturday? Most especially the latest news about the Florida State Seminoles. Who would be the trouncers and the trouncees on the NFL broadcasts in the afternoon? Martha had the kids rap a bit about football, then they did a little Luke and John. Next they sang a folk song, then they kicked around why cheating on tests was bad. Another break and another lesson. By the end of the session, these kids were laughing and excited. By the way, they even remembered some of the ideas. And they started applying them to little puzzles and problems that clever Martha sneaked into the conversation. On that Sunday morning, Martha rolled through the South better than Sherman ever could. Against their natural antischool instincts, these kids were actually beginning to learn and internalize things.

Wait. It gets better. The weeks pass. Over hominy grits and sugar-cured ham at Sunday breakfast, what's the table talk? Are the kids bickering about whether Roger Staubach will be sending Calvin Hill up the middle or around the end? No, they're debating the morality of stealing Twinkies from somebody else's lunch box. They were warming up, you see, for Miss Rogers' ethics seminar later that morning. Youngsters start bringing their friends to Sunday school! Fifth-grade boys, smitten by their first crush, mob the local drugstore for dime bags of valentines to see who can send the gaudiest number to this darn-sure-ain't-she-purdy Miss Rogers. Teachers down the hall in the other classrooms hear the giggles and songs from Martha's classroom overwhelm the deadly silence in their own. Something not altogether wholesome is going on here.

Patience snaps. One of the school overseers comes to her after class and says to Martha, "Child, there's been more than a trifling concern about your class. I'm afraid we're going to have to ask you to step down and not teach anymore. It's mighty different from the way our church is used to doing things. Now, be sure you bring back your teacher's guide to choir practice, and mind those cookie crumbs on the floor. That's a dear."

"At the time, I was devastated. It may sound trivial, but I had worked very hard," Martha recalls. "The lessons had registered, and I had met the curriculum requirements."

"When you look back now, what is the biggest lesson you have carried with you from this experience throughout your life?"

"Harvey, interestingly enough, it's not about teaching. It's about volunteer work. Any overseer or manager has special obligations to people who do volunteer work. And sometimes even paid people do volunteer work. That's true when you ask them to handle things outside their job description or to do it more than the usual forty or forty-five hours a week. When that happens, you need to be appreciative of that work. I'm far from perfect myself today, but since my experience I have made a conscious effort to try. When people volunteer their time, correcting them or even taking the drastic step of removing them takes a special kind of graciousness."

"How about you, Martha? Were there mistakes you made that did you in back then?"

"We had way too much fun, Harvey. I should have gone to the people in charge of things and given them a *fun warning*. It was *my* job to explain that it was okay we were having fun. After all, we were still getting the expected work done—even more and better than before. I should have kept better in touch with the people who were responsible for what I was doing. Communication 360 degrees is a good thing. You can win people's minds if you win their hearts. But sometimes you have to get permission to win their hearts."

"And for you, Martha: Did the experience make you rein in how you behaved as a teacher?" I ask.

"Not on your life! The experience made me *more* likely to take risks. It taught me that you had to break out of the dry routine if you want to make an impact. Today, I can't imagine teaching or speaking publicly about something I don't believe in passionately. I need to feel that I *have* to share this message with somebody so that it touches part of their brain, their gut, or their heart. That means you want them to take some of the message away with them. To make that impact you have to break the rules from time to time. If I have one piece of advice to young people, it's to break rules. Let's first assume you are delivering way more than what is expected of you. You have to do much more than the expected to compete today, because there are plenty of people out there happy to do the minimum. If you are already overdelivering, and breaking a rule will help you deliver more, then go ahead. Ask yourself a question: Will breaking a rule really help everyone out, not just myself? Is the answer yes? Then go ahead and break the rule. I'm not talking about doing anything criminal or unethical. I mean not following some stupid policy or convention. You'll have more fun and everyone will learn more. Most of all, you'll *deliver* more.

"James Bond had *his* license," I observe. If you are delivering way more satisfaction to customers than they should expect, then you have a 'License to Break Rules.' "

- Break the rules, especially if you're delivering super results already. It's the people who lean back and play it safe who are likeliest to fall out of their chairs.

- If you think paid time is gold, then volunteer time is platinum. Give your own volunteer time selflessly. But shower others with appreciation when they give their time to you. When your luck is down, energized volunteers are the kinds of community leaders business executives remember.

- Moments of great stress can bring to light skills and confidence we never knew we had.

MACKAY'S MORAL:

When it comes to make or break, breaking the rules
can make your career.

DOWN AND UP #4

- **Elvis Presley** was fired by a music studio in 1954. He was told, "You ain't goin' nowhere, son. Go back and drive a truck."

- **Ray Romano** got fired from the pilot of a TV show called *News Radio* while it was still in rehearsal. His spectacularly successful *Everybody Loves Raymond* TV show has since won a fistful of Emmys and Golden Globes.

- **Clint Eastwood** was fired off a Hollywood set in 1959. His Adam's apple was too big and he couldn't talk fast enough. His bankbook talks plenty fast enough today, after he acted in and/or directed dozens of blockbusters . . . and won three Oscars.

- **Burt Reynolds** was fired from one of his acting jobs. "You can't act," they told him. Afterward, he became the number-one box office draw for five consecutive years.

- **Madonna** was fired as the hatcheck girl at New York's prestigious Russian Tea Room restaurant for wearing fishnet hosiery. She is today the icon of popular music with eighteen gold and platinum singles.

- **Johnny Cash,** known as "The Man in Black," was fired from the Grand Ole Opry and went on to a legendary career that spanned four decades, and he ended up in the Songwriters, Country Music, and Rock and Roll halls of fame.

- **Suzanne Somers** was fired by the hit TV show *Three's Company* after she asked for a raise at the beginning of the fifth season. The tireless actress, singer, jewelry designer, and *Candid Camera* host is also an accomplished cook, bestselling author, and huge hit in the exercise-video market.

- *Baywatch,* the television show, was canceled after its first season. David Hasselhoff, the show's lead actor, bought the show's rights. The show—which annually went through 306 pounds of body makeup and 575 swimsuits—ran eleven years and aired in 140 countries, in thirty-two different languages.

DON PEPPERS

Founding Partner, Peppers & Rogers Group

"The whole idea behind executing a termination is to have the person agree with you."

In January 1992, Don Peppers was president of Perkins/Butler Direct Marketing in New York City. Perkins/Butler was the direct-mail division of the prestigious ad agency Chiat/Day/Mojo. Chiat was reeling from severe financial reversals that had run up over eight months. "Big accounts had left," Don explains. "While our own little corner of the business was marginally profitable—and performing according to our budget—I had been asked before the holidays to come up with a plan for cutting staff to save costs. My first order of business, returning from the break, would be to implement this grisly task."

Enter two agendas: the state of Chiat/Day's books vs. the race to write Don's own book. Don had been an author since his youth. As a teenager, he had actually sold to a publisher some spacey sci-fi he had written. Then there were various novels he had started and put aside. As an advertising and marketing maven, Don had penned countless proposals. He was gifted with the word, to say the least. In parallel to the financial pressure Chiat/Day/Mojo was experiencing, Don was feeling an exhilarating drive of another sort. He and a colleague of his, Martha Rogers—who was not at Chiat/Day—had been engaged by the publisher Doubleday to write a book on marketing. "It was no secret at Chiat/Day that I had an advance from Doubleday and that I intended to write the book on my own," says Don. "It wasn't going to be a Chiat/Day book. It would be a Don Peppers and Martha Rogers book. We had been working on it since before I joined the company."

Two days after returning to work in January, Don was summoned to a conference room for a meeting with Chiat/Day's president. Don knew it was cutback time. He grimly pulled together the paperwork that he and his finance director had assembled. "Included was a list of several people we could live without if we had to, and a plan for getting their work done without them. When I got to the conference room," Don recalls, "my boss and his planning director were sitting at the table, and I sat down opposite them. Before any discussion of my plan, however, my boss nodded at a sheet of paper his planning director had in her hand. She handed it across the table to me. My boss said he thought it would be a good idea to begin the meeting by having me read this. It was a press release announcing that I had resigned to pursue other interests, including writing a book."

Don didn't get why this document was being handed to him . . . because he hadn't resigned! "It took me a few seconds to get my bearings. At first, I thought it must be that they didn't like the idea of my writing a book," remembers Don. "They must want me to give it up. Or maybe this was a ruse to throw off our competitors. It took me a full minute after finishing my reading of the press release before I actually realized that I was being fired. For real! Me! Incredible! When I did finally realize what was happening, my face flushed, my heart raced, and my stomach churned." While Don had been grappling with the tough task of how to save money for the firm, his boss's team had been doing the same thing. They had decided that a simple way to lighten the budget was just to shed Don himself.

"The boss said I should sign this release and I'd get four months' severance instead of the standard six weeks. Also, the agency had to have a cover story for Chiat/Day's clients. The firm didn't want them to know I was being asked to leave. The press release provided that cover story blind. In reality, my position was being eliminated because the overall company had too many highly paid managers and needed to consolidate and streamline. My position would not be filled after my departure. Instead the whole executive staff would be consolidated into the bigger agency. Oh, yeah, and they would probably still make the additional cuts my CFO and I had identified, so thanks."

Don had never been fired before—only promoted. I asked him if the agency handled his departure professionally. "Harvey, Chiat/Day had been regarded as the agency of the decade back then. By the summer of 1991, however, the firm was on rocky times. All the officers had taken a 10 percent pay cut. My firing was typical for industry. They wanted to minimize potential resistance. The whole idea behind executing a termination is to have the person agree with you. The truth is, I would not have fired me in any other manner. Procedurally, they were right on target."

Don may have been pulling down a hefty income, but living in the New York market is no cheap ticket. "We had three children at home," Don says, "and my wife Pamela's career as a television producer would be very hard to restart after a four-year hiatus as a full-time mom. We had borrowed as much as we could without committing fraud. My wife and I could barely afford everything we were paying. I had a big alimony–child support payment from a previous marriage. We had a mortgage on a home in Connecticut."

"Don, how did you feel when you woke up the next morning after you got this punch in the stomach?"

"Harvey, you won't believe this. I was absolutely ecstatic. Inside, I was convinced the book Martha and I were writing was revolutionary. Have you ever seen the movie *Alien*? I had something living within me: a different life-form with its own reason for being. Only the alien within me was friendly. It wanted to burst out of me and spread itself in a positive and creative way. But there's more. You see, there was something that Chiat/Day didn't know."

"What was that?"

"No one could possibly have known that I *couldn't* quit because I was two months in debt. Had I quit to work on the book, I wouldn't have gotten any termination settlement. Because I was fired and they wanted to keep it secret, I got four months' pay. I was then two months ahead at the bank. It was providential."

"So, your firing fit smack into your grand design?"

"Partly. It fit right into my plan to write the book. Neither Martha nor I knew what would happen after the book was published. We did not, for example, write the book to start a consulting or speaking business. Perhaps I would become a talk show host, I thought. Harvey, we honestly had no idea of what would happen after the book came out. We didn't plan anything after the book was written. We never even talked about it. We didn't calculate what would happen as the result of this sea change. We only knew this book would have an impact. We were literally consumed to get down on paper this marvelous, interesting perspective that was eating us up. Early on, when my wife, Pamela, and I talked, she asked, Wouldn't it be a good idea to take a job? My only answer was 'I have to write the book.' Pamela remained supremely confident I could do what I had set out to do."

"Don, how did you know this book would be a tidal wave? It sounds like you were sitting on the secret formula for Coca-Cola."

"Harvey, that was simple. I gave speeches on the topic of the book. Jaws would drop when I gave my speech. Every time. I have always enjoyed amazing people, and this time I sure did. In his book *Whatever Happened to Madison Avenue*, Martin Mayer called that talk the most fascinating presentation he had ever witnessed. Martha's and my book described what would happen to marketing in the world of the web before the web took off. In those days, there was no World Wide Web. Fiber optics linked to the home were considered feasible in twenty years. Nobody knew what interactivity would really mean. They all thought it meant: You would see a TV commercial, you'd punch a button, and the peanut butter would be sent to your house. Nobody really knew."

"But Doubleday must have known what they were sitting on, Don."

"For a long time, they didn't know because we didn't know. Our editor Harriet Rubin saw this as a technology book, and that was her problem with the proposal. She didn't doubt what we were projecting would happen. Technology was rapidly changing and would be soon outdated. She wanted to know what the technology meant for business. How should business now think about *business* differently? Great challenge, but I had no idea how to revise the proposal. So for months the book just sat there," Don explains.

"This is around 1990–91, while you were still with Chiat/Day. What finally broke loose your vision of the book?"

"There was a moment of revelation. You'll recall I was president of Chiat's direct marketing agency—Perkins/Butler. One of our clients was American Express. They had hired us to do all their mailing programs for their Gold Card members. American Express had Green, Gold, and Platinum Card divisions. Each of these divisions was managed as a separate business. When you quit your Green Card and took a Gold Card, you got two letters from American Express. The first was an upbeat mailing from the Gold Card welcoming you aboard. It praised the card, and it commended you for choosing it. The second letter was from the Green Card. It was grave and asked urgently: What did we do? How do we get your business back? Can you imagine how crazy customers thought this was? We wanted American Express to solve this dilemma. Instead of limiting us to the Gold Card, we asked: Why don't you give us some customers instead? We'll handle all the mail for those customers. That way we can coordinate your interactions. We searched for a way to put this across to the client. Then we hit on it. American Express had thought *they* were interested in expanding their market share. Wrong!"

"What's wrong in going after share of market, Don? Isn't that how businesses compete?"

"Not in the Internet age. American Express should have been paying attention to *share of customer* not *share of market*. They needed to manage their customers, not think about managing their products like the individual cards. This was revolutionary. If you accept this change, then a series of dramatic consequences fall out. That night Martha and I wrote down the ten chapter headings and then we tinkered with it. Here were the consequences to business driven by the interactivity, which was about to happen big-time with the web. We sent one page to Harriet Rubin. She said great. Here's $50,000 and said we were set to go. Those chapter headings opened the gates for our first book. We finished writing it. Doubleday ordered an unusually large printing of 50,000 copies, and the book appeared in August 1993."

"So when the book hit the shelves, it was a colossal success?"

"No, not exactly. In fact, when *The One to One Future* came out, we couldn't get any attention in the business press at all. We didn't get a single review. You couldn't get arrested for talking about one-to-one marketing. I went on a book tour with Doubleday and appeared at bookstores in front of audiences of four or five people. The *Wall Street Journal, Business Week, Forbes* and the *New York Times* hadn't noticed us. At the end of November, we got a mention in *Fortune*, which called our book 'obnoxiously glib.' You know what they say: Any press is good press. I guess I'd rather be obnoxiously glib than anonymous."

"Things are not looking good at this point. It seems that the Alien Within was turning into the Alien Without a Future."

"You're right, Harvey, so it seemed. But then lightning struck. One day, someone faxed me to ask if I had seen Tom Peters' column in the newspaper. I hadn't, but I was floored when I did. Peters' verdict: 'Tom Clancy couldn't keep me awake on an overnight flight to New York from California, but Don Peppers and Martha Rogers sure did. This is the best business book I have seen in ten years. It's not just the book of the year, it's the book of the decade.' We immediately put that quote on the book jacket cover. George Gendron, the Editor of *Inc.* magazine, invited me to speak at a session. He introduced me saying that our book was not just the book of the decade. More than that, he praised it as one of the best business books ever written. By the end of 1994, the book had sold close to 150,000 copies. A decent showing. It wasn't ever a bestseller, but it was a respectable book. Martha and I have written six books since. We are writing a seventh. It promises to have all the excitement of the first."

"Today you have this huge consulting practice and are one of the most-sought-after marketing consultants in the world. But if you look at how this all evolved over the past twelve years, Don, hasn't it been a lot of shoestring innovation and a good dose of luck?"

"Granted, Harvey, I know I've been lucky, but I've been unlucky more than once, too. I have started six other businesses in my life. They all failed. I had half the money raised for an all first-class airline. I was going to put fax machines into people's homes and pay for them with advertising. I was the executive vice president of a group legal services firm. New business development skills are a real asset to have when you leave a business and strike out on your own. The time I had my own business lasted literally only four months. I got a few pieces of business. More importantly, I knew what it meant to make calls on my own. That gave me great personal confidence."

Don's advice to young people in business: "Study the basics. But what is really important is learning how to learn. I have degrees in engineering and political science/international affairs. I've never held a job for which I was actually educated. I was a director of accounting at an airline, and I never took a single accounting course. I was a director of marketing and am now thought of as one of the world's fifty most important marketing gurus. I've never taken a single marketing course. It's not the education you have, but your open-mindedness and a continuous willingness to learn. And keeping the corners of your mouth turned up in a smile. In every problem, there is a hidden opportunity."

- When you are asked to draw up a plan to cut back staff in your organization, always assume your boss has been asked to do the same thing . . . and that you could be one of the people who will be cut.

- If you have found a new idea you really believe in—an idea that you have tested in advance—getting fired may be a gold mine!

- The Internet has changed how *everything* is marketed, and that includes people looking for a job.

- The biggest thing school teaches you is not a subject but how to learn effectively for the rest of your life.

MACKAY'S MORAL:

Before you write off somebody's achievements to luck,
look for all the unlucky hard work that came before.
As Wendy's founder Dave Thomas put it,
"The harder I worked, the luckier I got."

OVER THE
BREAKFAST TABLE . . .

What's a leading reason people get fired? The people who hire them don't make *hiring* decisions thoroughly enough. Some wise man or woman once said there is something much finer, rarer, and scarcer than ability: that's the ability to *recognize* ability and compatibility. Strangely enough, we seem to learn this in other aspects of life:

- Let's say a man dates a woman for two years almost every day and every night. You would think they would know each other well. But let them marry each other and they will know more about each other in sixty days than they did in the previous two years of dating.

- Two married couples can live side by side for twenty-five years. They are best friends. One day one of the couples calls the other couple. "Hey, we've got a good idea. Let's go to Europe together for six weeks." Upon their return, they never talk again.

Ain't it the truth! But when it comes to hiring, we don't see things the same way.

You are interviewing a person for an IT position at your company. You can interview the candidate for six months and give them every test known to humankind. You would think that you would know the candidate well, but this is not necessarily true. Hire the person and you will know more in the first thirty days watching them on the firing line than you did the previous six months of interviews.

It is extremely difficult to pick the right person. If you have a system and commit yourself to it, the odds skyrocket that the match will succeed.

When a marriage, a friendship, or a job relationship goes on the rocks—the loss is serious, painful, and often expensive. It's in the best interest of all parties to reduce the potential risk. Hiring management is matchmaking. That's why it's good for *both* the candidate and the potential employer if:

- The candidate goes through psychological testing to see if there is a genuine fit with the job and between the people.

- There is socializing with the candidate to make sure there's a chance to talk about values and goals. It's also a great way to learn about relevant lifestyle, tastes, and habits.

- Multiple interviews are conducted—and not with just the person's boss or boss's boss. Include peers and sometimes even subordinates or outside suppliers.

- Thorough deep-background and reference checking takes place.

- And a tough question must be asked. This question is darn tough to answer when you need a body and somebody needs a job, but here it is: How would I feel about this person working for the competition? If you have any serious doubts, keep searching. Chances are a competitor will hire the candidate you don't. Remember that it's a lot better and cheaper for you, and more costly for your competitor, if they have to fire the guy or gal than if you do.

MACKAY'S MORAL:

Without safeguards, matchmakers get burned.

DEBORAH ROSADO SHAW

Founder of Umbrellas Plus and Dream BIG Enterprises

"Just about any soup you put me in, I can cook."

"Wellesley has just withdrawn my full scholarship after my freshman year. I'm back living in a New York City ghetto I had fought for sixteen years to get out of. I have hit rock bottom. I'm trying to find a job in New York City. I go on seventy-two job interviews over a stretch of three months. I'm frantic about what I will do and how I can redirect my life. I see an ad for an opening in the administrative offices at NYU and go in for an interview with a supervisor in the payroll department. He is literally drunk. He keeps staring out the window during the conversation and talking about the things he sees there. 'Do you *really* want this job?' he asks. 'Yes, yes!' I answer. 'Will you come to work every day on time?' 'I will, I will!' I pledge. He gives me the job, walks out into the reception area, and tells all the other applicants to take off. The job is filled. I start two days later."

Has the seventeen-year-old Deborah Rosado—with an ailing mother and a brother with a life-threatening kidney disease—just been saved from the brink of personal disaster? Maybe not . . .

"I know nothing about how to do this job," Deborah continues. "I am the worst payroll clerk on the planet. NYU has a huge payroll system. My job is to handle payments like supplemental hours. I can't type. I can never seem to squeeze the numbers into those tiny boxes. I decimate checks right and left for four months. Then my supervisor comes out of his office and tells me that this is absolutely the last check I am going to ruin. I'm fired."

"Wow! Deborah," I say to this vivacious and energized woman, "I definitely want you to trace your steps forward from the final check you massacred at NYU. Before we go there, though, why don't you tell me about how you lost your scholarship to Wellesley? For women, Wellesley is the school of schools. Madeleine Albright went there. So did Hillary Clinton. My wife, Carol Ann, went there, too. Young women give their eye-teeth to get into Wellesley."

"You hit the right point, Harvey," Deborah replies. "The amazing thing may have been *how I got into* Wellesley in the first place. As you know, my mother was ill and my brother had a life-threatening kidney disease. I lived in a traditional Latino home. It was okay for a girl to get married and leave home but not to leave home to go to a fancy university. That would be like leaving the galaxy. I had to deal with my parents' objections. Then I had to manage a war on another front, and that was at school. My high-school guidance counselor told me I was kind of bright, but that I would never get into an elite school. 'Deborah, you should consider a two-year community college. Instead of becoming a lawyer, why don't you think of becoming a legal secretary?' She refused to process the applications to my schools of choice. I had to go to the Board of Education to force them to send my transcripts. When I made these applications, I was just fifteen years old. I had entered high school at the age of twelve. I was only sixteen when I won a full scholarship and started my freshman year at Wellesley. It was a tremendous win for me."

"What didn't work out at Wellesley, Deborah?"

"Just about everything . . . and right from the beginning. Consider my background. I'm Puerto Rican. I grew up in the Bronx. Look where I came from. Imagine me walking to my high school in the morning. On the way to school, I would see crack deals done on street corners. Sometimes I'd watch guys fleeing down alleyways and hear the pistol shots of drug lords trying to finish them off. More than once, I stepped into the girls' room at school and found a drug-overdose victim writhing on the floor."

"So, Wellesley was your Camelot?"

"Exactly. It was my dream from the day I started to have any dream about going to college at all. There's just one big problem with that. The larger your vision, the larger the monster you may have to encounter. I walked into my room at Wellesley the first time. My new roommate's parents were just leaving as I got there. I was a little surprised and commented that I hadn't had the opportunity to meet her parents. Will I see them later? I asked my roommate. 'Well, frankly no,' she said. 'They actually want you *not* to be my roommate. They want you to move out.' She had been admitted to both Harvard and Wellesley. Her parents were so conservative they forbade her going to Harvard because they thought it was too radical! You can imagine what they were thinking: Here was the Latino girl from the slums of the Bronx. This was devastating."

"You had just clawed your way out of the ghetto into your dream world. How could the sixteen-year-old Deborah accept this?"

"As a parent, I now understand my roommate's parents' concerns much better than I did then. Three days later, the dean of students actually called me and asked me to move out to another room. I was reminded I was there on a full scholarship. I reached out to black law student friends I knew at Harvard Law School and asked them if I could really be made to move out or lose my scholarship. They told me to stand my ground. The other girl moved. I actually won that battle, stayed put, and got a new roommate. I couldn't imagine that my dream of Wellesley had turned into such a nightmare. I had thought that I had arrived where I really belonged, but that wasn't at all the case. Later on in life, I learned that the only home we really have is within ourselves. I was not emotionally prepared for what I encountered. This was the greatest disappointment of my life: to realize my dream and not have it be what I imagined.

"So there was no emotional support for you at Wellesley?"

"Nearly no one at Wellesley could fathom the many planets I had to travel through to get to that school. The only support person I found was a professor of religion who sensed I was really struggling. He was a renowned international scholar who called me to his office and read me the book *The Little Engine That Could*. I'll never forget the time he took. 'You know what,' he said, 'I know what you have been going through has been hard for you.' That encouragement was enough fuel for me to go on for the balance of the year."

"Did the entire burden rest with Wellesley, Deborah?"

"Oh, I contributed to the situation, too. I was troublesome and defiant. I had all kinds of problems in my dorm with roommates and housemothers. I refused to attend tea and crumpets on Friday afternoons. I was an immature sixteen-year-old. But, I learned that I could survive extreme rejection. I continued to develop tremendous emotional muscle enabling me to bounce back. And I trained that strength to be better and tougher."

"So you're back home for summer break. One day you get a letter in the mailbox with some very unhappy news? How do you explain this to your parents?"

"I didn't tell my parents what really happened until many years later. They just knew I had decided not to go back to Wellesley. I was embarrassed with my family. Three hundred people in the congregation were saying, 'I told you so! You should never have gone off to that fancy school in the first place.' The real reason I was not invited back was not because of my grades. Clearly they were poor, and I was not prepared. Even at the top of my game in high school, I wasn't even at the middle of what Wellesley expected in academic performance. I had a lot of learning to do. When they withdrew my scholarship, it was the same as not inviting me to return. The real reason that the scholarship vanished was that I didn't fit in and they didn't want the hassle of putting up with me."

"So, that was the end of your detour through the ivy-covered citadels of prestige schools, wasn't it? No more of the so-called Seven Sisters for you."

"Wrong. I applied to the prestigious Barnard College at Columbia as a transfer student. Barnard is a Seven Sisters school right in Manhattan. They refused to admit me. When I applied to Barnard, they told me to go to a small school, get straight A's, and come back to them. I did a year and a half at Hunter Community College at night while working during the day. Barnard accepted me with a full academic scholarship, but I still had to support myself. I attended four colleges over ten years before I finally got my diploma from Barnard in 1987 as a political science major."

"Now back to the work issue. Last we heard, you were out on your ear after bungling your job in the payroll department at NYU."

"Harvey, I found my next job through someone whom I had met at NYU. It was one of my first successful networking initiatives. That may have been the biggest silver lining in being fired. I had moved to New Jersey and shared an apartment with young women I had met in the university payroll department. The next job was a milestone for me. Sometimes you don't know why a particular good thing happens at a particular moment in your life. The pay was enormous."

"What exactly is enormous, Deborah?"

"During this period, I started working part-time for an attorney whose wife was senior vice president of an umbrella manufacturer. When I advanced from part-time clerk to full-time account executive, I was making $100,000 a year. I actually made close to $100,000 when I was nineteen and a half."

"Incredible! You're still in college and pulling down a hundred grand a year selling umbrellas. You can't possibly add any more spice to this story."

"How about matrimony, Harvey? The umbrella firm that hired me turned out to be my future husband's father's family business. My husband's family owned an umbrella-manufacturing concern. They had hired me away from a competitor. We were married fifteen years and have three sons."

"Then you didn't stay with the family business?"

"I was challenged reconciling my ambitions as a woman and my responsibility as a mother, as many women are. That business was counter to my values. The only way I felt I could reconcile my professional and private roles was to have my own business where I could play my game my way."

"By this point you had abandoned your dream of ever attending law school?"

"I was still applying to law school. At that point, I didn't think being a businessperson was a real job. When I didn't get into law school number eleven, I figured that maybe I should do something else. 'You know, you're not so bad at this business stuff,' I realized."

"So you decided to found your own company?"

"I had graduated from Barnard and was living in California at the time. I started Umbrellas Plus. My former father-in-law's company made rain umbrellas. Living in sunny California, I saw the opportunity for beach umbrellas. I asked my father-in-law if they were interested in pursuing the business. He said no, go ahead and do whatever you want to do. I didn't quit my job until I had my first order. I landed an order for $100,000 from the Nature Company. That's when I sent in my letter of resignation. This was in 1987."

Umbrellas Plus grew and grew to become a multimillion-dollar wholesaler to some of the most demanding retail buyers in the country. In an industry where there are few women, Deborah was and is a visible and distinctive success story.

As you would expect, Deborah aimed for big clients. Wal-Mart and Costco were prime candidates. "I wanted to pitch the mega-retailers," she recalls, "but I had no relationships. At Costco I introduced myself by writing the CEO a letter regarding things happening in Costco stores that he really ought to pay attention to. We had never met. I learned that I had to open an avenue when I couldn't pitch my merchandise. To do that, I needed to deliver value in some way to a top exec. He found my insights valuable and answered my letter with a phone call. I explained I was a vendor. He said, if you are ever in Washington State, come in and say hello. I asked him if he had his calendar handy. I made an appointment on the spot. There began a relationship that has lasted many, many years. The odds for that kind of approach working might be a hundred to one, but every once in a while it works. You have to focus on *their* concerns when you write. What can you do for him or her? I make it a point to always look at the issues and concerns of my potential customers. And there's even a bonus. To this day, every Christmas, their CEO sends me a big box of luscious Washington State apples!"

"You have the most downpour-repellent approach to setbacks and closed doors I have ever heard, Deborah."

"Just about every soup you put me in I can cook! I've learned the biggest monster in my life is confronting myself and trying to answer the question, 'Why do you want what you want, Deborah? What makes you think you can possibly get it?' When we have that conversation with ourselves, we often forget what we have accomplished."

"Somebody told me that you keep a list of the personal wins in your life posted up on the wall. Do you look at it when you hit a brick barrier?"

"You got it. My story is real. And I can list down the wins

one by one. I'm a single mom with three teenage sons. I came from nowhere. I had to really learn to speak English well enough to have this conversation."

In her book *Dream Big!*, Deborah has another nifty suggestion for people who are sometimes hesitant about being assertive. She thinks it can be especially useful for women. Each week decide to do one assertive thing you might not want to do. Do it to get something done, of course, but also do it to build confidence. What phone call have you been dodging because it's confrontational? What line at a bank or deli do you avoid because you always seem to get nudged to the back? In the book, Deborah described a major speech she was going to give the next week. She needed a favor from the chairman of a major firm. In a real piece of daring, she decided she would ask the chairman for it in front of an audience of hundreds. Talk about chutzpah on the part of the diminutive daughter of a Methodist minister!

Persistence. "I always remembered what my father would preach about us all being God's children," says Deborah. "I have never felt like I was acting alone even in my loneliest, gutter-roaming moments. Our worst enemy is the private conversation competition we have with ourselves. Does that ever register with me! We *do* talk to ourselves, and the messages we tell ourselves are influential. When I deliver a speech, I often ask the group how many of them talk to themselves. About half raise their hands. For those who *didn't* raise their hands, I say, I can hear you saying to yourselves, 'Who me? I don't talk to myself.' Talk to yourself. Coach yourself."

How does Deborah keep herself on track when she meets rejection? "You have to keep something very important in mind: You'll never encounter a greater foe or obstacle than yourself. As for discrimination, I have had all of it—almost everything that the world can target in a person's direction. I have been excluded from meetings. 'Skirts not allowed in this room.' I've had that hinted to me, and I've had it said outright.

Well, what matters most for me is what *Deborah* decides to do. There is only one Deborah, I remind myself, in the history of the universe.

"I also remember not to take myself too seriously. In my purse, I carry around a little blue rubber 'universe ball.' I can barely make out the planet Earth on the ball. Deborah? You couldn't hope to find her on the little dot called Planet Earth in a million years. Who are you kidding? I say to myself. Who even cares? I, too, get scared, but then I realize I had it easy compared with my brother. My brother struggled through his lifetime of thirty-five years with two kidney transplants. Scraping to get by is rough, but it's something different. I spent my entire early life hoping to *have* hot water in the morning . . . and fishing my clothes out of rummage bins at church. I would actually snip out designer labels from other pieces of clothes in the bins and stitch them into my own duds. But, I will tell you this: If all my assets disappeared tomorrow, I know I have the capacity to do it again and get back where I was."

MACKAY'S MORAL:

If life has a knack for raining on your parade,
it's not a bad idea to be in the umbrella business.

KICKED UPSTAIRS

*"I've seen too many guys who were kicked upstairs
and then found out they were working in
a one-story building."*
—Johnny Kerr (who initially opted to join the Phoenix
Suns rather than take a front-office role with another team
and is now a broadcaster with the Chicago Bulls)

How Links
Saved Links

When folks think of Minnesota, they're sure all we swing here are
hockey sticks. In fact, Minnesota has more golf courses *and*
golfers per capita than any other state. A vestige of the old boys'
club working the links? Well, Minnesota also has more *women*
golfers per capita than any other state. It's one factor why Minnesota women have shattered the glass ceiling in business so well.

At the University of Minnesota, I played varsity golf for
three years. I first met my coach, Les Bolstad, when I was still a
senior in high school. He was the major reason I could hardly
wait to get to the university. Les was a master at developing talent. He launched the career of Patty Berg, one of the first national women's sports stars. Les did not teach golf. He taught
life. If you learned a little golf on the side, well, so much the better. He was a second father to me. After graduating, I kept taking lessons from him for the next thirty years. Does it sound like
a hefty part of my soul is wrapped around the woods and irons
of my Minnesota golf days? You don't know the half of it.

One day in April 2002, disaster descended on Gopherville.

I came back from my morning run, poured myself a glass of orange juice, and opened up the morning paper. Front-page banner headlines proclaimed that then U of M president Mark Yudof was set to announce that golf at the University of Minnesota was *fired*. The program would be terminated. Devastated couldn't begin to describe how I felt. A legacy would be demolished. Not only would men's golf be banished, so too, women's golf *and* men's gymnastics. I knew gymnasts and women golfers who felt about their university experiences as I did. They owed much of their success in life to the strength of these character-building programs. It was payback time. It was time to mobilize.

That evening, I called President Yudof. I offered to spearhead an effort to save the three teams. He would condone it, *but* only if our fund-raising wouldn't hijack pledges to academic programs. We had to raise $900,000 in mere weeks from the announcement of the campaign. For this stay of execution, a total of $2.7 million had to be amassed within nine months.

At the same time, Athletic Director Tom Moe and Athletic Development Director Mike Halloran set out on the same wavelength. They asked me to co-chair the campaign with former Gopher All-American football star Bob McNamara. By this point, we not only had to save the teams from the budget axe; we had to save them from themselves! Panic had set in . . . especially among the golf teams. Entire programs and scholarships—the very lifeline to an education—would vanish. The talent would surely go elsewhere.

U of M men's golf team coach Brad James brought the entire men's team over to my office at Mackay Envelope Company for a summit meeting. I urged the members to stay put. Don't change schools, I counseled. I guaranteed in blood we would raise the $2.7 million, and long term there would be golf at Minnesota. Then I rushed over to the U of M to give the same message to the women's golf team. Unfortunately, a couple of team members abandoned ship, including the coach.

Athletic programs are perishing across the nation right and

left. Staffs are being fired. Educations are being undermined. Vital skills training disappears. We could not permit this to happen. The University of Minnesota has always been the state's crown jewel. When you trim non–revenue generating teams like this, you still diminish the University's national status. At the innovative suggestion of U of M star and NHL great Lou Nanne, we mounted a pioneering telethon campaign and raised $670,000. Throughout the campaign, money poured in from U of M grads who had never swung a golf club. It also came from Minnesotans who had never even attended the University! Seventeen hundred donors in all. The fund-raising itself became a model for public campaigns across the nation. The $2.7 million goal was surpassed, and critical athletic scholarships were even endowed. The U's new president, Robert Bruininks, has praised the program as "a tremendous positive for our athletic department."

This book focuses on the plight of individuals being fired. Believe it or not, it's also possible to fire a team or a program. It's actually *easier* to defend a program from being fired than it is individuals. Solidarity and innovation are the means.

By the way, the enthusiasm of saving the teams spilled over to the greens themselves. The throbbing energy that went into saving the men's golf team electrified the players in competition. The athletes were out to prove that they were worth saving. A mere six to eight weeks later, the men's golf team won the Big Ten championship for the first time in thirty years, and then the NCAA golf championship for the first time since teeing it up in 1921. It was also the first championship for a northern men's golf team in forty-five years. That takes the cake, but let's not forget the icing. The team followed that up with another Big Ten championship in 2003.

In the 1980 Olympics, former U of M coach—the late—Herb Brooks led a U.S. hockey team anchored with nine Minnesotans to the Miracle on Ice. In 2002, we had a comparable Miracle on the Links. The University's current athletic director,

Joel Maturi, said, "Trying to eliminate the three non-revenue sports was the best thing that ever happened to Gopher Sports. It awakened a sleeping giant."

Shining brightly on my ring finger is the NCAA/Big Ten championship ring that the men's golf team voted me for my efforts. Were it a Super Bowl or World Series ring, it couldn't mean more.

Each of us has organizations that we dearly love. It could be a school . . . a club, an athletic team . . . or a charity. When the string-pullers or bean-counters try to fire a program close to your heart out of existence, you don't have to take it. But, you *do* have to:

- Seek an up-front understanding with the powers-that-be and avoid making them an enemy.

- Link arms. Mobilize your network of friends and colleagues who share the same passions that you do.

- Chart a clear and practical course of action.

- Point out to the broader public why it's in everybody's interest to give your cause a lease on life.

- Be willing to try fresh and dramatic fund-raising measures.

MACKAY'S MORAL:

When fired upon, there really *are* ways to fire back.

LEE IACOCCA

Former Chairman and CEO, Chrysler Corporation

"It was salami-slicing time—one slice at a time. . . .
Each day I found another part of my body missing."

Lee Iacocca left Ford world headquarters in Dearborn, Michigan, for the last time in 1978. It was his fifty-fourth birthday. He says he was "filled . . . with rage" at "the despot whose name was on the building." The "despot" was Henry Ford II (whom I'll simply refer to as Henry Ford), known wryly in the industry as Hank the Deuce. Iacocca wrote: "It's like the lioness and her cubs. If the hunter knows what's good for him, he'll leave the little ones alone. Henry Ford made my kids suffer, and for that I'll never forgive him."

The suffering that Iacocca is referring to is the stress and pain his family experienced after having been fired from Ford after some thirty-two years. Suffering for the family it might have been, but Iacocca's digs at Ford headquarters were one velvet torture chamber. "The office of the president," he recalls, "was the size of a grand hotel suite. I had my own bathroom. I even had my own living quarters. As a senior Ford executive, I was served by white-coated waiters who were on call all day." When Ford fired him, however, the company moved his office to a little cubicle in a warehouse, and—on his last day—he was offered a cup of vending machine coffee. "This final humiliation was much worse than being fired. It was enough to make me want to kill—I wasn't quite sure who, Henry Ford or myself. Murder or suicide were never real possibilities, but I did start to drink a little more. . . . I really felt I was coming apart at the seams." This, despite the fact that Iacocca was already well heeled enough to "play golf" for the rest of his days.

His late wife, Mary, advised Iacocca: "Don't get mad. Get even." No doubt both the pain he perceived his family to have experienced as well as his personal humiliation became powerful prods to get back at Henry Ford in Ford's own Detroit backyard. Iacocca left Ford for Chrysler. Aided by government loan guaranties, but relying most of all on gifted leadership skills and extraordinary marketing prowess, he staged the most memorable turnaround in American business history. After he retired from Chrysler, Iacocca—the proud descendant of Italian immigrants—went on to lead the restoration of Ellis Island, the landing point for so many newcomers to these shores over so many years.

Iacocca had been fired before. By the U.S. Army. He had a history of rheumatic fever and that made him categorically ineligible for military service during World War II. "Being burdened with a medical deferment during the war seemed like a disgrace, and I began to think of myself as a second-class citizen," he contends. The embarrassment was driven home by a doctor giving him a life insurance physical shortly afterward. The physician eyed Iacocca and asked pointedly, "You're a healthy young fellow. Why aren't you overseas?"

After Lehigh University, Iacocca started a remarkable career at Ford, marked by a steady stream of successes and innovations. These included both the Mark III and the Mustang. In 1968, he became the front-runner to be named president of Ford. Two years later, he was anointed. With that elevation, he also climbed a scaffold that seated him right next to raw power in the Dearborn headquarters known as the Glass House. Officed next to Henry, he felt the tremors daily. In Iacocca's words, Henry Ford "held the power of life and death over all of us. He could suddenly say 'off with his head'—and he often did." Iacocca recalls Henry Ford telling him to fire an executive for wearing trousers that were too snug. Iacocca was astonished at his boss's contention that the exec must be gay. Ford prevailed, and the head rolled. This insecurity and intimidation was part of a general management outlook. "If a guy works for you," Ford counseled his president protégé, "don't let him get too comfortable. . . . Always do the opposite of what he expects. Keep your people anxious and off balance." Iacocca concludes, "Henry got a little paranoid about some things."

Henry Ford got especially paranoid when Iacocca's successes started to stretch out from the States and turn global. A watershed was reached when Iacocca's Ford Fiesta model was a success in Europe. Henry considered himself to be a European at heart and didn't appreciate the Ford spotlight there being turned on Iacocca. Worse yet, in 1973–74, Ford Motor Company started making a ton of money. I'd put it this way: You might live next door to Henry Ford on the old homestead, but heaven help you if your lawn starts to look greener than his does.

Letting the air out of Iacocca's tires didn't happen overnight. "In 1975," Iacocca recalls, "Henry Ford started his month-by-month premeditated plan to destroy me." While Iacocca was on a trip abroad to meet with the royals in Saudi Arabia and talk about the price of oil, Henry Ford—convinced a massive depression was in the making—demanded that $2 billion be scrapped from the company's budget, especially in product development. The net effect: Ford was years late in coming to market with the smaller, fuel-efficient, front-wheel drive cars that higher oil prices necessitated.

Henry Ford's personal peculiarities started to intervene as well. Iacocca's secretary came to him and said: "I've just learned that every time you make a call on the company credit card, a record of it goes to Mr. Ford's office." According to Iacocca, Henry Ford gave "a speech in which he announced: 'I am the captain of this ship.' Our management, he said, was going about things all wrong." Dealers started to attack Hank the Deuce. In the minutes of one of their meetings, the record read: "Henry Ford II is not at this time offering the type of quality leadership that his dealers expect from him."

Beginning with investigating a Ford vendor who just happened to be Italian . . . and who, Iacocca maintains, Henry Ford suspected of having Mafia links . . . a series of inquiries were launched. Iacocca contends he was the real target of these probes. "Under the guise of an audit of the travel and expense accounts of top executives," Iacocca says, "Henry conducted nothing less than a full-scale investigation of both my business and my personal life." The result: a goose egg. "After spending $2 million and coming up with nothing, a normal person might have apologized," Iacocca recollects bitterly. Of course, that, didn't happen. Looking backward, Iacocca thinks he made a mistake: "That was the atmosphere in the Glass House in 1975. And that was when I should have quit."

The tension continued. Hal Sperlich, a highly regarded product designer, had a vision of the future that differed from Henry Ford's. One day after a product committee meeting, Ford dressed down Iacocca one-on-one and told him: "I hate that goddamn Sperlich, and I don't want him sitting beside you. He's always pissing in your ear. I don't want the two of you ganging up on me like that." Despite Iacocca's feeling that Sperlich was the best Ford had, Henry Ford compelled Iacocca to fire him. Sperlich moved to Chrysler and, within two years, Iacocca himself joined up with him at their new employer.

Incident after incident occurred. "It was salami-slicing time—one slice at a time," remembers Iacocca, "Each day I found another part of my body missing. I put out the word that I wasn't going to take it." When the decision was finally made,

Iacocca actually learned about it first from *Automotive News* publisher Keith Crain. Iacocca suspects that Henry had arranged for word to be leaked to the press first. When the inevitable meeting took place, Henry didn't use the word "fired," Iacocca recalls. Instead, he said, " 'It's been a nice association . . . but I think you should leave. It's best for the company.' " Although he was actually fired in July, he would be kept on to his birthday in October so that he wouldn't lose some valuable benefits. But, at their encounter, Iacocca looked at the bigger picture of the money Ford had been making and the contribution he had made to the bottom line. Iacocca showed no restraint and said to his boss: ". . . [M]ark my words, Henry. You may never see a billion eight again. And do you know why? Because you don't know how the f—— we made it in the first place!"

Iacocca left in loneliness, but also with a clear understanding of why his departure was destined to be so lonely. ". . . [M]ost of my company friends deserted me. It was the greatest shock of my life. . . . To some extent, I can understand their attitude. It wasn't their fault that the corporation was a dictatorship."

Lee Iacocca's firing at Ford has monumental lessons:

- Zebras don't change their stripes. Iacocca had ample opportunity to observe Henry Ford at close range.

- The more you do to make a tyrannical boss look good, the bigger the threat you become, and the greater the boss's need to undercut your importance.

- Life at the top is tough. You get used to sharp elbows. The hardest thing to sort out is this: Are these just the rough edges you have to live with, the price of playing at the top? Or, is this part of a concerted campaign to either grind you down or to dump you? By his own admission, Iacocca saw the design of the plot too late and should have acted on it sooner.

After the career fiasco at Ford came the test of fire at Chrysler. The Japanese nameplates were chowing down on Detroit's lunch bucket as though it was stuffed with sushi. Ford was hurting. Chrysler was reeling. Drowning in battleship-sized, gas-guzzling cars, Chrysler could never survive the new era of high oil prices. Teamwork? Chrysler had never heard the likes of it. Iacocca overhauled how Chrysler designed cars. The Le Baron, Chrysler announced, was the first computer-designed car. While attacking the onslaught of Japanese industrial competition, Iacocca remained a wily competitor. As early as 1983, Chrysler installed Japanese-style robotics in one of its plants. Iacocca sped the development of fuel-efficient autos from blueprint to assembly line. The front-wheel drive K-car and the minivan were early innovations. The Voyager MPV became the first "people-carrier."

Faced with plummeting passenger car market share, Chrysler took a sideways whack at the market and emphasized the van. Vans and small trucks had always been considered commercial vehicles. Iacocca positioned them as consumer autos. Customers put sales through the roof. That thinking bridged over to the Jeep, which had started life as a military reconnaissance vehicle with an eighty-inch wheelbase. In 1987, the Iacocca-led Chrysler acquired Jeep and added another power hitter to its lineup.

To turn itself around, Chrysler needed concessions from its workers. Underlining the need for everyone to sacrifice, Iacocca cut his own pay to $1 a year. He made an unprecedented appeal to the federal government to help Chrysler avert bankruptcy. In 1980, the U.S. Congress guaranteed $1.5 billion in Chrysler loans, provided that Chrysler raised $2 billion more on its own. In 1981, Chrysler reported a small profit. Solvent again,

Chrysler settled accounts with the government in 1983. "We at Chrysler borrow money the old-fashioned way," he declared. "We pay it back." In 1984, Chrysler blew out the scoreboard lights with record profits of $2.4 billion.

Iacocca's wizardry extended to showmanship. He was one of the earliest CEOs to become a TV spokesman. And no CEO anywhere since has ever filled his tire tracks. Over a span of fourteen years, he did sixty-one Chrysler commercials. Sylvester Stallone may be the Italian Stallion, but Lee Iacocca has horsepower plus under the hood. And, he's willing to change horses. In 2002, ten years after his retirement from Chrysler, Iacocca appeared in San Francisco plugging the virtues of nonpolluting vehicles. Five years earlier, he had launched an electric vehicle firm called EV Global Motors in Los Angeles.

I don't know if Lee Iacocca would admit that getting fired at Ford was the best thing that ever happened to him. In fact, he has said about his move to Chrysler: "I went from the frying pan into the fire. . . . If I'd had the slightest idea of what lay ahead for me when I joined up with Chrysler, I wouldn't have gone over there for all the money in the world." Somehow I doubt that's really true. Iacocca's ouster and move to Chrysler transformed him from a great manager into a management legend. He has inspired and will continue to inspire millions and millions of young managers that the impossible is indeed doable if you shoulder up to challenges in a clear-headed, straight-talking, common sense, creative way. For immigrants, there is the Statue of Liberty to inspire them. For managers tasked with enormous challenges, there is the image of a determined and defiant Lee Iacocca.

Life lessons learned from Iacocca:

- Working with a despot, no matter how good you may be at it, can have only two possible endings. Either you become a despot, too, or the despot is going to turn on you.

- You might live next door to the person with the power, but heaven help you if your lawn starts to look greener than his does.

- Even if you're feeling desperate, be careful about whom you hook up with. The old phrase, "Lie down with dogs, wake up with fleas," still holds true in business.

- Look for bosses who are buoyed by your success. If they seem threatened by it, it's time to grab a life preserver and swim for shore.

- If you just can't move forward, go sideways. Sometimes just creating movement is enough to shake an enterprise—or a career—out of its doldrums. Only when Iacocca side-stepped the passenger-car market and emphasized the minivan did he send sales through the roof.

- Don't ever let your love of success justify staying in the wrong place too long.

MACKAY'S MORAL:

He who has the gold not only makes the rules,
he can break the rules.

JAMIE DIMON

Chairman and CEO, Bank One

"It's not my net worth. It's my self-worth."

There are some compelling similarities between Jamie Dimon and Lee Iacocca. Both have been powerhouses in their respective industries—Jamie Dimon in finance and Lee Iacocca in the automotive world. Both have turned around huge companies—Bank One for Dimon and Chrysler for Iacocca. We have already seen what Iacocca did for Chrysler. In March 2000, Jamie Dimon joined Bank One. For fiscal 2000, Bank One lost $511 million. It was an express train hurtling from being Bank One to Bank Nothing.

In 2003, under Dimon's incredible leadership, Bank One earned a record $3.5 billion. Today, Bank One is the nation's sixth-largest bank with $325 billion in assets. It's the third largest in credit cards issued, and it has branches in fourteen states. Bank One's stock price is up 85 percent since Jamie Dimon became the company's CEO. Not only that. In January of 2004, Bank One announced plans to merge with J.P. Morgan Chase & Co., with Morgan agreeing to pay more than $55 billion for Bank One. Or was it for something more? What were they really buying? As one respected market expert put it: "This deal's about Jamie. That was the price of J.P. Morgan getting Jamie Dimon to be the next CEO." In an interview with *Fortune* magazine, Arthur Levitt—the former chairman of the SEC—praised the scrupulous and demanding Dimon this way: "Jamie Dimon is the un-Enron." Just as Iacocca was the management icon of *his* era, Jamie Dimon, now forty-eight, is the signature manager of ours. Both are dynamic, charismatic, and gifted.

And you know what? Both were unceremoniously fired by strong-willed bosses.

Jamie Dimon's relationship with Sandy Weill was every bit as complex and intriguing as Lee Iacocca's with Henry Ford II. Dimon's professional contact with Weill actually began much earlier in life, when Dimon was still an undergraduate student at Tufts. He had written a college economics paper about the takeover of the brokerage firm Shearson by another Wall Street house—CBWL-Hayden Stone. Jamie's father—and his Greek immigrant grandfather before him—worked as a broker with Shearson. In fact, the family had developed a powerful niche as brokers serving the Greek American community. Weill was the architect of the Shearson takeover. The Weills and Jamie's parents socialized. Jamie's mother sent Weill her son's paper. He liked it enough to give Jamie a summer job at Shearson. Several years later, after Jamie graduated from the Harvard Business School, he sped on line as Sandy Weill's assistant.

Then followed one of the great adventure stories in the history of high finance as Weill and Dimon whisked from transaction to transaction.

Back when Weill recruited Jamie for a full-time job, Sandy Weill had already succeeded in selling Shearson to American Express. When it was clear Weill would not be the ultimate successor to American Express's CEO, Weill bolted the company and Jamie went with him. The two spent more than a year looking for a new launching pad before settling on a Baltimore outfit known as Commercial Credit. They revitalized this sagging consumer loan business. With a strengthened base in 1988, they bought a conglomerate named Primerica, including the brokerage firm of Smith Barney. (You remember those classic Smith Barney TV ads by the *Paper Chase* movie star John Houseman—"We make money the old-fashioned way. We eeeaaaaarrrnnn it.")

At the age of thirty-five, Jamie became president and COO of Primerica. Travelers Corporation was Primerica's next target, and the new company became Travelers Group in 1993. Four years later, Travelers bought Salomon Brothers and merged it with Smith Barney to create the Salomon Smith Barney subsidiary. But the biggest fish of all came after Travelers stock had risen 78 percent in the single year of 1997. Travelers acquired Citicorp in 1998 and created Citigroup, a well-matched financial powerhouse.

Through all their deals, Jamie Dimon and Sandy Weill continually created a larger, more profitable company. Yet these two were decidedly different personalities. For example, Weill was a seasoned gourmet eater. I'm talking big league and deep dish. Weill referred to the resplendent Four Seasons restaurant in Manhattan as his company cafeteria. Then there was highbrow music. A leading fund-raiser for the restoration of Carnegie Hall, Weill used socializing around this fund-raising as a business trump card. As Weill's virtuoso violinist friend Isaac Stern put it: Carnegie Hall was the "Fifty-seventh Street version of a golf course." Dimon, a determined jogger, would have preferred life to be a container of low-fat yogurt rather than a bowl of cherries jubilee.

Over sixteen years of working together, Weill and Dimon had their share of spirited discussions, loud arguments, and even shouting matches. For many years, Dimon was no longer Weill's assistant, but an executive in his own right. In addition to his executive titles, he served on the Travelers board for seven years. He was to be president of the combined Citicorp and

Travelers organization but was not named to the corporation's board of directors.

Over the previous few years, there had been tension between Dimon and Weill. As the Citicorp deal came together, the tension continued to grow. Weill "yelled and screamed a lot, but I didn't think anything about it, Harvey," Jamie recalls. "This seemed like nothing out of the ordinary. In hindsight, it's clear our relationship was in trouble," said Dimon. "The problem was we were working so fast, and doing so many deals so quickly, that we ignored the fact that our relationship was deteriorating. By the time I realized how bad it had gotten, it was too late."

On November 1, 1998, Jamie was summoned to a management retreat center in Armonk, New York. He expected that Weill and co-CEO John Reed wanted to ask him to get more involved in steering the company. Instead, Weill and Reed told Jamie that they wanted him to resign. Jamie's iron nerve came to the fore. He turned to his bosses and said, "You've obviously thought this through, and there's nothing I can do about this."

While he was surprised and wouldn't wish this situation on anyone, he also knew there was nothing he could do. It was time to move on. When he realized this one was for real, Jamie called his wife and "told her that I'm going to tell you something and I don't want you to tell me I'm kidding. I thought she'd say, 'Oh, stop that.' I said, 'I've been asked to resign, which I'm going to do.' I got home an hour later and sat down with my three girls, who were about twelve, ten, and eight. I thought it was important how I dealt with them. I said I'm resigning but basically being fired from my job. My youngest asked, 'Do we have to live on the streets?' 'No. We're going to be fine.' Then the middle one asked, 'What about college?' 'I can still handle college.' 'They are taking this right in stride,' he thought. How did he know everything was golden? When his twelve-year-old said: 'Good, Dad, then can I have your cell phone?' "

In a TV interview, broadcaster Jeff Greenfield asked Jamie about what he did during the time off. "I did eight or nine of the ten things I promised myself to do," Jamie recalls. "I went to the store and bought and read about a dozen books—books about Teddy Roosevelt and Abe Lincoln. Just read some of those experiences and you say to yourself, 'My God, are you going to feel sorry for yourself?' George Washington lived in a tent for seven years during the Revolutionary War!"

Jamie left Citicorp with a reported $30 million severance package. For most people on the planet that would mean: 'Roll out the caviar, Jeeves, nonstop, if you please.' Not for Jamie. Jamie used every free moment with the passionate time economy of a workaholic who no doubt knew he would soon be back in the fray. "I refused to think about my career for six months," he said. "I went to see friends, Harvey. I drove across the country. I took our family to Europe. I asked myself a lot of questions. Do I want to write, teach, be an investment banker? I explored a lot of things. Bottom line, I decided that I would love to build a company. I like working hard. I love a challenge and motivating people."

It would be March of 2000 when Dimon was named to head Bank One, sixteen months after leaving Citigroup.

In between—in December 1999—an event of great import happened. So important that the article headline in the *Financial Times* read: "Season of Good Weill as Feud with Dimon Ends." Jamie Dimon had dialed up Sandy Weill and proposed lunch at the "company cafeteria"—the Four Seasons. Not only that, Jamie apologized for being impetuous. Since then he has praised Sandy Weill and acknowledged that he learned a lot from him. Jamie is a great believer in learning by walking in another person's moccasins. It would be hard to find a bigger pair of moccasins than Jamie's own.

"Jamie, what else did you do after you were fired?" I asked him.

"I took up boxing, Harvey. I had wanted to do it for decades. Literally, I called up the trainer the weekend I was fired. For the year and a half I wasn't working it was great. Forget jogging and tennis, this was really tough."

"What did this suggest to you?"

"Pick up something different. It changes your perspective. Boxing totally focused my mind. It is truly a sweet science. Learning boxing is physically, emotionally, and intellectually exhausting. It's a tough sport. It teaches a real sense of perseverance."

"You and Sandy Weill reconciled. You were the initiator, Jamie. How and why did you do this?"

"It was close to the one-year anniversary, and I had mellowed by then. Sandy wasn't going to call me. I knew it was time. I was ready to say thank you for what he did for me. I also knew he and I should talk about what happened. I wanted to get this event behind me so I could move on. Part of me said I had spent sixteen years with him. Twelve or thirteen were pretty good. You can't just look at one side and not the other. I made my own mistakes. I acknowledged I was partly to blame. Whether I was 40 percent or 60 percent to blame really didn't matter. I felt very good about my meeting with him."

"So, Jamie, this was a memorable reconciliation with a mentor?"

"Sandy was never really the mentor type, Harvey. He didn't sit down and help you think. He was more a sink-or-swim type. Look at the people who surrounded his career. Some survived, and some didn't. Other managers might sit down and help their subordinates and point out mistakes.

"I was a protégé, but I don't think he was ever a mentor. I learned by watching and being around Sandy. Nonetheless, he left me hanging in the wind several times. I just happened to be the best shortstop, second-baseman, or pitcher at the time."

"It seems to me, Jamie, that one of your great strengths is an invincible commitment to clarity of thought."

"Hold yourself above the fray. At Citigroup, I reacted just

because he punched. You owe yourself better. It's not my net worth. It's my self-worth. You live and learn and keep going. You can't be owned by the past. Try to keep life in perspective, and always remind yourself what you are there to do."

"Jamie, do you think that this conflict with Sandy could have been averted?"

"Perhaps I should have said quietly to Sandy that we need to meet every Sunday for a couple of hours to talk about the week and what we are both trying to accomplish. It might not have worked, but perhaps it could have."

Lessons learned from being fired? Jamie has some memorable ones:

- Perseverance is central. Life is full of ups and downs, and you must learn from these experiences.

- No career has a straight trajectory. How we respond during the tough times says more about us than how we handle the good times.

- Educate yourself every day.

- Surround yourself with people you trust, admire, and respect.

- Always do the right thing, even when it's not the easy thing.

- Problems don't age well—especially those involving people. If you are having a problem with a co-worker or a boss, take the time to address it.

MACKAY'S MORAL:

Advising others? As Jamie puts it,
"Eat your own home cooking."

Don't Demolish: The First Lesson to Learn

Heaven help you if you don't learn this lesson early. I call it the *demolition lesson.* If you learn the demolition lesson late in your career, you'll turn into a Ralph. A Ralph is somebody who lands his carcass in the land of no return.

Ralph was a terrific employee. He brought in a lot of business for his company, a firm that I knew well over many years. Unfortunately, Ralph had a tremendous work ethic. It was *too* good. So good that he felt justified in setting standards for his boss. Ralph thought the guy he worked for was inept, took too much time off, had no leadership ability, played favorites, promoted a bevy of unqualified cronies, and overlooked countless screwups and goof-offs. All of this, Ralph calculated, was costing the company big bucks.

Finally, Ralph couldn't take it any longer. The biggest stakeholder in the business made it a point to visit each division a couple of times a month. When the principal owner made his rounds of Ralph's division one September morning, Ralph made his move. He requested a meeting with the owner away from the office. Ralph then delivered chapter and verse. Righteous Ralph. "I've got a stake here," he said. "My profit-sharing plan is the biggest investment I have. Of course, your stake is a lot bigger than mine. But if my direct boss keeps running this division, he'll bankrupt the company. He'll bankrupt my future. And he won't do your balance sheet much good either. No doubt about it."

Business is business, and Ralph was dead sure his meticulously documented report would open some eyes. Was he ever right! In mere days, it was obvious the owner had passed on Ralph's complaints to Ralph's boss. Ralph may have been dead right; he was also dead meat. Up till then, Ralph may have been enraged. He was now about to be disemboweled. He had acquired an archenemy in a high place with a single-minded intent: mounting Ralph's head over the fireplace mantel.

Ralph took it in the neck. What hadn't Ralph known? Long before he was hired, the owner and the division boss had gone through some tough times together. Their relationship was both professional and social. Every Wednesday afternoon, Ralph's boss was goofing off on the golf course, wasn't he? Oh, yeah? Ralph never realized the boss's golfing partner was the owner. The time on the golf course was actually their weekly briefing.

Banished, Ralph started his own business. Many small firms get their biggest hunk of business from a former employer—assuming the parting is amicable. This parting was acrimonious. Ralph never landed the profitable jobs. With nearly suicidal glee, Ralph would take grunt assignments from his former employer. In his own mind, they were victories. In reality, they were the troublesome roadkill nobody wanted.

It's a lot of fun telling the boss where to get off. Short term. It's fun only if you're sure that your boss won't land on your backside first. And if you risk it anyway, you better have a plan to leave the company if forced. Ralph took neither precaution. By the way, Ralph's boss didn't bankrupt the company. But he darn near bankrupted Ralph.

Mackay's Moral:

Unless you work in demolition, don't burn bridges.

ROBERT REDFORD

Academy Award–Winning Director, Actor, and
Founder of the Sundance Institute

*"A certain amount of failure can be a
wonderful education."*

Robert Redford was once a roustabout at a Standard Oil refinery. His father was an accountant with Standard and helped get him the job. Bob was less than a zealous oilman. He was caught sleeping in an oil tank instead of cleaning it. After this incident, the oil company put Bob on probation. They moved him into the bottle-washing department in the chemical building. "To make these jobs more interesting, I always played games," Bob says. "When I had to recondition barrels, I learned how to drive a forklift, but I would always stack an extra load on the lift. I played games to amuse myself. I would devise patterns for my driving the lift. I'd do loops and figure eights. I met my doom because I was so bored.

"There was a gigantic load of twelve cases of empty bottles on that forklift truck. I was hauling the bottles onto a freight elevator. I wanted to see how close I could push the load to the edge of the platform. Zooming into the elevator, I nudged the cases right to the edge, but I stopped too quickly and the momentum tipped the entire load all over the dock floor. Every single bottle crashed and broke," he recalled. "All the windows opened in the administration building. Everyone in the offices—including my dad—looked down and saw all the broken bottles. I knew it was the end of my career in that business."

The list gets longer if you turn the clock back earlier. "Another guy in the neighborhood and I didn't have any money. We were sixteen years old. 'Go out and collect Cadillac hubcaps,' a guy told us, 'and I'll give you $15 apiece.' We didn't know he was a fence.

"By the time I went to college, I realized I was probably not going to be in school too long. My grades were not as good as they should have been and that had to do with my mind being elsewhere. I blew my baseball scholarship at the University of Colorado because I spent too much time at the local beer parlors," Bob admits. "For a time, I was a carpenter's apprentice, but I was finally let go. My foreman was a demanding guy. I thought that he was creating jobs for me that I believed were a waste of time. When I challenged the efficiency of what he wanted done, he said that he didn't need my lip. I was through."

After the refinery jobs, Bob worked down in the garment district of New York City supporting himself while in acting school. "I had to put shipping department papers into a giant machine to sort them out," Bob recalls. "I jammed the machine and destroyed all the papers. Then I was a theater janitor at the American Academy of Dramatic Arts from 10:30 to 1:00 in the morning. I just swept up. I didn't get fired from that because there was nobody around to see me do anything wrong."

"Did you deserve what you got?" I ask Bob.

"I got fired from jobs I *should* have been fired from. I took these jobs to earn money. The lesson I learned was that I wasn't meant to do any of those things. I was never meant to be in the labor market."

Lack of serious commitment was at the heart of Bob's meandering career. "In the early days, I could only take what was available. I would become distracted and my concentration would wane," Bob says. "I couldn't apply anything I felt strongly about to the jobs I had. It was only a means to keep me going until I could figure out what my path was. That occurred when I went to Europe and studied art. During that year and a half I realized that I had to do something dealing with art. Art led to acting and everything else. I started out in the theater in New York, grinding away like everyone else did, competing with thirty other people for auditions. Broadway led to appearances on the tail end of live dramas on television. In 1963, I alternated between TV in New York and Los Angeles. The success of the movie *Barefoot in the Park* led me to my ultimate path."

While Burt Reynolds, Clint Eastwood, and Harrison Ford were all fired from Hollywood film jobs early in their Hollywood careers, Bob was never sacked as an actor. Since his film career started, Robert Redford has acted in over forty movies, directed six, and produced twenty-three. Among his classics are *The Way We Were*, *The Sting*, and *Butch Cassidy and the Sundance Kid*. He won his first Oscar as a director with *Ordinary People* in 1980.

With all these great achievements, none will probably rival what Bob has done to advance opportunities for young filmmakers through the Sundance Institute in Utah. He founded the institute in 1981. Filmmakers go to the June Lab at Sundance to learn from the best, most experienced, and, not coincidentally, most famous professionals in the film industry. It is the only enclave of its kind in the world and, as a result, one of the most difficult to get accepted into. It's an opportunity for aspiring young directors, writers, cinematographers, and editors to learn and experiment with the best tools of the trade. Most of all, there is access to such talents as Sally Field, Sydney Pollack, Jake Eberts, Sigourney Weaver, Ed Harris, and Bob Redford.

For a young filmmaker, developing a script at Sundance also raises the profile of the project and adds huge credibility. It increases the chances that an independent project will get made into a movie. Numerous June Lab projects have gone on to become feature films—films such as *Reservoir Dogs, Requiem for a Dream, Boys Don't Cry,* and *The Laramie Project.* Bob launched the Sundance Film Festival in 1985. Today, its only rival in debuting new films is the Cannes Film Festival. In 1996, he began the Sundance Channel, a cable network devoted exclusively to independent film.

In my twelve years on the Sundance Board, I couldn't believe I got to rub elbows with the likes of Denzel Washington, Jodie Foster, Sally Field, and Glenn Close. I also had the chance to observe Bob firsthand and learned that what you see is what you get. He skis, rides, and plays tennis out of sheer enjoyment, not just to stay in shape. But, it's astonishing that a guy who is regarded by so many women as the heartthrob of his era has so little vanity. While many of his Hollywood contemporaries have succumbed to the plastic surgeon's scalpel, Bob has refused. "I am what I am," he says. "People do it to just hold on to youth. The trade-off is that something of the soul in your face goes, too. You end up looking body-snatched."

Bob thinks about his life dream very seriously. His grandfather was an accomplished violinist who turned down a chance to study music in Vienna and ended up working at a boat company in Connecticut. "He figured he blew it," Bob once said, "and he taught my father *not* to dream, that to dream is dangerous. It leads to disappointment."

No one in cinema has done more to help young people. Bob has some very clear advice for anyone considering a career in this intensely competitive and at times treacherous business. "You have to want it more than anything else in the world," he says passionately. "Here's an analogy: Let's say you are right-handed. A career in film is not something you can do with your left hand."

Although he conceived something as mammoth an enterprise as Sundance, Bob does not see himself as a businessperson. "I was not meant to be a business executive," he explains. "My day job in the arts is to make films. If you step into that other area of being a businessperson, you have to be very careful that those decisions are the ones that would support your own goals."

On firing people, Bob has equally clear views. He says that problems often arise from poor hirings in the first place. "Don't let other people make firing decisions for you," he says. "Do proper due diligence on the people you bring in. Be sure that they understand what your vision is rather than converting your vision to their own agenda."

And if a young person encounters failure early in their career, take this from the voice of experience: "It's all about focus," Bob reflects. "A failure isn't the end. A certain amount of failure can be a wonderful education. Don't take it too hard."

- Find out what your passions are in life, then pursue them tenaciously. Bob Redford went through a long list of career missteps before he landed on the right track. The trick is to do that learning early in life, and then to be willing to pay your dues learning your real craft.

- Embrace a dream. We all have at least one. For Bob Redford, those dreams have included acting, directing, and creating the Sundance Institute. Bob's grandfather and father had their own "scripts" that dreams were bad. Have you been living out someone else's script that has squelched your dreams for the future?

- Link your thinking. Sundance led to a film festival. It also was the cornerstone of a movie network. In 1970, Bob built a gourmet restaurant in Sundance called the Tree Room. Once you find your primary channel in life, it can sprout opportunities in a hundred different directions.

- Give back. Robert Redford could have rested on his laurels. Instead of Sundance Institute, he could have taken a stroll down Sunset Boulevard. Not Bob. He became one of the great energizing forces to inspire and enable the filmmakers of tomorrow.

MACKAY'S MORAL:

The people who give back the best are the ones who push things forward.

RISING FROM THE ASHES

Ancient clans of long ago who wanted to eliminate someone without killing them would burn their houses down—hence the term "to get fired."

DAVID MACKAY
A PERSONAL EXPERIENCE FROM MY SON
Feature Film Director and Producer

Editor's Note: Everyone is entitled to have a chapter contributed. There is an old European adage: The acorn does not fall far from the trunk of the oak. David Mackay has his father's characteristic writing verve, and it's a pleasure to showcase his talent in this chapter. One recalls a 1943 concert when a young Leonard Bernstein stood in for Bruno Walter at the podium of the New York Philharmonic. The rest is—as they say—musical history in the key of A major!

It was the summer of '85. My last summer as a student, a kid, a freewheeling partier. The following fall I would become a Stanford senior, and the summer following that I'd be in the workforce, full-time, somewhere—probably in New York starting out as an analyst, or an overeducated gofer. So this was my last summer to let loose, my last hurrah.

That summer I was going to live in San Francisco. What better way to have a good, carefree time in the city than to work as a waiter, five to six shifts a week. I'd have plenty of free time and, as I calculated it, enough earnings to really enjoy all those leisure hours.

I was always pretty driven, so my sights were set high. Although the job description "waiter" is mundane, the restaurant I was pursuing was not. I interviewed at a brand-new establishment called Stars. So new, in fact, it had not opened yet, but would in three weeks. The location of Stars was impeccable, across from the Opera House on Van Ness Avenue. It was poised to attract San Francisco's elite. And the head chef, Jeremiah Towers, had established a track record that included a top-ten eatery in Berkeley called Chez Panisse. Wolfgang Puck was the leading chef in the entire gourmet restaurant industry at the time. Little known to me, Jeremiah Towers was the Wolfgang Puck of the Bay Area. At my tender age of twenty-one, I couldn't appreciate Towers' stature in culinary society, but believe me, every VIP in town did. All I knew was that Stars was poised to be one of the top restaurants in San Francisco. And for me, that meant $200 to $300 per night—cash money.

The new staff would be critical to the restaurant's success. Knowing that, there was really no reason why Stars should have hired me in the first place. I was too young and I'd only had one job waiting tables before. That three-month experience was in Minneapolis at Winfield Potters—a step up, make that *a half* step up, from TGI Friday's. I suspect the Stars managers looked at my résumé and all they could see was visions of potato skins and nachos. I was hardly the kind of black-tie waitperson they were seeking out, and moreover, I was a kid!

But what I lacked in experience, I made up for in enthusiasm and education. I played the Stanford card. I told them I had just graduated from Stanford and that I wanted to pursue a career as a restaurateur. What better way than to learn from the best and work my way up? I was in it for the long haul. So I said. Had they known the truth—that I was going back to school in only three months and that they'd be training me for three weeks to work for twelve—they'd have laughed me out of the interview. The unlikely prevailed. My infectious attitude and a glowing letter of recommendation from David Webb, the owner of Winfield Potters, got me the job.

I started training a few days later surrounded by proud, sophisticated men twice my age with histories at some of the best restaurants in the country: 21, Auberge du Soleil, Le Dome. The service procedure at Stars would be consistent with those blue-chip, white-tablecloth establishments—a team of two for each table, a front waiter and a back waiter, each with very specific responsibilities.

The front waiter would welcome the guests, take drink orders, rattle off the numerous specials from memory with precision and detail, make recommendations and handle all communication with the table. The back waiter would interface with the kitchen and the cooks, schedule the orders, deliver all the food, refold napkins when a patron stepped away from the table, and act as a full-time busboy, rarely talking to the customers. The front waiter was the showman; the back waiter was the worker bee. The two split tips evenly and had to communicate well to make everything look seamless. This was a far cry from Minnesota where "Hi, my name is David and I'll be your waiter" was my mantra. Stars was the kind of place where imposing patrons would answer, "Do you mind if I just call you 'Waiter'?"

There was absolutely no reason why the owners should have positioned me as a *front* waiter, and yet they did. I lacked credibility, I was too young, too green, too everything. And the rest of the waitstaff agreed. They never said it, but I later suspected that was the case. What could they have seen in me?

After three weeks of intensive training, we opened with two days of free meals to the SF glitterati. The pressure was on for us to provide top-notch service when we really should not have opened yet. There was confusion and chaos behind the scenes. The menu was still in flux, furniture was still arriving, and the waitstaff—all very experienced except for me—was still working out many kinks in the high-tech ordering system.

On the second night of the shakedown, Herb Caen landed at one of my tables. Herb, who has since passed away, was the most prominent columnist at the *San Francisco Chronicle*. Herb once wrote, "Cockroaches and socialites are the only things that can stay up all night and eat anything." His review could make or break a new restaurant. He told me how he once discovered a quiet, charming little café, mentioned it in his column, and ended up standing in a long line the next time he was there. We got along great, and I put everything I had into serving him. His notice in the paper the next morning was at once a blessing and a curse:

"The food wasn't very smart, but my Stanford waiter was."

Hey, I did my part!

Stars' management reeled from Herb Caen's comments. They consoled themselves, saying how any restaurant was going to have growing pains. All the while I continued to rake in 20 percent tips. One night I served the owners of Charles Krug Winery, the makers of the finest champagne in the world by some expert accounts. In that one seating, the Charles Krug people purchased over $1,000 of their own champagne and tipped me more than a month's rent. I was on easy street.

That same night the headwaiter, a rigid, detail-oriented (make that anal) little man came over to me and pointed out a classic service error I'd been making. On occasion, he said, I was failing to clear unused glassware. If someone wasn't drinking wine, he said curtly, their glass should be removed from the table. Likewise, if they were not drinking water: flat bottled water, sparkling water, or even, God forbid, tap water, their glass should not remain on the table. This is easier said than done considering that each place setting had three glasses even before anyone sat down—add cocktails to that and a table of six would start out with twenty-four crystal glasses jammed in the center. Many people ordered both red and white wine, some reds requiring special oversized "balloon" glasses, and before you knew it there were enough filled and half-filled glasses on any given table that it looked like a ready-made glass harmonica. You could lick your fingers and play the theme song from *Chariots of Fire*.

So, needless to say, finding the one or two unused glasses on a table was like finding a needle in a haystack, and besides, from my perspective, that was the back waiter's responsibility.

After being open to the public for a week or so, my parents were going to be in town, and I'd planned to go out with them to dinner one night. We discussed several of our favorite places: L'Etoile, Trader Vic's, and the Empress of China at Ghirardelli Square. Then my mom had the great idea! "What about Stars? What better way for you to learn about the restaurant than to experience it from the other side, as a customer?" she said. I'd have a chance to sample some of the food I hadn't tasted and that would improve my knowledge of the menu. As a customer, I would be able to assess the service and, in turn, become a better waiter myself. Great idea, Mom!

I cleared it with the managers, and on a busy Friday night my parents and Pat Shannon, a good friend of mine from Stanford, and I showed up at Stars. We were greeted by the short, gruff headwaiter and Miles, the host, who got a crisp, green handshake from everyone that night but me. We got the best table in the house and sat down to a flurry of confusion right off the bat. Apparently, it wasn't clear who exactly was waiting on our table, and I had to make a trip to the board to find out what team was assigned table number seventeen. Once I let Jim and Kevin know that we were in *their* section, things were smoother.

My mom got her master's in cooking . . . and a doctorate in ordering; she usually conjures up between five and ten questions regarding the menu selections. (That's *not* including the ten-minute conversation with the sommelier.) To her credit, let me add that her questions are always well founded and exactly framed. Needless to say, Jim was put through the ringer. "Is there beef stock in the soup?" "Is the salmon farm-raised?" "Is the beluga from Kazakhstan or Uzbekistan?" By the time our order was in, the Q & A with our waiter had lasted twenty minutes. But the good news is, among just the four of us and with my mother at the helm, we'd ordered almost everything on the menu. Jim, who, believe it or not, actually had other tables to wait on, was scrambling to keep up. Meanwhile my mom's taste buds, along with her uncompromising opinion, had us all salivating.

The first course arrived without delay. My mom pointed out that the dressing on the salad was particularly oily—much less vinegar than normal vinaigrette. Then when the entrées came the food was not very hot, tepid at best. This bothered even me. I actually tend to eat my food quickly in fear that it will get cold and taste, well . . . cold, which I hate. I practically had to wolf mine down before my throat got frostbite. The entrées that night were edible if not spectacular. However, it was my dad's veal stew that we all universally panned at the table.

The next day at work I went right up to Jeremiah Towers and briefly reintroduced myself since he didn't know the wait-staff personally and probably didn't know my name. I explained the little experiment I'd done.

First off, I asked him about the "oily salad dressing." He explained that he thought that a heavy vinegar dressing was too hard on the pallet, too early in the meal, so he created a dressing that was "soft on the pallet." "Great, great!" I said, "This will be very helpful to know as a front waiter."

As he turned to leave, I continued, "One more thing, Jeremiah, the food wasn't very . . . hot. Are you concerned that people might burn their tongues?" "What?" he exclaimed. "The food should be piping hot, and it's *your* job as a server to get it out there quickly!" "Yes, sir, you got it. I will. I will get it out piping hot, sir!" So now I'm thinking, I'm two for two in valuable, practical observations.

Jeremiah again turned to leave, but I stopped him in his tracks. "Oh, ummm, one more thing, Jeremiah, I wanted to talk to you about the veal stew—I found it somewhat bland." Mr. Towers looked me in the eye for a beat, then spun on his heals and marched into the kitchen. Well, two out of three, not bad, from my perspective. Did I forget to mention that Herb Caen had already told all of San Francisco that I was smarter than Jeremiah Towers' food anyway?

My shift that night went well—more 20 percent tips and seemingly very satisfied customers. At the end of the night, I was tallying up my earnings, and tipping out the back waiter and bartender, when the headwaiter came up to me and took me aside. He mentioned that twice that evening I had failed to clear glassware. I had been warned once before, and he said he would not tolerate the same mistake twice. I was fired, effective immediately.

I was crushed. I loved that place; I'd poured my heart into it. I went out of my way to study the restaurant to improve my service. And, after all, I was complimented by the city's most prominent columnist!

I hung my head low and said my good-byes. I walked out the back door and down the alley to the cable car that would take me home, unemployed. As I zigzagged aimlessly between puddles in the cobblestone, I heard a voice shout out my name from behind. I turned around to see the headwaiter, jogging up to me. He looked upset, almost tearful—strange for this stuffy, uptight guy. And he quietly, almost furtively, said to me in the dark walkway, "David, it wasn't the glassware. Next time, just be careful what you say to the head chef."

MACKAY'S MORAL:

Don't tell the Ayatollah to shave his beard.

THE DAY GOLIATH
SLEW DAVID

A head chef fussing over truffles may not look like Goliath. But, he is Goliath if he presides over the fate of your career. I asked David what he learned from the experience. In the family, the story has been encrypted as "How Mom Got David Fired." David learned plenty from the experience. And it was a lot more than handling head chefs. More importantly, he *only* learned the bigger lessons over time. That's what made this experience— he'll tell you—the best thing that ever happened to him.

First, he learned something about honesty. Honest input is something you absorb, not always something you dish out.

It's great to play the role of being a customer to the firm where you work. You can learn oodles. File the information away and use it tactfully. *Don't ever feel that you are entitled to the same rights as a customer. Especially if you want to go on enjoying the rights of being an employee.*

If you're in the learning mode, always ask why, rather than be judgmental. "*Why* was there more oil than normal in this salad dressing?" or "*Why* was the veal stew constructed on the mild side?" That way you both make the point and deliver your message without affronting somebody in authority.

No matter how tempting, steer clear of wisecracks. You might have to bite your tongue *not* to say: "Are you concerned that people might burn their tongues?" Bite hard . . . or burn in hell.

Never use what you learn as a chance to show up the boss. Especially if the boss is the founder of the firm.

David really did *not* want to lose this job. I'm glad he did because today he is a successful feature film director and producer in Los Angeles. The pain of his Stars defeat made the lesson so indelible. In David's case, it wasn't just a matter of what he learned. It was **when** he learned it.

No one in this book wanted to be fired. They may have been thankful they learned the lessons, but these are not lessons you *choose* to learn.

FINISHED OR FINISHER: THE CHOICE IS YOURS

"It's not those who start. It's those who finish," famed Boston Celtic coach Red Auerbach told sportscaster Lesley Visser. There are those who finish and those who *believe* they are finished: that is life's great divide.

When I was twenty-six, I quit my job as a salesman and bought a run-down, ramshackle envelope company. I had fired myself from a steady paycheck. I fretted. I stewed for months. Was this the right decision after all? I was frantic for a parachute. Before I quit, I had bit my lip and slinked back into my boss's office. "If this doesn't work out, can I have my old job back?" I had asked in a soft, slightly shaky voice.

"Sure, Harvey," he'd warmly reassured me, having little confidence—as I did—that I would make it on my own.

Dueling with the banks. Covering bad debts. Learning that salvaging the cutting-floor scraps would decide if I would be using red or black ink . . . on my profit-and-loss statement, that is! Confronting and resolving an intense and bitter strike. In the months and early years after I set out on my own, I can't tell you how often I thought of throwing in the towel and yanking the cord on that chute.

During those years, it was hard to find inspiration. I looked for it in an unlikely place. Down Mississippi River Boulevard—not far from the shabby tenderloin district in Minneapolis, where our old plant was—stood the Shriners Hospitals for Children. Several times I walked up and down the floors. I saw toddlers on crutches and children in wheelchairs. Little patients struggling in braces. I'd say to myself, "Harvey, what are you worrying about? Your tiny trials—c'mon, you idiot—you think *you* have worries!"

In 1987, I ran the first of my ten marathons in New York City. We gathered on the Staten Island side of the Verrazano Narrows Bridge for the gun. My daughter Mimi was with me. Kenyan Ibrahim Hussein won the race in two hours and eleven minutes. I wasn't even halfway through the course at that point! I finished, but I don't remember that part much. My memory of the race has to do with the race itself. I recall looking down while I was running. Right down at the pavement. There was a guy propelling himself with padded "handshoes" bound to his wrists with leather straps. His rippling arms were pumping him forward. He saw me glance at him, and he flashed me a smile. Seeing him made it easier for me to finish because I knew *he* would.

Bob Wieland had lost his legs in 1969 in Vietnam while trying to rescue another soldier during a mortar attack. Four days, nineteen hours, and seventeen minutes after we started that 1987 race, Bob crossed the finish line. On his hands. One year earlier, in 1986, it took Bob three years and eight months to cross America coast to coast. On his hands. Just recently, at fifty-seven, Bob finished the 2003 Los Angeles Marathon. On his hands.

How long is a real marathon?

Over the past forty years, I have mentored some 500 young people who have filed through my office as they have entered or reentered another kind of race: the race of their life. Every one of my visitors has walked away with a piece of advice—mostly it's what you've read in this book. Nearly every one of them has followed it to some degree, the only difference being the time it took them. To cross the finish line? No. *To realize that there is no finish line.* There is always a race and you are still in it. The only finish line in life is when you *believe* you're finished.

If you have thoughts, comments, or ideas about this book, I'd love to hear from you. (Please, no requests for personal advice.) Write to me at the following address:

Harvey Mackay
Mackay Envelope Company
2100 Elm Street Southeast
Minneapolis, MN 55414

I also can be reached electronically. My e-mail address is Harvey@Mackay.com. My website address is www.mackay.com.

Name Index

21 (restaurant) 321
60 Minutes 168

ABC 30, 99, 144, 159–160, 165
ABC Sports 158
Adler, Bob 243–244, 249
Adrian-Lewis, Inc. 194
Aesop 251
AFC 71
Aguilera, Christina 186
Albright, Madeleine 281
Alco Standard Corporation 194
Alessandra, Dr. Tony 189–190
Ali, Lonnie 254
Ali, Muhammad 254–259
Alien 271
All the President's Men 145
Altshuler, Michael 189–196
America's Cup 242
American Academy of Dramatic Arts 314
American Express 156, 272, 273, 303
American Gladiators 195
American Heart Association 91
American League 126–127
American Management Association 22
American Red Cross 84–89, 91
American Society of Association Executives 114
Amsterdam Admirals 73
Anderson, Sparky 122

Anthony, Carmello 162
Apple Computer 241
Apple IIc 108
Apprentice, The 14, 16
Architectural Digest 153
Arena Football League 73
Arizona Republic 179, 181
Arkansas, University of 37–38, 40–42, 46
Armstrong, Lance 144
Army, U.S. 295
Art of the Comeback, The 15
Art of the Deal, The 14
Ashrawi, Hanan 31
Associated Press 3, 178
Association Management 114
Atlanta Braves 120–122, 124
Atlanta Falcons 71
Atlanta Hawks 178
Auberge de Soleil 321
Auerbach, Red 164, 329
Automotive News 298
Autry, Gene 122
Avis Rent-a-Car 156

Bach, Richard 227
Bain, Bill 110
Bain Capital Funding 110
Baker, George F. 106
Bally's Casino 193
Baltimore Colts 61, 72
Baltimore, David 89

SUBJECT INDEX

A subject index is inevitably *subjective*. This list is an attempt to highlight some of the key concepts in the book. It's purpose is to help you find and put to work advice quickly. The guide is not exhaustive. It highlights some of the key ideas. Take a couple of minutes to browse this list. It may help you to tailor the reading of this book to your personal needs.

HARVEY MACKAY is the author of four *New York Times* bestsellers. His first two books—*Swim With the Sharks Without Being Eaten Alive* and *Beware the Naked Man Who Offers You His Shirt*—were #1 *New York Times* bestsellers and are also listed by *The New York Times* among the top fifteen inspirational business books of all time.

Dig Your Well Before You're Thirsty made the *New York Times* bestseller list twelve days after its release on April 20, 1997. His *Pushing the Envelope* cracked the *New York Times* Top Ten list shortly after its release in January 1999. His books have sold more than 10 million copies worldwide, been translated into thirty-five languages, and distributed in eighty countries.

Harvey is a nationally syndicated columnist for United Feature Syndicate, whose weekly articles appear in fifty-two newspapers around the country. He also is one of America's most popular and entertaining business speakers, having been named one of the top five speakers in the world by Toastmasters International.

In addition, Harvey is chairman of Mackay Envelope Company, a $100 million company he founded at age twenty-six. Mackay Envelope has six hundred employees and manufactures 25 million envelopes a day.

Harvey is a graduate of the University of Minnesota and the Stanford University Graduate School of Business Executive

Program. He is a golf fanatic and former #1-ranked senior tennis player in Minnesota.

In April 2004, Harvey received the prestigious Horatio Alger Award. He was inducted into the Minnesota Business Hall of Fame in 2002. He is the past president of the Minneapolis Chamber of Commerce, the Envelope Manufacturers Association of America, and the University of Minnesota National Alumni Association, to name only a few of the organizations in which he is involved.

He played a key role in bringing the 1992 Super Bowl to Minneapolis, along with serving as the catalyst in bringing an NBA franchise (Minnesota Timberwolves) to his home state, serving as chairman of the task force in getting the Hubert H. Humphrey Metrodome built, bringing in Lou Holtz to coach the University of Minnesota, and many more.

All of which is why *Fortune* magazine refers to him as "Mr. Make Things Happen."